TIMELESS QUESTIONS

How World Religions Explore the Mysteries of Life

Timeless Questions

How World Religions Explore the Mysteries of Life

JAMES R. DAVIS

SUNSTONE
PRESS

SANTA FE

The publisher cannot verify the accuracy or website URLs used in this book beyond the date of publication.

Sunstone books may be purchased for educational, business, or sales promotional use. For information please write: Special Markets Department, Sunstone Press, P.O. Box 2321, Santa Fe, New Mexico 87504-2321.
Printed on acid-free paper
∞
eBook 978-1-61139-641-6

—————————

Library of Congress Cataloging-in-Publication Data

Names: Davis, James R., 1936- author.
Title: Timeless questions : how world religions explore the mysteries of
  life / James R. Davis.
Description: Santa Fe : Sunstone Press, [2022] | Includes bibliographical
  references. | Summary: "The timeless questions that nag us all, those
  that ask about our origin, essential nature, way to live a good life,
  and final destiny, are explored through the ancient traditions of world
  religions in a probing dialogue between a knowledgeable professor and a
  persistent, unidentified questioner"-- Provided by publisher.
Identifiers: LCCN 2022004927 | ISBN 9781632933621 (paperback) | ISBN
  9781611396416 (epub)
Subjects: LCSH: Religions. | LCGFT: Dialogues (Literature)
Classification: LCC BL80.3 .D38 2022 | DDC 200--dc23
LC record available at https://lccn.loc.gov/2022004927

—————————

WWW.SUNSTONEPRESS.COM
SUNSTONE PRESS / POST OFFICE BOX 2321 / SANTA FE, NM 87504-2321 /USA
(505) 988-4418

This Book is Dedicated to Julianne Davis Robinson, PsyD.

※

Contents

Acknowledgments ∴ 8

Preface ∴ 9

Before: The Guide for the Perplexed ∴ 11

1 / God: Playing Hide and Seek with the Ground of Being ∴ 20

2 / Creation: Myth, Science, and the Survival of the Fittest ∴ 42

3 / Human Nature: The Game between the Devils and the Angels ∴ 62

4 / Social Order: Building Community Out of Political Chaos ∴ 76

5 / The Good Life: Stumbling along the Path to Virtue
    and Happiness ∴ 97

6 / Suffering and Death: Asking Why and Feeling Worse ∴ 115

7 / The Fate of the World: Extinction, Plague, Atom Bombs, and
    Astronomical Disasters ∴ 134

8 / Expansion: Growing Bigger and Spreading Out ∴ 159

9 / Division: Fighting over Truth and Goodness ∴ 175

10 / Observance: Certainty, Belonging, and Proper Dress ∴ 203

After: Founder's Day at the New Life Cafe ∴ 228

Readers Guide ∴ 254

Acknowledgments

When I started to write this book, I shared some chapters in the early stages with my grown daughter Julie, and she became very interested in the project and began to offer unsolicited edits and comments on the subject. I was delighted but surprised at her interest, and as it turned out she became the perfect first reader and editor for this book. She is a fine example of a well-educated person (undergraduate Phi Beta Kappa, summa cum laude, earning a Graduate Doctorate of Psychology Degree), who through no fault of her own knows little about the field of religion but is eager to learn. She was able to identify places in my writing where I was being unclear, making assumptions about what readers know, employing language that might be too technical or inappropriate, running on with too much detail, or using humor that wasn't funny. She not only made criticisms but supplied new language much of which appears in this final copy. In other words, she made this book user friendly, and we all have her to thank for that. Therefore, this book is dedicated to Julianne Davis Robinson, PsyD, and her family: the legacy of grandchildren and great grandchildren that she and her husband Scott have provided for me.

I also want to acknowledge the continuing help of my wife Adelaide B. Davis, who proofed the entire manuscript and added all of those pesky diacritical accent marks for words from languages other than English. She managed the computer complexities that often baffle me and also provided the cover and author photos.

Thanks also to Carl Condit and James Clois Smith, Jr. at Sunstone Press. I've published many books, and I know how rare it is to be able to pick up the phone and work through details informally with such competent, easy-going, and friendly publishers as they are. Thanks also to Lindsay Ahl for the beautiful cover design.

Preface

This is an unusual book. It contains the interesting research of many scholars presented in an informal question-and-answer style. The idea has been in my heart and on my mind for a long time. The pandemic gave me the isolated days needed to write it. To understand this book better, you may wish to take a moment to learn something about me as the author. So, let's get acquainted.

After earning an undergraduate degree in history from Oberlin College, I studied for three years at Yale University Divinity School, preparing to be a Christian minister, and I actually served as parish minister of a Congregational Church (United Church of Christ) in Springfield, Ohio. I left after two years to teach at the nearby historically-black (HBCU) Wilberforce University, serving there for six years as an assistant professor of religion and academic dean as well as a minority white person in the black community during the Civil Rights Movement. My career had taken a turn away from preaching to teaching and administration, and I went on to earn my Ph.D. in Higher Education Administration at Michigan State University with related studies in religion. At Wilberforce I commuted fifty miles at night once a week to Miami University in Oxford, Ohio, to take four graduate seminars in world religions, one each in Hinduism, Buddhism, Chinese Religions, and Islam; and those studies changed my outlook on religion and life completely. The remainder of my career was spent as a professor, administrator, and eventual dean of the adult education college at the University of Denver. My fascination with the study of religion as a window into the meaning of human existence never ceased. I am not affiliated with a church or religious organization; I just continue to read and ponder life.

When I think of how much I have been able to learn about religion, the sheer fun of it, and the importance it has had for examining my own life, and then notice how little acquaintance the typical adult has with the world's religions, I am inspired to try to provide a resource to stimulate more contemplation and eventual discussion of life's mysteries.

I am an experienced writer, having written eight academic books on college teaching, training, and university leadership, as well as two novels published by Sunstone Press.

Note, however, that I am not an academic specialist in religious studies, and the true scholars in the field may scowl at the sprawling scope of this book and its oversimplification of complexities. But the goal is not to provide either a comprehensive or specialized book on world religions, but to present a more general book that enables the reader to discover relevant knowledge for exploring life's fundamental questions while experiencing a sense of joy in learning something new.

Religion is a personal matter—I understand that—but being better informed is always helpful on the journey from shallow convictions to reasoned preferences. Going through life without having thought deeply or talked seriously about life's mysteries or timeless questions is like skiing down a steep mountain in the dense fog of a sudden whiteout blizzard. (I've done that on Aspen Mountain in Colorado.) You know that the goal is to "get down safely," but you don't know what trail you are on, what turn to take, or exactly where you will end up. You can only see a few feet ahead, so you slip and slide along slowly, taking it a few feet at a time, hoping not to fall off the edge of a cliff. Life should be more than going downhill blindly in a blizzard. Although life will always involve navigating the unexpected, the person who wishes to live more deliberately, with greater insight, clarity, and understanding, will surely profit from pondering carefully the mysteries of life and timeless questions.

Before: The Guide for the Perplexed

Some readers don't like introductions and skip over them. So to replace "Introduction," I have stolen a title for this chapter from a famous Jewish philosopher, Maimonides: *The Guide for the Perplexed*. He was trying to help Jewish followers understand Aristotle. (See Chapter 9.) The more modest goal here is simply to help you understand this book. I can guarantee that if you skip over this brief chapter, you will not only be perplexed, but confused, puzzled, baffled, bewitched, bothered, and bewildered—and maybe even flummoxed.

If you read this very brief guide, you will know what is meant by "mysteries of life" and "timeless questions." You will understand which of the world religions are explored and why. You will meet the questioner and the narrator-professor. And you will know what can be learned from reading this book. Without this guide, you may need to read several chapters to discover that no one is trying to convince you to "believe" anything, although knowing what to believe surely keeps us perplexed. You will probably figure things out by the fifth or sixth chapter, but why be perplexed at all when you can begin here?

Timeless Questions and the Mysteries of Life

What is meant by *timeless questions* and *mysteries of life*? Certain mysteries surround our human existence, which people in all cultures have been trying to explain for centuries. The way they describe the mystery may be quite different from culture to culture and their explanations often vary widely. We might call them "unsolved" mysteries (not to be confused with unsolved crimes) because the explanations provided don't settle the issue once and for all, so that people continue to regard the mystery as a mystery. A human mystery is by definition unsolvable although some explanations seem more reasonable and attractive than others.

Timeless questions grow naturally out of the mysteries of life and support the human quest for answers. We might say they are the questions asked to try to solve the mystery, comparable to the persistent questions of a skilled detective. They are timeless because generation after generation of human beings keeps asking them. This is not so much because the answers are poor, but because the questions cannot be answered easily or satisfactorily. So, people continue to ask them, and have for thousands of years. That's what makes them timeless.

What are some examples of unsolved mysteries and timeless questions?

Mystery: Some people seem to be very kind and generous while others appear to be quite selfish and even evil. Some people are like saints and angels while others are like monsters and devils. It's hard to explain why.

Questions: Are people basically good or basically evil? Does human nature lean more toward the good or the bad? Is there such a thing as universal human nature?

You can see why this mystery is basically unresolved. The questions are timeless because people continue to ask them even after tentative answers are given. Consider another example.

Mystery: Suffering is everywhere, and it is difficult to understand why there is so much suffering associated with life. It is especially difficult to comprehend why some apparently good people suffer greatly while some bad people appear to avoid it almost completely.

Questions: Why do good people suffer? Why is there so much suffering associated with life? Can suffering be eliminated or at least reduced? If so, what is the best way?

The world's religious traditions, particularly in their ancient and original form, have had a lot to say about timeless questions and the mysteries of life. In fact, we might say that these mysteries and questions are what give rise to religion. Some people like the answers provided and become followers of a particular faith. Others aren't so sure and keep looking. The religious traditions formulate and frame the questions as well as suggest options and solutions. By reflecting on these options, we can examine our life and decide what we do and don't believe. And we can do so in an informed way, having walked in the footsteps of others who have thought deeply about the unsolved mysteries and timeless questions.

What are the faith traditions that have been drawn on in this book to explore the mysteries of life? Hinduism, Buddhism, Confucianism, Daoism, Judaism, Christianity, and Islam are usually recognized as the "world religions." There are, of course, many other religious traditions. *The Penguin Handbook of the World's Living Religions* lists16 religions with a chapter on each one. Many valuable ideas can be found in religions that are not as well known, but it is not the goal here to scan all of the religions or provide a comprehensive review, but to select the more widely known faiths and delve deeper into those, keeping in mind the reader's challenge of understanding what may be new material. (Notable omissions include Jainism, Sikhism, Zoroastrianism, Baha'ism, Shinto, and Native American religions.)

The religions explored in this book are not presented with a single chapter for each one, as is often the case in a book about world religions, but on an "as-needed" basis to speak to the mystery being explored in that particular chapter. Not all religions are brought into the discussion in each chapter, and the door is opened little by little on each faith, so that at the end, the reader will know not only what that religion says about the various mysteries, but will have a fairly good grasp of several religions. The focus, however, is on the mysteries and questions, not the religious traditions in themselves.

Serious Talk and the Big Silence

Oddly enough, the timeless questions of human existence are not discussed very much. It seems natural to have conversations about world events, sports, work, travel, or fashion, but the timeless questions aren't on the radar for most people. In fact, when they come up, it can be downright uncomfortable. Why is that?

Usually, the timeless questions and mysteries of life are perceived to be associated with religious beliefs. If a question should surface, such as one of the following:

Is there a God?

Where did the world come from?
What is the good life?
What happens when people die?

The natural tendency is to associate these questions with religious belief, which is understandable, if not always correct.

People are generally very reluctant to discuss religion because they don't want to offend anyone by saying the wrong thing. Some people hold their beliefs strongly (some non-believers do as well), and to avoid an argument, people prefer to keep to themselves. It becomes a matter of politeness, of etiquette, not to discuss religion, a contract of respect for each other's beliefs: I won't ask you what you think, if you don't ask me. Unlike politics, which seems to get constant comment, religion is hardly mentioned.

Furthermore, religion is a subject where many people, to tell the truth, are not very well informed. In countries where there is a sharp separation of church and state, there is little opportunity to learn about religion, except through brief classes through a religious school or after-school affiliation. Such hit or miss instruction, limited to a few hours a week, usually reaches only a small subset of the population. For most people, through no fault of their own, there is a sizable gap between what they know about most school subjects and what they know about the subject of religion. If religion comes up, they stay out of the conversation, not for lack of interest, but because they don't know what to say. Unfortunately, otherwise well-educated people in our society, have never had the opportunity to learn about religion.

Apart from the religious dimension of timeless questions, there also appears to be a widespread cultural aversion to serious discussion at all. Death? Suffering? Human nature? Who wants to get into a discussion of that? We seem to have created a cultural taboo around serious talk. Some people just push the timeless questions away and try not to think about them very much. Others would like some serious conversation but don't know where to find it, surrounded as they are by the big silence. The result is that many people go through life thinking at a very elementary level—in a way that is not very helpful to them— about life's most important questions. Shouldn't the most basic issues of human existence deserve serious talk instead of the big silence?

Well, you might say, what difference does it make that people don't know much about religion and don't discuss serious subjects? We seem to be getting along fine this way. Maybe, but maybe not. When the subject of religion and the timeless questions are avoided, the deeper issues of life go unexamined. Centuries ago, the Greek philosopher Plato reminded us that the life unexamined is not worth living. An important consequence of the big silence is that the basic issues of life, the timeless questions we face as we try to live our lives each day, are not examined, studied, or explored with depth and intensity. They might, nevertheless, nag us persistently, whether we are conscious of them or not. Our lives go unexamined as the timeless questions are avoided or repressed under the culturally-constructed norm of silence. To raise children in the big silence can be downright embarrassing at times, as when they suddenly break that silence and begin asking difficult questions such as "Where did grandpa go?" and "Where did I come from?" and you realize that you need better answers than "Hell" and "Ohio."

But religion is different, you may say, because it is about believing, and believing is a personal matter not up for discussion, and besides religion is certainly not a subject. Religion may be *more* than a subject, but it is a subject, one that is taught professionally in most colleges and universities, both public and private, in an objective and scholarly manner. As for "believing," it is really not the point here. It is neither the prerequisite for nor the intended outcome of reading this book. Being well-informed, a reasonable aspiration of any educated person, is useful and necessary both for those who see themselves as caring about religion and those who don't. This book provides an opportunity to explore what religious traditions have had to say about the timeless questions and mysteries of life, whether you do or don't have "religious" beliefs.

Furthermore, it provides information about religion that will help you support or question your beliefs and appreciate the beliefs of others. It will help you examine your life. If you believe in something "spiritual," it is good to know why and what the alternatives might be; and if you don't believe, it is always valuable to know about what it is exactly that you don't believe. The emphasis of this book is not on believing in a particular faith—or believing at all—but on discovering what each of the religious traditions contributes to the discussion of human existence. When you know this, you are in a better position to make up your mind about what you do and don't believe.

Learning from this Book

The author assumes a reader with an open mind, ready to question and eager for new information, interesting ideas, and occasional light humor about the human predicament. What will be gained by reading this book?

First of all, literacy. By using the world religions as a vehicle for studying the mysteries and questions, we learn about a huge academic field pursued by scholars all over the world. Religious studies might be thought of as an important part of a basic general education. As you fill the knowledge gap in religion, you become more literate, a better-educated person. Another word might be *conversant*, which means being familiar enough with a subject to be able to have a conversation about it, as opposed to remaining silent. Reading this book should make you feel more comfortable with serious talk about life, more willing to engage in discussion of timeless questions, and eager to hear what others have to say.

Second, the reality is we *do* live in a global village in which we regularly encounter people who represent the religions of the world: a man with a long beard and turban, a woman in a black robe and headscarf, a young boy with a little round cap, an elderly woman in a gold sari with a red dot in the middle of her forehead, a young woman with a cross hanging from a chain at her neck, or a monk with a shaved head dressed in a saffron robe. They may be people who are just passing through our world on their travels, or we may be the traveler in their world; but either way, we will meet people who were born into or chose to be part of a particular religious tradition: Buddhists, Muslims, Christians, Jews, Hindus, Daoists, or followers of Confucius, as well as many others. As human beings, we all have unsolved mysteries and timeless questions. By exploring life's basic issues through several religions, we are in a better position to talk to a person of another faith, understand them, and learn from them.

Third, and most important, what a person learns about the mysteries of life and timeless questions will be helpful in developing a so-called philosophy of life, an outlook on life that comes from grappling with serious issues through a world religious perspective. In fact, there are very few subjects so directly applicable to life as religion. If a child is born with serious handicapping conditions, if a loved one dies young, if a relationship turns sour, or a career becomes stale, we often find ourselves confronting challenging questions: Why me? What am I supposed to do now? Why must people suffer so much? Is this all there is? Is life completely pointless? What will happen when I die? Sometimes these questions become more pressing as we work through a difficult experience or face the challenge of moving to the next phase of life. These are the "big picture" questions, and even though the study of religion may not provide direct and satisfying answers, it can at least help us to realize that we are not the first to ask these questions. Religion is a sturdy vehicle for examining life because it has been dealing with perceptions of the "big picture" in every culture for over 3,000 years.

Learning from this book may contribute to your literacy and conversancy, it may help develop cultural understanding, but the most important benefit is the perspective it provides for examining life. Religious perspectives on life's mysteries may not solve all of our problems, but they may keep us from freaking out when life's next catastrophe strikes.

Concept and Format of the Book

I have considered for some time how to write a book that would address the mysteries of life and timeless questions while at the same time introduce readers to what they may never have learned about the world's religious traditions. It must present the questions and mysteries in a clear, concise, and readable format, using the intriguing ideas of the world's religions as illustrations. It should not be a book that persuades people to believe, but rather offers an exploration of the key mysteries and questions that have given rise to belief. Reading it will be like a leisurely stroll at a reasonable pace, neither a sprint nor a marathon, so that the reader can pick the book up, read a chapter, ponder it, discuss it, and perhaps re-read a section of particular interest before moving to the next chapter.

What would be useful to know if a person wants to better navigate the mysteries of human existence through various religious traditions? In addition to the mysteries and questions, taken up chapter by chapter, other topics will surely need to be addressed, such as the nature of scientific and religious language, the concept of myth, the idea of the sacred and the holy, the critical study of scriptures, and the diversity of religious experience and practice. These "topics" do not appear separately as they might in a textbook, but are introduced and woven into each chapter as needed, gradually presenting the skills and tools used by those who study religion.

The exploration of each mystery, the main topic of each chapter, should be objective, introducing the religious traditions in an unbiased, and appreciative way, as a university professor would do, using the evidence-based historical and critical research from the field of religion to present the subject. The material for these chapters must be drawn from classic and recent scholarly texts on each religion and related subjects. (They are listed as references at the end of each chapter.)

The goal here is to draw value out of each faith tradition without favoring one over another, with the hope that readers of differing faiths, or those of none at all, will feel comfortable reading this book and learning about other religious traditions from it. The author has a watchful eye out for bias, but the problem is not so much bias, but familiarity, often resulting in a fuller treatment and more detailed presentation of certain topics, such as Biblical criticism or modern Christian thought, growing out of the author's upbringing and professional training in the Judeo-Christian tradition. Keeping this in mind, the author continues to strive for balance and neutrality, presenting all sides and bringing up interesting options, as an experienced professor would, while hoping to convey a deep appreciation of how various religions speak to and illuminate the mysteries of life.

The organization of the book is in ten chapters that address the mysteries and questions dealt with in religious traditions. The chapters explore such things as the concept of God, the idea of creation, human nature, the need for social order, the good life, suffering and death, the fate of the world, the expansion and spread of religions, the divisions within religious traditions, and religious observance. These translate into the chapters listed in the Table of Contents. A concluding "After" provides an imaginative fictional description of a hypothetical breakfast meeting of Moses, Jesus, Muhammad, Buddha, Confucius, Zhuangze (representing Daoism), and Rāmakrishna, a Hindu saint who appears to be both convening and facilitating the gathering. Naturally, they have a lot to say about what their followers "did" to them and what has happened through the ages to their teachings.

Each of the chapters uses a question-and-answer format to assure that the book speaks to pressing questions that readers have about life and to avoid a textbook coverage of the subject of religion. The professor who tries to respond to the questions is a fictional teacher, not the author, but a person crafted by the author. The hypothetical questioner is definitely not you, the reader, but is meant to raise the questions you might want to ask. The questioner functions as a fictional "someone" with a unique personality, independent mind, and quick sense of humor. You can decide whether this person is female or male, young or old, and what type of background they might have. The questioner, whose words are in Italic, is there to be watched, appreciated, and enjoyed, and is the one who keeps the discussion serious, challenging, and relevant. As someone with genuine curiosity and a keen desire to examine life, the questioner sometimes has the voice of a skeptic, often filled with genuine doubts. But it is also the expectant voice of the persistent inquiring mind that seeks answers to the timeless questions and unsolved mysteries of life.

References

Hinnells, John R., Editor, *The Penguin Handbook of the World's Living Religions*. New York: Penguin Books, 2010. See Table of Contents.

Shapiro, Fred R., *The Yale Book of Quotations*. New Haven: Yale University Press, 2006. The quotation from Plato (Socrates speaking) is actually, "Life without this sort of examination is not worth living." Apology 38a. The editor notes that it is frequently quoted as "The life which is unexamined is not worth living." Commonly, one also hears it as "The unexamined life is not worth living."

1

God
Playing Hide and Seek with the Ground of Being

I don't know exactly how to begin. Life has been going along okay for me, but suddenly I have a lot of questions. Big questions. I don't know where they are coming from, but I can't stop thinking about them. My father suggested that I might enjoy talking to you. I don't have people in my life to talk to seriously.

That's not uncommon. The timeless questions, growing out of what I call the mysteries of life, often get neglected. We try to live our lives without much discussion of these questions, but there is in fact an accumulated wisdom about them in the world's religions that can be very useful. I'm happy to share what I've learned through the years if that will help.

Yes, that's what I'm seeking, some wisdom, insight into—what did you call them?—the mysteries of life. I know that you are a professor and I'm eager to have you tell me what you know because at this point, I really want to learn about life. But assume that I don't know very much about religion. Try to put it in terms I can understand. I might interrupt once in a while. Is that okay?

It will be wonderful and I would love to know what you think about what I am sharing. And thank you for meeting here in my office. It's not only convenient for me, but as you can see, I have my personal library here.

Wow! It's quite a collection.

Yes, I have some older classic works that I still enjoy and value very much, but also some newer titles by respected scholars with up-to-date information and commentary. Meeting here allows me to pull a book off the shelf from time to time to show you something or read you a passage.

Should I take notes?

My students usually take too many notes. It's better to listen and try to understand. Think of it as a discussion. Where shall we begin?

Well, I might as well just plunge right in with a really big question. Lately, I've been wondering if there is a God, and if so, what God might be like. Some of my friends say they believe in God and others say they don't. When I ask them to explain, they don't say much. Some of them look at the world and say, "What you see is what you get, and there's nothing more." Others say, "I think there's something more out there beyond what we see."

We might begin by asking your friends what they might mean by "nothing more" or "something more." From the earliest times individuals and their societies have looked around at the world and found some things in it that they called sacred. *Sacred* is the word used for "the manifestation of something of a wholly different order, a reality that does not belong to our world..." That's an observation by Mircea Eliade, a man who spent a lifetime studying the sacred in ancient, pre-modern societies, and the author of a book I have right here called *The Sacred and the Profane.* What he discovered is that in most of these societies the sacred was identified in trees, rocks, or mountains, in sacred places and at sacred times, and remembered in sacred rites and rituals. Sacred spaces have sacred doors or ladders to get in and out, and they have a sacred center. The sacred space, or holy place, is the foundation of order in their world, and what they fear most is chaos which "corresponds to a terror of nothingness," Eliade tells us. The interesting thing about this sense of the sacred is that it appears again and again, almost universally, in ancient cultures, and Eliade has tracked down many of them. He tells us that a completely profane society is a "recent discovery in the history of the human spirit" and that only "modern man has desacralized his world and assumed a profane existence." The word *profane*, by the way, is not about profanity; it is simply the absence of a sense of the sacred. *Sacred* is used to describe that "something more" that people see and have been seeing for a long time in many different cultures.

That's an interesting way to think about the "something more." But that's what I'm asking about. What is it?

The Romantic poet William Wordsworth also referred to a sense of "something more," but he never quite called it God. Wordsworth found it in nature and in the later pleasurable recollections of moments spent within natural settings. When Wordsworth describes a field of daffodils, the reader has a sense that there is something more than daffodils there.

I have a poetry anthology here. Let me read for you a few lines from Wordsworth's poem, "I wandered lonely as a cloud."

> I wandered lonely as a cloud
> That floats on high o're vales and hills,
> When all at once I saw a crowd
> A host of golden daffodils;
> Beside the lake, beneath the trees
> Fluttering and dancing in the breeze.
>
> Continuous as the stars that shine
> And twinkle on the Milky Way,
> They stretched in never-ending line
> Along the margin of a bay:
> Ten thousand saw I at a glance,
> Tossing their heads in sprightly dance...

Some of my friends would say "It's just daffodils, William, nothing more. The poor man was overcome by natural beauty, but that's all it was. Let's not get all carried away by a field of yellow daffodils on a windy day.

Yes, that's what many people would say. Others would suggest that Wordsworth saw something else and put it into poetry for the rest of us to see it, too. Some people tend to see just the daffodils. Others see something sacred in a dancing field of flowers. They wonder why daffodils are constructed as they are and why the human brain is able to perceive them as beautiful. Perhaps you have had similar experiences, but not with daffodils, such as reaching the peak of a mountain to find miniature wildflowers blooming on the tundra after a winter of snowpack, hiking through a dense forest in autumn with colorful leaves swirling all around, or paddling across a serene lake with the shoreline reflected in the glassy surface.

Yes, falling leaves on a sunny day with blue sky. That's special.

Another way to describe the "something more" is as an experience of holiness. I have an old classic here by Rudolph Otto. It's called *The Idea of the Holy*. He describes the human encounter with what he calls the "wholly other." He identifies it as an experience with the *"mysterium tremendum"* (tremendous mystery), filled with awe, astonishment, and a sense of dependence, but also an entrancing fascination. Some people (both mothers and fathers) have an experience like this in the birth of a baby, in the mysterious and awe-inspiring beginning of life. Others find it in their unlikely survival of a disaster, that head-shaking moment of wondering why you are still alive. Others feel it as they watch a handicapped child triumphing over challenging disabilities, somehow remaining cheerful and persistent as if plugged into a mysterious source of energy.

Otto gives us a stronger, more concentrated sense of "something more," often filled with deeper, almost overpowering, emotion. At times, this experience is a bold encounter with something numinous (supernatural) that surpasses the tangible physical universe. It goes beyond the exhilarating walk along a bay lined with dancing daffodils. Many people say that they have never had an experience like this; others say they can relate to it.

Some of your friends might insist that living in a desacralized world, without any sense of the sacred, is exactly what we are meant to do as thoroughly modern human beings of the twenty-first century. The time has definitely come, they would say, to throw off any lingering beliefs in sacred stones or trees and shun any mysterious experience of the numinous wholly other. A daffodil is a daffodil is a daffodil.

Yes, that's exactly what they would say. It's as if you know them.

Isn't it interesting that people tend to divide into those who see "something more" and others who see the natural world as "nothing more" than just that? Some people understand the sacred and holy; some people don't, and that's okay. But this is a good starting point for thinking about God: the sacred and the profane, the beauty of nature, and the mystery of the holy encounter.

So, some people have this sense of "something more" that goes beyond physical reality. But how do we get from this "something more" to the idea of God? Isn't God more than "something more"? I don't know much about other religions, but it seems like there are a lot of different ideas about God.

The notion of God is certainly one of the central human mysteries, and yes, there are many different ideas about God. Some that are more familiar to you may be more understandable, so let's begin there. Then we will discuss the ideas of God in other faiths, but in their earliest and purer forms before they became complicated by later traditions. Along the way it will be necessary to slip in some basic information about each of these religions in order to understand the early historical settings from which these particular ideas of God emerged. I hope that's okay.

That's fine. I don't know much about religion and I need all the background I can get. Maybe you could start with the Bible.

The Bible? Okay. It is usually thought of as a book, but it is more like a library, consisting of several books and many different genres of religious literature. Christians usually refer to the Old Testament and New Testament, but the former might better be referred to as the Hebrew Scriptures (sacred writings) because they are the founding documents of Judaism. Keep in mind that Christianity grew out of Jewish traditions as a new religion. Jesus himself was a Jew and when his followers began to create a religion around him that grew into Christianity, the Jews who said "no thank-you" continued on in their own direction. They evolved a distinct religion based on the Hebrew scriptures and their later interpretations in the Talmud.

Let's begin with the concept of God in the Hebrew scriptures. That's not as easy as it sounds because there are conflicting pictures of God in these scriptures and even two names for God: Jahweh and Elohim. But let's take a stab at it and say that the idea of God in the Hebrew scriptures is that of a strong power that influences human destiny, a God that looks out for his people.

That's always a nice feeling, knowing that someone is looking out for you.

The Hebrew scriptures are not completely identical with the Old Testament, but they are a close match. The traditions found there go back as far as 3500 BCE (Before the Current Era) to the legends developed around Abraham, Isaac, and Jacob, the earliest leaders of the people of Israel, and to Moses whom we might think of as the founder of the tradition that became Judaism. The Jewish people, originally twelve tribes, went through many trials and tribulations, and after a successful kingdom under the reign of David, eventually ended up being conquered by Babylon and taken there as captives in 597 BCE. It was there in Babylon, in the experience of exile from their temple and their land, that the central portions of the Hebrew scriptures were edited, combined, and reshaped, drawing on much older written and oral sources, to tell the story of the people of Israel.

Most of us have had the experience of wondering why certain

things happen. Was it chance? Coincidence? Some kind of plan? The hand of God? Destiny is one of the mysteries of human existence. How do people meet, become acquainted, fall in love, and get married? Why do things turn out as they do? Why do some nations rise and others fall? One way to view the Hebrew scriptures is as the extended religious explanation of a people's history. Out of this arises a view of God as involved with human destiny, a God that brings a people into existence, makes an agreement (covenant) with them, helps set up and develop a series of governments with them, and then appearing to grow disillusioned, permits them to be conquered by Babylon and taken into captivity. And yet this God still holds out hope for them. This was a people, as set forth in its scriptures, that needed to explain how it had come so far through its glory days, only to end up as prisoners in another country.

Rather than thinking of the God of the Hebrew scriptures as a divine Spiderman who jumps into human history to manipulate events, it might be better to think of a people who believed in a force, knowable at times, but at other times remote and mysterious, that nonetheless guided them through its leaders, kings, and prophets, holding them to high standards of justice and righteousness. God as the explanation of destiny—that's one idea of God.

What about the idea of God in Christianity? Christians still value the Hebrew scriptures, but they have a different idea of God, right?

If the Jewish God provides an explanation of *communal* destiny, the Christian God is presented as an explanation of *personal* destiny and salvation. Some people are deeply troubled by the timeless question: What happens to the individual after death? Christianity links personal morality with immortality, urging each individual to be a better person, but knowing that only God can save a soul. Salvation might be thought of as referring both to the afterlife and the ability to live a better life on earth now.

The Western calendar is ordered by the birth of Jesus, although some scholars today mark his birth at around 4 BCE. We once used B.C. to refer to the years and centuries "Before Christ," with everything coming after as A.D., meaning in Latin, *Anno Domini,* in the Year of our Lord. Historians today prefer to use BCE to mean "Before the Common Era" and CE as "Common Era," but the demarcation of centuries and millennia still hovers around the historical figure of Jesus.

We can discuss Jesus more later if you wish, including the controversy that continues to swirl around his life and teachings. For now, I can tell you that he is described by scholars today as a humble Jew who spoke Aramaic, who believed that the world was soon to come to an end, and who had a profound impact on those who encountered him and his difficult teachings. Jesus ran into problems, both with the Jewish priests and Roman authorities. After Jesus was crucified, a common practice in the Roman Empire of the time, some of his followers believed that they had encountered him alive or as a spirit and began to build a movement around him that turned into a faith that he was not only the Jewish Messiah (Christ), but that he was the Son of God. One of these followers was Paul, who nurtured the new churches that were springing up in the Mediterranean world, and he developed in his letters to these churches, particularly in his letter to the Romans, the idea that Jesus played a key role in the salvation of individual souls.

The dominant belief in early Christianity was that humans are sinful and if they have any dreams about a life after death, the Christian God holds the key to their salvation both from sin and death. This God has the power to forgive sins, transform lives, and save souls—a second idea of God. Sometimes the Christian idea of God is expressed in a simpler way by just saying: "God is love" and "Love your neighbor."

I like the simpler way, because I'm not exactly sure how this salvation process works. We will definitely need to come back to Jesus in some future discussion, but for now, I understand that this is another idea about God. What does Islam say about God?

Judaism and Christianity are thought of as the "monotheistic faiths," because their followers believe in one God (mono/one + theism/belief in god). Islam is also a monotheistic faith. The idea of God drawn from Islam is of a strong power responsible for everything and upon whom human beings are deeply dependent.

Islam develops somewhat later than most of the Western and Eastern faiths, through the revelations to the prophet Muhammad in 610 CE, beginning with his frightening "Night of Destiny" that made him the messenger of Allah. Allah was the high God of Arabia, already identified with the God of the Jews and Christians, and many of their traditions are included, but often modified and restated, in the scriptures of Islam. But let there be no mistake, Allah, is the one God and the Muslim creed is: There is no god but God (Allah).

Muhammad was a businessman and when he looked around, he

saw a lot of robbing and stealing, raids and wars, and he thought the Arabs deserved a quiet place to trade in peace. Worshippers already gathered around the Kaaba, a huge square stone structure in Mecca, a holy site in today's Saudi Arabia, so why not create a space of twenty miles in radius around it, free of violence, a kind of free trade zone, not quite akin to the Duty-Free area at the airports today, but a similar idea. When things didn't work out exactly as Muhammad had hoped, he left with his followers and settled in Medina, 250 miles north of Mecca. It is here that the community and teachings of Islam were developed. Muhamad was a peace-maker and by his death in 632 he had brought an Islamic peace to war-torn Arabia.

Although the Quran (sometimes written Koran) is held by many Muslim believers to be the inspired words of Allah delivered directly to Muhammad, it is more likely, as with many scriptures of the world's religions, that it came together over time, was recited aloud at first, and then written. The Quran has no main narrative but consists of many verses for meditation, often beginning with the word "Recite."

Although Islam is generally inclusive of other traditions, it makes clear that there is only one God, Allah, who embodies the unity of the entire world. One might say that Muslim monotheism means more than belief in one God. It is the God of Oneness. God is Unity. God is indivisible, unique, and nothing exists apart from God. There is no division between this world and the world of hereafter, no natural and supernatural, because God is One. God has no attributes, no "three persons," because God is beyond description.

So, don't try to paint any pictures of God or cartoons of Muhammed. I know Muslims don't like that.

Human beings are dependent on this one God for everything, and part of Muhammad's mission was to remind people not to forget this dependence. Islam means "surrender" or "submission" and much of Islamic worship is designed as a constant reminder of God: recite the obligatory prayers five times a day, face toward Mecca, recite Quranic verses while bowing forward face to the ground, and visit the Ka'ba at least once in your life on pilgrimage. Islamic practice centers the believer around the unity and oneness of Allah, the all-powerful God upon whom people are all totally dependent. One God that unifies everything and complete human dependence—a third idea of God.

That's interesting. I didn't know about the close relationships of those religions in the beginning or the idea of God as the unity of everything. Now I think I would like to know about the idea of God in other religions, particularly those of Asia.

China has three major religious traditions: Confucianism, Buddhism, and the lesser-known Daoism, which is not much of an "ism," but a tradition based on a collection of philosophical writings. It is debatable whether any of them in their earliest forms had an idea about God that matches the Western theistic notions of a transcendent deity, but Daoism has an interesting concept to consider. The Daoist teaching was a rebellion, to some extent, against the Confucian preoccupation with society and the best way to govern. The movement against it was well under way about a century after the death of Confucius in 479 BCE, and the founders of Daoist teaching began to turn attention away from the state toward the individual by focusing on how a person can learn to lead a satisfying and responsible life.

Daoism is called the religion of the Way (dao = way), but just as we have many meanings for the word *way* in English, so, too, in Chinese for *dao*. It is difficult to tell exactly what Dao is, but images used to describe it often come from nature. Water, for example, nourishes all living things, does not favor one plant over another, and everything can use it. Water is weak, so weak you can run your hand through it with little effort, but water can wear down the hardest rocks. Water won't fight, but it can drown you. Dao gives birth to things. Like the root of a plant, Dao is our foundation.

Is Dao just mother nature?

Probably all of that and much more. Dao is certainly natural, often being compared to uncarved wood, the tree before it has been cut down and made into boards. It is "the opposite of anything artificial and constructed." Where is it? Everywhere. The pathway for living life can be found in the simplest stream or in the vast cosmic process. Some scholars call Daoism a type of "intraworldly mysticism" because it is not looking for something beyond but within the world. "Daoist mysticism brings a new perception of the everyday, where we see everything in a different way." Why? Because we see "something more" as the Way within nature. So, if there is a God in Daoism, it is not a God beyond the natural world but within it.

In the United States in the 1960s and 1970s Daoism became interesting to the counterculture activists (so-called hippies) who were enthralled with a translation of one of the great Daoist texts, the *Dao De Ching*. It is through them that the phrase "go with the flow" became popular. This is regarded now as a superficial summation of Daoism, but there is, indeed, within this tradition the idea of alignment (going) with the natural Way (flow) built into the universe. Is Dao God? Some would call it that, others not, because Dao is within, not beyond. Daoists are reluctant to say very much about Dao, insisting that "those who know don't talk and those who talk don't know." If we were to summarize this view of God, perhaps we could call it the mysterious guiding force embedded in nature—a fourth idea of God.

I like these different ideas of God, but I'm stuck on something you just mentioned about a religion without God. I had not heard of that previously. Is that really possible?

The other two Chinese religious traditions, Confucianism and Buddhism, may be examples of religions where the concept of God is even less developed although scholars who study such matters don't always agree on this point. Confucianism grew up around a historical figure Kong Fuzi (551–479 BCE) whom Westerners call Confucius. His pupils began to bring together his wise sayings to put in an anthology, and although these maxims were attributed to Confucius, the volume we call *The Analects of Confucius* probably took several centuries to reach its final form. Confucius focused on what we would call the ethical life of the orderly society. He thought it was normal for people to cooperate, and he may have been the first to make a statement that parallels the "Golden Rule" of which there are several in the world's religions. His was "Do not impose on others what you yourself do not desire," a more cautionary statement than the familiar "Do unto others..." Although he was a modest figure without great influence in his own time, he became a sacred figure in Chinese history, and a religious tradition of reverence was built around him. He was a teacher of a way of ruling, and he traveled widely searching for a ruler who would follow his way but never found one. When he died, most people considered him a failure, but his followers made him into a religious hero of Chinese culture. But Confucius didn't have much to say about God. If his followers made him into one, as some did, he would have been shocked.

As for Buddhism, it was an outgrowth of Hinduism and in its earliest development stressed meditation and insight as important for reaching the spiritual state of *nirvāna* to break the chain of continuous rebirths. *Nirvāna* is a state of emptiness and supreme enlightenment, not to be confused with a rock group going by that name. Although Siddhartha Gautama (c.485–410 or 400 BCE) known as Buddha or "Enlightened One" focused on reaching *nirvāna,* his later followers believed that the Buddha existed before Gautama and lived after him through *boddisatvas,* human incarnations of Buddha-like figures. But the earthly Buddha, whom we would call the founder, has little to say about God in the theistic sense, because he is focused on human efforts to reach Enlightenment.

If some religions have no God, are there still some with many Gods? I've heard that there are.

We would call that *polytheism.* (poly/many + theism/belief in god), and the best example of a long-established religious tradition with more than one God is Hinduism. The word *Hindu* was used by the British colonialists of India to distinguish the original people of India and their faith tradition from late settlers like Muslims and Sikhs, so Hindu really means Indian as distinct from other people. There is another theory that the name goes far back into the Aryan people who lived across the Indus River, pronounced (or mispronounced) as Hindu River. Either way, the name refers to a people and culture with a very old religious tradition based on ancient scriptures called *Vedas* and *Upanishads* and great epics such as the *Mahābhārata.*

It is true that one finds in Hinduism many gods, incarnations (embodiments) of gods, and avatars of gods appearing in human form. The best known are Īshvara, Brahmā, Vishnu, and Shiva. There are also semi-divine male and female shining bodies and rishis who are sages. People within monotheistic traditions are often shocked by this idea of so many gods, but while the shocked ones are arguing about and possibly slaughtering each other over who follows the one true god—the Christian Crusades against Islam would be a good example—polytheists are able to say: "Well, there is my god, and your god, his god, and her god, and their god, and we can each have our own god, the one who best fulfills our needs, without having to fight about who is right. Thus, Hinduism with its many gods is also very inclusive—well, until recent times.

The local gods of Hinduism, which are sometimes set up as household shrines, small statues, icons, or good luck pieces for a spare pocket, are all part of a larger unifying concept of *brahman,* the energy that pervades the universe, and *ātman,* the sacred self that dwells within all of us. In other words, the many gods are manifestations of one deeper spiritual reality, the underlying force behind the gods. One of the early Hindu theologians in trying to explain *brahman* to his son, had the boy mix salt into water, and when it had dissolved asked him to taste it. You can't see the salt, but you can taste it. *Brahman* is like that. In some ways, Hinduism has the best of both worlds: local gods who take care of human needs, and the abstract power that is the invisible source of the energy and "breath" of the entire universe.

We might say that Hinduism provides multiple snapshots of God, not only close-ups of the local gods, but panoramas of a universal spiritual source of power and energy that animates the universe and dwells within the self—a fifth idea of God. Or is it gods?

I like your description of these different ideas about God, and I'm learning many things I never knew. But now I have a different question. Is there a way to prove through reason that God exists, or will God always remain a mystery to us?

A number of famous philosophers have tried to prove that God exists. I can share a few with you and you can see what you think. They are cast as arguments with proofs. They come from philosophers such as Plato, Aristotle, Augustine, Anselm of Canterbury, and Thomas Aquinas. The "proofs" of the existence of God can be boiled down to three primary arguments:

Cosmological Proof. If we look at the cosmos, we see cause and effect, operating as chains of cause and effect going back to the first cause, which is God.

Teleological Proof. The universe seems to be going somewhere, moving toward an outcome with purpose and God is both its goal and the "orderer."

Ontological proof. Humans are able to imagine a being so huge that it is impossible to think of anything bigger, and if humans have this idea of such a being, then that being must exist, and that being is God.

If these proofs of God sound a little medieval to you, it may be because they are. People of recent times don't make these arguments anymore. But this does not mean that reason is not important in thinking about belief.

Is it possible to make proofs that God doesn't exist? Is that what atheists do?

The proofs against God are not much better than the proofs for God (at least as proofs), but several great thinkers have certainly made the case against God and religion through strong arguments.

Karl Marx (1818–1883) called God the "opiate of the people," meaning that people who are poor—enslaved by the capitalist system—latch on to God like an addict to a drug fix. Born a Jew and raised as a Christian, Marx eventually became an atheist and the founder of a political ideology for redistributing wealth that came to be known as Marxism. For Marx, God does not exist, but lives only in the minds of the people as a consolation offered by their oppressors.

Sigmund Freud (1856–1939) thought and taught that God is an infantile illusion. Although Freud was raised in a religious family—his mother was Jewish—later in life as the founder of psychoanalysis, Freud had very critical things to say about religion. Children fear but need the protection of parents, and as they grow up, they carry their fears and needs into adulthood, nurturing the illusion of God as a protector. In Freud's view, there is a neurotic element in religion. God is just an illusion, a fantasy.

Ludwig Feuerbach (1804–1872) believed that God was nothing more than man's projection of himself. Baptized as a Catholic and brought up as a Protestant, Feuerbach was on a path to becoming a Protestant pastor, but got sidetracked by his love of philosophy; and he, too, became an atheist. Christians taught that man was made in God's image, but for Feuerbach that process was reversed: God is made (up) by man in man's own image. Feuerbach tells us that God is nothing more than the personified nature of man with the human attributes of love, justice, and wisdom. Man is the projector and God is his projection. We might say that Marx, Freud, and Feuerbach all thought that God was an illusion, just in different ways.

Perhaps the most dramatic point about the non-existence of God was made by the philosopher Friedrich Nietzsche (1844–1900). (Don't get all caught up in the "tzs." If you say "neat/she," you will be close.) Young Fred lost his father by the time he was five years old and in his upbringing was surrounded by his mother, a sister, a grandmother, and two maiden aunts—enough to drive any man mad, which, sorry to say, is exactly what happened to him near the end of his life. Let's not hold that against the kind women who raised him or discount his ideas as coming from a madman, for he was a deep and influential thinker, and a prolific writer who continues to draw broad comment. His most famous point was that God is dead. We might say that "God" as a concept doesn't have meaning anymore; it's as good as dead. The death of God in people's minds had already happened in the scientific revolution of modern times. It was not necessary for Nietzsche to make an argument against the existence of God, because this had already been done. There was no longer any need for an idea of God.

The twenty-first century has witnessed a resurgence of atheist writing by a group known as the "New Atheists." The books come with titles such as *The God Delusion* and *The End of Faith* and *God Is Not Great: How Religion Poisons Everything.* Although the writers differ in their approach, they share the common position that religious faith is blind trust without evidence. A religious belief, they say, like everything else, must be based on scientific evidence. Their insistence on empirical (observable) evidence is called "evidentialism." Not only is there no evidence for God, God is unnecessary because science can explain what religion once tried to explain. Some of these authors call religion "poison" and advocate active opposition to those who believe in God.

Do you think science can explain everything? It seems to be doing a good job with many things. But asking for observable evidence for God seems a little unfair because the whole point is to look for what we have been calling "something more." If it is "more," it won't be observable in the usual way.

Good point. Science, as the direct empirical examination of the physical world, took a long time to develop and is highly valued for its research on the scope and workings of the physical universe, from sub-atomic particles to the farthest galaxy. We would not want to suggest anything that would curtail that research or disparage its findings, as some people are doing with science today. But when the "New Atheists" turn to science as the method for explaining all things, they have jumped from "science" to "scientism," making the claim that science provides not just a path to the truth, but the *only path.* Scientism wants to reduce all phenomena to the natural and material—the mind to the brain and the brain to cells and the cells to molecules—leaving no room for other perspectives. All real knowledge, they claim, is contained within the boundaries of science.

Although science has produced fantastic results when focusing on its realm of investigation, the natural world, many questions go unanswered, not because science fails, but because the questions are not the type where science can be of much help. Science tells us little about the timeless questions: "who we are, where we come from, why we are here, what we should be doing while we are here (if anything), and what happens to us when we die." These are the questions that give rise to religion, and no amount of empirical investigation will provide answers because the questions don't lend themselves to the methods of science. The "answers" provided tentatively in the world's religious traditions may not be such great answers, lacking both consistency and specificity, but these are the questions they grapple with and seek to answer. How could science possibly address these questions?

I'm beginning to see why these timeless questions have such importance for the way we live our life. I think I heard fairly convincing arguments to support both the idea that God exists and doesn't exist. What am I to do if I'm not sure what to believe.?

The debate about whether God exists or not continues on, probably because there is no convincing way to resolve it. One suggestion, perhaps a bit humorous sounding today, was made by the French philosopher, mathematician, and physicist, Blaise Pascal (1623–1662). It is called "Pascal's Wager" and is summed up in his own words:

> Let us weigh the gain and loss in wagering that God is. Let us estimate these two chances. If you gain, you gain all; if you lose, you lose nothing. Wager, then, without hesitation that He exists.

Since we can't prove God's existence, Pascal tells us, we have to make a bet. If we behave as if God exists, trying to live a godly life, but in the end discover that we have made the wrong choice—that God doesn't exist when we thought He did—it's not much of a loss, just our efforts at the godly life. But if we were right in choosing to believe that God exists, and He does, we gain all. It's hard to know exactly what Pascal means by "all," but he probably has in mind the traditional Christian belief of the time, the idea of eternal life.

So, we have to go to Vegas to make a bet on God? Was Pascal serious or just teasing us?

Keep in mind that he was a mathematician who understood probability. For him the choice was what we today would call a "no-brainer." But wouldn't it have been nice if after dying, Pascal would have slipped back into existence to tell us which way to bet? All we have is his marvelous wager. Does it help?

Not really, but I like it, especially the idea of living as if there were a God, whether you believe or not. It provides a safety net for doubters. Could you tell me about a really sophisticated idea of God that might convince the atheists?

It might be a waste of time trying to convince an atheist, but I know what you are seeking. The question to ask an atheist is this: What God do you *not* believe in? Maybe I don't believe in that God either. Is it the bearded old man on a cloud? That's a simpler idea of God that is easier to attack. You might be looking for a more sophisticated idea of God that is not so easily taken down.

Consider, as one example, the idea of God as Being-Itself. Paul Tillich, a world-famous Christian theologian of the mid-twentieth century, set forth this idea of God in his book, *The Courage to Be*. I have an old copy right here. Let me get it. He suggests that God is not a being like other objects or living things in the universe, but is the ground (foundation) of being that we can call "Being-Itself." By this Tillich means that God brings all things from non-being into being, gives the world its being, including our being, not so much as the architect of creation, but as the power of being itself. Tillich refers to the "God above God." The mysteries associated with birth and death are the mysteries of being. When we see, or believe, that our being, our very existence, is rooted in the ground of being, Tillich says, that gives us the "courage to be," not only to live life boldly but to face death calmly. Thus Being-Itself is both what brings us into existence and sustains us.

Yes, that's a really abstract idea of God, But I like the suggestion that God is not just another being like the rest of us. Some people might find the Ground of Being to be too impersonal, but even so, it does seem to have implications for how we are to live our lives: with courage. What I'm concluding is that we may be able to get some interesting ideas about God, but we can't really know what God is like for sure. It's like we poor humans are playing "hide and seek" with the ground of being without ever catching up to Him...or Her...or Itself.

In the Hebrew scriptures, God seems to appear from time to time in different forms: as an angel of the Lord, in a pillar of cloud or fire, in a burning bush, in a fierce storm, or out of a whirlwind, but in those stories and others, the general idea is that humans don't see God directly and live to tell about it. An important power seems to be guiding the destiny of Israel, but as a hidden, mysterious, and unknowable God. The temple was so important in the Jewish tradition because the essence of God was represented in a very special place in the temple in the Holy of Holies behind a veil. Yahweh, the hidden God of the Hebrew scriptures is hard to pin down or describe in detail. What God expected of the Jews is one thing; who God is, can be quite another.

Consider the Christian idea of the Trinity—Father, Son, and Holy Ghost—which does not appear in the Bible, but was formulated by the early church fathers of the fourth century, two brothers, Gregory and Basil, and another Gregory, bishop of Nanzius. In their version, Father referred to the source of being, Son gave a glimpse of the divine essence, and Spirit suggested an immanent divine presence, but what is seldom understood is that these were concepts developed to describe how the unknowable Godhead made itself known. Behind the Trinity is a surprising effort to describe an essentially unknowable God.

Saint Thomas Aquinas (1225–1274 CE), who some call the founder of theology (speech about God), laid out proofs of God's existence and then undercut his own work by insisting that we don't actually know God because grasping God lies beyond the human mind. The highest knowledge, he noted, is to know that we don't know God.

In the Chinese tradition of Daoism, one learns the fundamental rhythms of life from the Way, but the endlessly evolving Dao itself is not to be described. Getting specific about Dao is impossible because Dao is unnamable, unknowable, and dynamic. The best one can hope for is being at home with one's self in the natural world.

Even in Hinduism, where there seems to be a god at every corner, the brahman behind the gods, the ineffable (inexpressible) higher force, cannot be apprehended directly. Who can know the awe-inspiring power that sustains the entire universe?

Meanwhile, those who sense "something more" keep seeking. One of the bishops of the early Christian Church, Saint Augustine (354–430 CE), suggests that we are meant to be searchers after God because that is how God made us. He speaks to God, "You have made us for yourself, O Lord, and our hearts are restless until they rest in You." That is one reason, we could say, why so many people in so many different cultures have searched for and tried to describe God.

Although it may be disappointing to come to the end of this discussion of ideas about God without clear knowledge of God, maybe it makes sense, actually, to conclude that God is only partially knowable. Perhaps that is the nature of God. Why would mere humans think that they can describe God clearly or even know enough about the divine to affirm or deny God's existence? I know, some people have a very cozy, personal relationship with God, talking to God in informal hip language, as if they can walk along together, holding hands, chatting comfortably. Some people achieve that, but we may need a less folksy idea of God now that we know about Yahweh, the Trinity, Allah, Brahman, Dao, and Being-Itself.

Joseph Campbell, the famous scholar of myth, put it this way in a television interview with Bill Moyer:

> "God" is an ambiguous word in our language because it appears to refer to something that is known. But the transcendent is unknowable and unknown. God is transcendent, finally, of anything like the name "God." God is beyond names and forms. Meister Eckert (a Christian mystic) said that the highest leave-taking is leaving God for God, leaving your notion of God for an experience of that which transcends all notions."

Perhaps we should not be disappointed in being the loser in the game of hide and seek with the ground of being. Maybe it is just expected that the striving to know God will tease and tug at us indefinitely, because God is the ultimate unsolved mystery of life. What we gain in the study of religion is a profound respect for the enlightened people of ancient times who used their creative imagination to describe the indescribable "something more."

Thank you for what you have taught me in our discussion today. I'm beginning to feel like it's normal to have these big questions spinning around in my head. But now I'm wondering where the world came from and if it was really created by God. Can we meet again?
Yes, of course. Maybe next week. Here?

References

To maintain the spontaneity of a question-and-answer discussion, I have chosen not to use footnotes, but I draw heavily on new and older sources as references and wish to credit them appropriately. For each source I describe how or where the ideas from that source are used, and when direct quotations of more than a few words are made, the pages are cited. References are listed at the end of each chapter. Some of these references may also be thought of as books for further reading.

Armstrong, Karen, *The Lost Art of Scripture: Rescuing the Sacred Texts.* New York: Knopf, 2019. This comprehensive new work on the scriptures of the major religions of the world is referred to frequently in this book and in this chapter, particularly for material on Islam, Daoism, and Hinduism. The direct quotations are the Confucian "Golden Rule," "Do not impose…" found on p. 114 and the British origins of the word *Hinduism* discussed on p. 423. The origin of the Trinity is elaborated on pp. 243-244. The discussion of St. Thomas Aquinas is on pp. 304-305.

Aslan, Raza, *No god but God: The Origins, Evolutions, and Future of Islam.* New York: Random House, 2011. A very readable recent statement of the development of Islam, which is drawn on frequently throughout this book. The description of Allah as Unity is from pp. 152-153.

Bashkarananda, Swami, *The Essentials of Hinduism.* Seattle" Viveka Press, 2002. This clear, brief guide is a very useful introduction. The alternate theory about the name *Hindu,* is on p. 2 and the names and descriptions of various gods and incarnations are drawn from Chapter VIII, God, pp. 65-78.

Campbell, Joseph, with Bill Moyers, Betty Sue Flowers, Editor, *The Power of Myth.* New York: Random House, Anchor Books, 1991. The quotation "'God' is an ambiguous word…" is from p. 56.

Collins, John J., *Introduction to the Hebrew Bible.* Minneapolis: Fortress Press, 2004. This valuable source on the Hebrew Scriptures is referred to often in this book and is the source of general background on the Hebrew idea of God for this chapter.

Cragg, Kenneth, *The Call of the Minaret.* New York: Oxford University

Press, 1956. A classic older study of Islam with sound basic explanations of the history.

Creel, H.G., *Confucius and the Chinese Way*. New York: Harper Torchbooks, 1949. Chapter IV, "Biography" provides a classic description of Confucius.

Creel, H.G., *Chinese Thought from Confucius to Mao Tse-tung*. New York; New American Library, 1953. An older basic resource on Daoism. Chapter 6, "The Mystical Skepticism of the Taoists" provides an overview. The quote about "Those who know..." is from p. 91.

Erdman, Bart D., *The New Testament: A Historical Introduction to the Christian Writings*. Sixth Edition, New York: Oxford University Press, 2016. The idea of salvation is found in Chapter 23, "The Gospel According to Paul," p. 401ff.

Eliade, Mircea, *The Sacred and the Profane*. New York: Harcourt, Inc., 1957. The key work for concepts of the sacred and profane. Direct quotations are "the manifestation of..." on p. 11, "corresponding to a terror..." from p. 64, and "recent discovery..." on p. 13.

Flood, Gavin, *An Introduction to Hinduism*. Cambridge, England: Cambridge University Press, 1996. A current scholarly work on Hinduism. The story of putting salt into water to teach about Brahman is on p. 85.

Harris, Ian, Consultant Editor, *The Complete Illustrated Encyclopedia of Buddhism: A Comprehensive Guide to Buddhist History, Philosophy, and Practice*. Wigston, England: Hermes House of Annes Press, 2011. Harris is joined by Helen Varley, Peter Connolly, and Stefania Travagnin in this visually delightful illustrated scholarly work. This author uses the name Siddata Gotama, for the name of Buddha, but you will also find Siddhatta and Siddhartha and Gautama, depending on translation from Pali or Sanskrit. I will use Siddhartha, which also matches the name used in the well-known novel of that title of the life of Buddha by Hermann Hesse. The dates for Siddhartha Gautama are on p. 14.

Hitchens, Christopher, *God Is Not Great: How Religion Poisons*

Everything. New York: Hatchett Group, 2007. Other books by the "New Atheists" include Richard Dawkins, *The God Delusions,* New York: Bantam Books, 2006, as well as Sam Harris, *The End of Faith,* New York: W.W. Norton, 2004.

Kaufman, Walter, *The Portable Nietzsche.* New York: Penguin Books, 1959. Selected writings edited and translated by Kaufmann along with a useful introduction to Nietzsche's life and ideas. Descriptions of his birth and family are on p. 7 ff.

Küng, Hans, *Does God Exist? An Answer for Today.* New York: Random House, 1981. The proofs of God's existence are summarized on pp. 530-531, including a fourth. Helpful extensive discussions of Marx, Freud, Feuerbach, and Nietzsche are found on pp. 192-403. This is a comprehensive work of scholarship by a Catholic Christian ecumenical theologian.

Lewis, Bernard, *The Crisis of Islam: Holy War and Unholy Terror.* New York: The Modern Library, 2003. A recent view of Islam in the modern world.

Morgan, Kenneth W., *The Religion of the Hindus.* New York: Ronald Press, 1953. A classic older study. See Chapter 2 "The Hindu Concept of God," p. 48ff.

Otto, Rudolph, *The Idea of the Holy.* Mansfield Centre, CT: Martino Publishing, 2010, originally published in 1923 by Oxford University Press. Otto provides and elaborates the concepts of "wholly other" and *"mysterium tremendum."*

Pascal, Blaise. For Pascal's Wager see Wikipedia. En.wikipedia. org/wiki/Pascal%27s_wager. This site provides background and the quotation. See also Britannica.com/topic/Pascals-wager.

Rainey, Lee Dian, *Decoding Dao, Reading the Dao De Ching and the Zhuangzi.* Malden, MA: Wiley Blackwell, 2014. In addition to unpacking two difficult texts, this is a comprehensive introduction to Daoism in its initial form. The description of Dao is drawn from Chapter Three, pp.49-68, and direct quotes are "the opposite of anything artificial..." p. 54 and "Daoist mysticism brings..." p. 212.

Smith, Houston, *Why Religion Matters*. San Francisco: Harper, 2001. Smith is one of the classic scholars and popularizers of world religions. In this later work, he attacks scientism extensively. The quotation about "the only path to truth" is actually taken by Smith from a review article by Timothy Ferris. The quotation that includes several religious questions—"who we are, etc."—is from p. 61.

Tillich, Paul, *The Courage to Be*. New Haven: Yale University Press,1952. Tillich was a well-known Christian theologian with a decidedly modern attitude, concerned about speaking to contemporary culture but within the Christian tradition. Ideas about God as Being-Itself and the "God above God" are found on pp. 184-186, but also elsewhere in Tillich's writing.

Waley, Arthur, *The Way and the Power: A Study of the Tao Te Ching*. New York: Grove Press, 1958. The text of the old Daoist classic with a useful introduction by Waley. The discrepancy between Tao and Dao derives from differing translation rules for Chinese.

Wordsworth, William, "I wandered lonely as a cloud" in Stephen Greenblatt, General Editor, *The Norton Anthology of English Literature*. New York: W. W. Norton & Company, 2006. The first two verses quoted here are on pp. 305-306.

2

Creation
Myth, Science, and the Survival of the Fittest

Y ou wanted to talk about creation this time. Thanks again for coming to my office.

No problem. It was a nice walk over here. The campus is beautiful at this time of year. I usually take a longer walk on the weekend and if there's a good view, I stop sometimes to take it in. I often wonder where it all came from and how we got here. I learned about evolution in high school biology, but the teacher covered it pretty fast. She seemed a little nervous. I know that there is still a huge amount of controversy between people with a religious view of creation based on the Bible, and those who hold to the scientific outlook of evolution. I don't know which side to take.

If you are asking "Where did it all come from?" you are asking one of the timeless questions. It's really quite mysterious, isn't it, and people have been asking that question for centuries. Before we take sides in the evolution controversy, let's explore the issues. Who knows, they could both be right. The Bible isn't the only place you will find religious ideas about creation, but before we examine any of the other religious traditions, let's review the scientific perspective to be sure that we have that account clearly in mind.

Good idea. I'm not sure I learned everything I was taught in biology. Besides, it's been a while.

Okay. Here we go. Evolution, though often called "the theory of evolution" is much more than a hypothesis, a theory to be proved. When sizeable sets of scientific findings begin to link together, the larger explanation that emerges is known as a theory. Evolution is that kind of theory, a well-established, comprehensive explanation of how human life began and developed. The theory continues to develop in its details as new evidence comes in, but the basic explanation is based on established fact. Scientists are good at that. Furthermore, the issues relating to the religious idea of creation range well beyond human evolution to the entire cosmos, a word used to describe the universe as an orderly system.

Let's begin with the Big Bang, not the TV show, but the idea that something dramatically forceful occurred (an expansion, not an explosion), setting in motion an outward movement in all directions from an "infinitely dense state" of "unimaginable tininess." Astronomers today are able to describe what happened "starting from the first billionth of a billionth of a second arriving at today, 13.8 billion years later." Eventually, from this intense inferno, a lot of stars were created and they formed into huge galaxies. As recently as 1924, Edwin Hubble—a telescope is named after him—demonstrated that "our" galaxy is not the only one, but that all around us, distant galaxies can be seen moving outward from a point of origin. We know that we live in an expanding universe and scientists once thought it would collapse, falling back in on itself, but now the evidence supports continuing expansion.

Our solar system (the sun and its planets) came into being around 4.5 billion years ago, the sun and the earth having approximately the same birthday. The Earth, a rotating disc of dust, eventually came together in a more solid mass, but then an accident occurred: a planet almost the size of Mars crashed into the earth, knocking off a piece that became the moon, and tipping the earth's axis of rotation, creating differing amounts of summer and winter daylight in temperate regions of the globe. Gradually, the earth cooled from a searing fireball into a more hospitable place with floating plates of granite continents, basalt ocean bottoms, and large liquid oceans—an arrangement unique in our solar system and (so far) in this universe. Scientists now speak of universes, in the plural.

So the earth itself evolved, not just life on earth. If we talk about creation, we need to think of the whole picture, and not just how the Bible conflicts with human evolution. This is much more than we covered in class. But go on, review the evolution of life for me.

In five minutes? Somewhere around four billion years ago, methane-producing microbes came into existence and everything thereafter descended from these earliest forms of life. The planet was ruled by these boring little singleton cells and microbial slime for over a billion years. Then 2.7 billion years ago—we know these years from scientific dating methods—something amazing happened: the microbes developed the capacity to draw energy from sunlight through a process of making food from carbon dioxide and water, which today we call photosynthesis. The process also produced oxygen, and the release of this new oxygen plunged the earth into a cooling crisis causing some parts of the earth to freeze—global cooling. Plants evolved and eventually simple animals. As more complex life forms developed there was an explosion of new life in what geologists call the Cambrian Age, leaving traces of some very odd-looking creatures in rock fossils. Then comes the first extinction, destroying 85% of marine life and two-thirds of terrestrial life. But enough life survived to continue developing new species, in particular forms of animals that eventually led to humans.

So it was certainly not six days or even 10,000 years. And we know this through scientific methods of dating fossils and other materials. I'm remembering from my class something about the first human originating in Africa. Didn't they find some young girl there?

You might be referring to Lucy, the remains of a small woman discovered in 1974 in modern-day Ethiopia. She was a pre-human ancestor called *Australopithecus,* and by using sophisticated dating methods, scientists were able to determine the astounding age of the remains at 3.2 million years. And yes, she gets her name from a Beatles song that was playing at the base camp that night, "Lucy in the Sky with Diamonds." I'm not kidding.

Maybe they were high on LSD or something. This story sounds just too fantastic: ordinary people finding their long lost three-million-year-old ancestor. Naming her Lucy. But it's true, isn't it?

The full story is this. Apes split into two separate species about six million years ago, one line leading toward chimpanzees, the other line heading toward...

McDonalds. I'm sorry, I just couldn't resist that.

You're right...toward McHumans. About four million years ago some of these descendants started walking upright, like Lucy and her *Australopithecus* relatives. About two million years ago, a larger brainy biped (walking on two feet) started using tools and was given the genus (classification) name *homo*, meaning man. Somewhere between 100,000 and 200,000 years ago, a new group within the genus *homo* evolved, an individual that was less heavily built, more mobile, and supposedly with greater cognitive flexibility. This group was given the name *homo sapiens.* That's us.

Other *homo sapiens* like Neanderthals became extinct, while our ancestors migrated all over the world from a small group in Africa. We know this from mitochondrial DNA lineages. There is some controversy over whether we are still evolving, but many scientists say that we are not, that we are in an evolutionary stasis. Darwin's great contribution was to suggest how the process of evolution worked and to show the relationship of mankind, *homo sapiens,* to other animals. If you deny this, you are doubting the foundation of modern medicine, which is based on the human connection to other forms of animal life. Think about how we test our new medicines on animals first.

When I go to a natural history museum, I often see the skeleton of a huge dinosaur, and it has those same two leg bones and same two arm bones that we have, so I guess we must be related. I like this scientific description of the world we live in, but where does religion fit in? It seems like Adam and Eve don't have a leg to stand on, so to speak, after the scientific description you have provided.

You are referring to the creation stories in the Christian Bible and Hebrew Scriptures: Genesis, Chapters 1 through 3. Actually, we find two creation stories there, one focusing more on the cosmos, the other on the creation of mankind. Both include differing accounts of the creation of humans. Let's review them.

The first account, (Genesis 1 through Genesis 2, verse 4a) describes the creation of the heavens and the earth over a six-day period that includes setting apart light and dark; separating upper and lower waters to make sky, then land, then vegetation; putting the sun, moon, and stars in place, and separating day and night; creating water, air, and land creatures and eventually humans along with vegetation for food. Then God rests, creating the Sabbath.

The second story (Genesis 2, verse 4b through Genesis 3) focuses on the creation of humanity, *adam* being the generic Hebrew word for human being. Not much is said about the cosmos. The setting for the dramatic scene is the lush Garden of Eden, where Adam is created by the breath of God and Eve through Adam's rib. The scholars who study these Scriptures note that the first story comes from a Priestly source, with its dignified language and majestic descriptions, while the second story, which uses Yahweh for the name of God, is of the Yahwistic source and presents a folksy and humorous account of the mischief of Adam and Eve as they are discovered trying to hide from Yahweh after their disobedience. He comes calling after them like a person "Where are you?" These are the basic creation myths of the Jewish, Christian, and, to a certain extent, Islamic traditions.

Hold on a minute. Did you refer to these stories as myths? Don't most people consider myths to be something that isn't true, like a rumor or the conspiracy theories that appear on social media.

Yes, most of us grew up with the idea that a myth is something that is not true: a widely held but false belief. "That's just a myth," we say. But the dictionary definition of myth suggests. "a traditional story of ostensibly historical events that serves to unfold part of the world view of a people or explain a practice, belief, or natural phenomenon." In the words of Joseph Campbell, perhaps the world's foremost student and collector of myths, these are the stories told "to interpret the mysteries of life." Myths contain "metaphors for what lies behind the visible world." We might say that myth is the story form of ancient religious traditions. But why myth? If you have no science, no concept of historical accuracy, no interest in the facts but only the meaning of experience, then you compose the most powerful and fantastic story you can to make your point. From the viewpoint of the story teller, a myth is true in its own intent as a story with a profound message about something mysterious or unexplained.

We today are children of the Enlightenment, a period of history marked by scientific discovery, empirical observation, and a new approach to language that matches words and concepts to observable reality. Blossoming in the 1600s out of the work of Descartes, Spinoza, Galileo, Francis Bacon, Isaac Newton, Johannes Kepler, and many others, it brought forth observation based on scientific rules of evidence. Eventually a new concept of history emerged as well, based on verifiable historical facts. The result was a new idea of truth, that made every other mode of expression "not true." Most of the progress made in modern civilization (to the extent that one sees progress) is due to the outlook and methods of the Enlightenment. To sum up the Enlightenment outlook, we might say "a tree is a tree." Oh, to be sure there were wonderful arguments about whether the tree really exists "out there' in reality or only in the perceiving mind. But in general, the Enlightenment philosophy was that the word *tree* corresponds (refers) to an actual tree that can be studied, examined, and understood. It was a huge breakthrough for civilization.

Did those who created the earliest religious traditions have the tools of the Enlightenment? Surely not! What did they have? Myth. The ability to construct clever, beautiful, and profound stories to try to explain the mysteries of life they didn't understand. Because we are children of the Enlightenment, it is not easy for us to comprehend the myths, legends, sagas, and epics of the ancient religious traditions. But one thing we don't want to do is to take them literally. Did God actually make the world in six days? Only if you are a literalist, reading religious writing as if every word were literally true, or even worse, dictated by God. And literalism is not just a problem for the readers of Hebrew and Christian scriptures; it is a problem for anyone who seeks to understand the religious literature of the ancient world. Many literalists still exist today.

Now you probably see more clearly the conflict between those who read the myths of the Bible literally and the scientific Darwinists. The pointless and unnecessary battle still rages, when it might be far wiser to say, "Once you understand science and once you appreciate myth, maybe they are in a sense both right, but on completely different terms." There need not be a battle of the survival of the fittest explanation here. They are both fit for different purposes and can be seen as complementary not conflicting.

Are there other creation myths? If I had some examples, maybe I could get a better understanding of what a myth is.

Some of the oldest come from the ancient civilizations of Egypt. One tells of a rising of land out of the waters of Nun, providing a primeval mound where the first deity could come into existence, taking the shape of a falcon, heron, or some other bird. Another myth from Egypt suggests that a primeval lotus rose up out of the waters and opened to reveal an infant god. Note a concept that differs from Genesis in these myths: an existing world creates god, not the other way around.

African myths from Mali and Zambia suggest that the universe came from the vibrations of a cosmic egg, a parallel to the Big Bang theory, perhaps, but much tamer and on a smaller scale. Another African myth suggests that in the beginning there was emptiness and that emptiness was filled with knowing, the prime creative force of the universe, and eventually became human consciousness. An abstract myth or profound philosophy?

Native American traditions of North America are rich in creation myths. The Pawnees describe how Tirawa, a primordial deity, ordered the sun and the moon to unite and produce the first man. The morning star and evening star were ordered to produce the first woman. Natives to the American Southwest tell how the supreme divinity created Mother Earth and Father Sky. Many Native American myths include animals, such as the idea that the earth rests on the back of a turtle, or that a spider wove a web that eventually formed earth. Another tradition suggests that the Earth Diver swam to the bottom of the primal sea and picked up a handful of mud which then expanded to form the earth.

A favorite story—there are many versions of this story—of the Ute Indians (residing in Utah and Colorado) tells how Sinauf, the god who kept the world in order, was preparing for a journey by packing a bag with sticks. His brother Coyote, curious and mischievous, cut a hole in the bag to peek. Sinauf threw the bag over his shoulder and started off. Unfortunately (or is it fortunately?) the bag had a hole in it and as he walked along, the sticks fell out; but they weren't sticks anymore, they were people scattered everywhere in families, bands, and tribes. In the end, Sinauf discovered what happened as he looked in his bag and found it almost empty. The remaining people, he lifted out carefully, naming them Utikes, and giving them a special land to have in the mountains.

In an ancient Japanese myth, at a time when the universe resembled floating oil drifting like a jellyfish, Izanagi appeared with his sister Izanami and they stood together on a Floating Bridge of Heaven. (Maybe a rainbow?) They stirred the sea below with a jeweled spear, and when they lifted it from the water, drops fell off and formed the first solid land. Even though they were brother and sister, they decided to procreate. Izanagi (the male) asked his sister Izanami how her body was formed. She told him there was one place where it was formed insufficiently, and he said that was interesting because he had a place that was formed to excess. He suggested that they unite these two points. Their first child Hiruko, the Leech Child, was deformed and as might be expected, the mother/sister was blamed, but when they tried again, she produced a series of gods and goddesses, mountains, trees, and winds.

Oh, I love these stories, but I know they are meant to be more than stories, so help me to understand them. How do I interpret myth?

The key word is *interpret* because we can't take myths literally. We have to take off our Enlightenment glasses and put on our spectacular spectacles reserved for reading myths, suspending our scientific use of language for the moment as we develop our ability to use the metaphorical thinking of the ancients to see what light they might have shed on the mysteries of creation. The question becomes: Is it possible to find the message behind the myth?

I need to go on a short detour here to explain something, so bear with me. The issue of myth was raised directly in a short essay (44 pages) by Rudolph Bultmann, translated from the original German into English in 1953 as *Kerygma and Myth,* kerygma meaning "the core message." He also delivered a set of lectures at Yale and Vanderbilt universities that were published as *Jesus Christ and Mythology* in 1958. Bultmann was a well-known Protestant Christian theologian from Marburg, Germany, who presented the idea that the New Testament message was set forth in myth, and that one had to "demythologize" to arrive at the central affirmation of faith apart from its setting.

Bultmann is aware of the "cosmology of the pre-scientific age" and regards it as an "obsolete view of the world" that we can no longer accept "in our everyday life." It is an age of miracles, a soon-to-end world, where Jesus atones for the sins of man through his own blood, and Bultmann regards this as primitive mythology. To get to the basic message, he suggests that we need to demythologize.

The analysis is sound and the need is great, but the task is not easy. Consider the comparison of demythologizing to peeling away layers of an onion, allowing the onion to represent the myth. How far do you go down into the onion to get to the core? It is not like a peach or an avocado, with an obvious stopping point. Maybe what is left as core is still onion—in this case, still myth. Maybe after much effort all you are left with is a pile of onion layers and dripping eyes. The onion comparison suggests that it is not easy to know which words and concepts to cut out or pass over in the account and which to keep. The remaining core may still be myth.

But this is not what Bultmann means by de-mythologizing. The main challenge of demythologizing is not cutting out certain passages (peeling the onion), but the task of interpretation. Leave the myth in place as the means of expression used at the time, and try to get behind, beyond, or around the mythological language to a meaning that makes sense in our world today. In Bultmann's own words—I have the book of lectures right here—"This method of interpreting the New Testament which tries to recover the deeper meaning behind the mythological conception, I call demythologizing. Its aim is not to eliminate the mythological statements but to interpret them."

Bultmann also had some useful comments about myth. "Myths express the knowledge that man is not master of the world and of his life, that the world within which he lives is full of riddles and mysteries and that human life is also full of riddles and mysteries." He said that "the real purpose of myth is not to present an objective picture of the world as it is, but to express man's understanding of himself in the world in which he lives." It is the "understanding of existence" that myth provides.

So, the emphasis should be on interpretation. Can you guide me through the process of interpretation? What should I look for and how do I get to the deeper message?

One place to begin is with the idea of an *explanation*, technically referred to as an *etiology*, usually a description of where something came from or why it is the way it is. If you go back and read the Adam and Eve story in Genesis, you will find in the text a lot of explanations. The maker of the myth, in telling us that Eve was born from Adam's rib, explains why men have one fewer number of ribs than women. One of the punishments for Eve is that there is pain in childbirth. Adam's punishment is that man has to toil his whole life with sweat on his face. Even the poor snake has to slither along in the dust. These are all etiologies, and you can learn to spot them in myths. Some of them are small matters that make you smile, but others deal with larger existential concerns: Where did all of this come from? Why am I here? Does it have any point?

The Japanese creation story provides a humorous etiology of physical sexual differences, but the larger message is about an almost magical creation of islands from droplets of ocean water, something rather different from the six-day project of Genesis. If you find yourself being disturbed by the idea of first ancestors being brother and sister, realize that incest is a problem in creation myths because there is no one else around to procreate with except for close relatives. Adam and Eve produced Cain and Able, and suddenly Cain has a wife (Genesis 4). Adam is probably wondering: Where did *she* come from? Did Cain or Able procreate with their mother, my wife Eve? In the Japanese myth, things don't work out the first time (sound familiar?) but after that, brother and sister create gods, goddesses, mountains, trees, and wind, a rather glorious and beautiful incestual procreation by siblings. Are these myth makers telling us that this creation, like all creation, took effort, starting from something small, resulting in initial failure, but eventually multiplying into something grand?

In the Ute Indian myth, on one of Sinauf's spontaneous journeys, humans fall out of a bag with a hole cut in it by the mischievous Coyote. This gives us an etiology of families, bands, and tribes, but is the story also telling us that our existence is accidental and random? (We know from studies of sperms and eggs just how random it is.) Or is the Ute myth placing humans in their proper place in nature? God went for a walk on a mountain path, unwittingly creating other tribes, and at the end of the journey pulled out the Utes, a special people made out of what was left? Myths contain explanations of mysteries, small, medium, and large.

Another thing to look for is the theme, the main point, sometimes shared with other myths. One of the main points of the first creation story in Genesis is the bringing of order out of chaos. Creation is considered to be the work of God, but there is the theme that it is an orderly creation, with everything reliable and working together, the sun and moon in place, night and day, not chaos. The Ute god, Sinauf, keeps everything in order. The additional mystery is that creation holds together and has order. It actually works, and on a grand scale. That takes some explaining.

Most of the creation myths also express a sense of awe and amazement. Even something as simple as the African myth of a gigantic vibrating cosmic egg has that sense of awe such as they must have felt as they saw "something more" in the hatching of an egg. As you dig deeper behind the myths, you begin to see that most of them provide explanations for our being, growing out of the fundamental human questions about the purpose and meaning of existence. It is not so much the answer they provide that catches our attention; it is the timeless question that prompted their answer.

Now I can see things in these myths that I was missing. I was wondering if there are creation myths in the major world religions. They do have creation myths, don't they?

Some of them more clearly than others. One has an elaborate cosmology (descriptions of an orderly universe) if not an actual creation myth. So, let's take a look.

Hinduism is a little complicated. Because there are so many

Gods and such a long tradition, Hinduism has more than one theory of creation. Remember that brahman is the one and only source and cause of everything, behind all of the gods. If we ask, "Who was there before creation?" it would be brahman. And if we ask, "What was brahman like before creation? Hindus would say "in a very abstract transcendental state...beyond our time, space, and causation." As such, God is not "he" or "she" but THAT, the Supreme Spirit. In the famous *Creation Hymn* of the Rig-Veda, we have a creation myth full of questions. Notice that brahman is referred to as That.

> Not non-existent nor existent was it at that time:
> There was not atmosphere nor the heavens which are beyond.
> What existed? Where? In whose care?
> Water was it? An abyss unfathomable?
> Neither mortal was there nor immortal then;
> Not of night, of day was there distinction:
> That alone breathed windless through inherent power.
> Other than That there was naught else.

Here we have a "before-creation myth" attempting to imagine what there was before creation, as if to try to answer what there was prior to the Big Bang. And what was God like before creation? Only transcendent and not yet manifest. Oddly, the "Creation Hymn" ends on a note of profound skepticism.

> This world—whence it came into being,
> whether it was made or whether not—
> He who is the overseer of the highest Heavens surely knows—
> Or perhaps He knows not!

Maybe even God does not know if the world was created or not. How's that for an example of an unsolved mystery? Even God can't solve it.

From this sublime and profound myth, we turn to another Hindu creation story in the later part of the Rig-Veda. It tells how the gods sacrifice and dismember a cosmic giant to use his body parts to create the cosmos, society, and even the verses of the Veda itself—winner, perhaps, of an Oscar for the most violent creation myth, but suggesting to us that creation itself involved struggle and violence.

One of the questions raised about Hindu belief is whether the created world is real. The concept of *māyā* as illusion, suggests that it is not. One explanation of this asks us to think of a magician who casts a hypnotic spell on his audience and induces them to see a tree on stage with him. The tree is an illusion, but it is real to the audience. To the magician it is not a real tree. To mankind under the sway of *māyā* creation is real, but from God's standpoint, He (That) has not created the world we perceive. It is not quite fair, therefore, to say that Hindus believe that the real world is an illusion. It is interesting to speculate, however, on the extent to which the so-called reality on which we base our daily life is real or illusory. "Reality" is the reality our human brain is able to perceive, which may be quite different from the reality perceived by a dog or an ant, or a Hindu god.

Another Hindu view of creation is that brahman in a transcendental state takes the form of a more personal God, Īshvara, who has three basic aspects: Brahmā, the creator God, Vishnu the preserver, and Shiva the destroyer. These are well-known gods worshipped in Hinduism and they play different roles in creating, sustaining, and, yes, destroying the universe. (Let's resist calling them the Hindu Trinity.) The interesting idea here is that creation is more than a one-time act in the beginning, but involves the follow-up work of keeping the universe running, along with the notion that a god needs to be in charge if and when the world comes to an end.

The idea of sustaining the universe is elaborated in a book by Mircea Eliade entitled *The Myth of the Eternal Return, or Cosmos and History*. After studying the myths of many ancient civilizations, Eliade was struck by the number of cultures that have myths about starting over and making new beginnings, with elaborate rituals for pleading with the gods to return. Eliade calls these the myths of eternal return, and they reflect not only the human concern for the sustainability of creation, but a sometimes, frantic effort to avoid desertion by the creator gods. Please come back for another year. Don't leave us here alone to perish. We need you to keep everything running smoothly. Hinduism has Brahmā the creator god, but also Vishnu, the preserver.

Would Confucianism be one of those religions without a creation myth?

Confucianism was primarily concerned about social structure, building the social order and governing properly. Although some rulers seem to have the blessing of Heaven, it is not exactly clear what Heaven is. A supernatural power perhaps? An impersonal force in nature? It seems safe to say that whatever Heaven is it deserves no credit for the creation of the universe. Let's just say that Confucius had other concerns and took creation to be what it was: primarily a mess during the Warring States period when he lived and taught.

As for Daoism, with its undefinable Dao somehow embedded in nature, Dao does not create the world as the theistic God of the Bible. Dao is compared to the root of a plant, implying that the root is a part of, not separated from the plant. So, the idea of God, standing apart from the world and then creating it, does not fit Daoism very well. Although there is no creation myth, there is a notable passage in the *Dao De Ching* that speaks to the process of creation.

> There was something formless yet complete,
> That existed before heaven and earth;
> Without sound, without substance,
> Dependent on nothing, unchanging,
> All pervading, unfailing.
> One may think of it as the mother of all things under heaven.
> It's true name we do not know
> 'Way' is the by-name we give it.

Dao appears to be part of creation, part of nature, not something that creates it. Perhaps it is best in Daoism not to worry about the source of creation, but to find the Way and follow it.

What about Islam?

Islam, as we have seen, tends to incorporate, selectively, ideas and practices from Judaism and Christianity, so from the Islamic perspective we must assume that Allah is the same creator God found in these earlier religions because there is no god but Allah. One small mention is made in the Quran that has a mythological ring to it, the statement that the Lord created man from clots of blood. Clots of blood? Scabs? Or is it the idea that the lifeblood itself is the source of human existence?

As for Buddhism, recall that Siddhartha Gautama, the Buddha, (485 BCE–410 or 400 BCE) was born into a thriving culture of Hinduism with Sanskrit oral traditions dating back to 1500 BCE. Buddhism draws many things from Hinduism, but it is more than a reform movement; it is a new path. Buddha appropriated many Hindu ideas, such as *samsāra* (rebirth) and *karma* (the accumulated result of good and bad deeds.) It is doubtful, however, that Buddha accepted Hindu ideas about creation. He saw belief in the all-powerful Hindu creator god Brahmā as a mistaken belief because such a god would then be responsible for suffering. It is said that Buddha searched but could find no evidence for the existence of a creator god or an eternal soul. What did develop in early Buddhism was a rather elaborate cosmology of places and times for rebirth, what some call reincarnation.

I have friends who often speak glibly about reincarnation, saying things such as "I'd love to have another shot at life" or "Wouldn't it be cool to come back as an eagle?"

This is not the *samsāra* of Buddhism. As a wealthy young man who had been sheltered from life, Buddha was shocked in his early wanderings as he came face to face with old age, suffering, and death. This was not a good life to be repeated, but a horrible existence to be avoided. The goal was to escape the endless cycle of rebirth, to be lifted up to another realm, or while remaining in this life, to be of help to those who are suffering.

In Buddhism, therefore, we find a complex cosmology of imagined extraterrestrial spheres and realms, a sphere being globe-shaped concentric shells into which suns, moons, and stars are set, and realms being regions (like kingdoms) within a sphere. It is possible to be reborn in any sphere or realm and be there for eons (thousands and thousands of years). The goal is to reach a state of Enlightenment where one no longer inhabits a sphere of existence. The extensive Buddhist spiritual cosmos not only requires considerable space but a lot of time as well. If Buddhism doesn't have much to say about the created world, it has a lot to say about extraterrestrial spheres and realms.

It would be easy to dismiss this description of spheres and realms as only myth, but let's promise ourselves never to say "only" with regard to myth and to look behind myth for some deeper meaning. What could this be with the Buddhist spheres and realms? Perhaps the human drama is played on a far larger stage than we realize, including the characters that come before us and those that come after, and we are all playing out our lives over a huge expanse of space and time. Could that be the Buddhist message? We are recycled through a world of realms and spheres over eons that make the creation of the natural world on earth almost irrelevant. In Buddhism, the drama of the individual life in its quest for ultimate release is of paramount concern and gives cosmic importance to human existence.

My head is swirling with so many interesting ideas about creation, I hardly know how to sort them out. But I guess that's the point: having more ideas to stimulate deeper thinking about the mystery of the origin and meaning of life. But what if I just stick with the scientific explanation? It seems easier to accept and more familiar, but I'm not sure it answers all of my questions about life.

It is natural to seek a resolution of the conflict over evolution and creation, to decide which theory is the fittest. If science and religion have not worked out a comfortable compatibility, at least there have been efforts in both domains to build bridges. The French Catholic Jesuit priest and theologian Pierre Teilhard de Chardin was also a biologist and paleontologist. He wrote extensively about evolution in *The Phenomenon of Man*. The scientist and mathematician Albert Einstein wrote about religion in *The World as I see It* and stated that he was a deeply religious man. It may be best to let each area do what it does best, knowing that science is good at theory-building from empirical observation and that religion does its best work through myth to raise and address the timeless questions of meaning and purpose.

Let me provide you with an example of an on-going scientific quest recently reported in the news. Scientists have been trying to figure out for a long time why there is matter (material substance). Instead of what? Space filled with energy but no solid substance. Apparently, it could have happened, and, of course, that would not have been good for us. Recent discoveries are helping to build the case that the presence of matter in the universe has something to do with neutrinos, ghostly, quirky little subatomic particles. It looks like neutrinos, in the first moments of the Big Bang, tipped the balance toward matter rather than energy without solid substance.

We could make a very bad pun and ask, "Does it really matter?" But, in fact, it does matter. It is a very important scientific question and no one should play down its importance or threaten to eliminate the funding that supports such research. We need to know. But let's assume that in a few years we *do* know; we establish with greater certainty that it is the slippery little neutrino that makes the difference between a universe with matter as opposed to one without matter. What do we know when we know that?

We know why there is matter. That's what you know if you stick with your scientific explanation. But we don't know the answer to the deeper religious and philosophical questions: Why is there anything? Why are there universes? Why is there a planet Earth on which complex life evolved? Why is there this puzzling creature named *homo sapiens?* Is our existence purposeful, accidental, or irrelevant? These are the timeless questions that give rise to religious speculations about cosmos and creation. Perhaps the religious traditions don't provide satisfying, modern-day explanations of the mysteries of life, but they surely sharpen the problem and demonstrate how inventive humankind has been in concocting explanations.

Yes, I'm impressed with how imaginative some of these myths are. Do we still use myths in our daily lives?

Science makes clear that we don't live on the second floor of a three-story universe with heaven up and hell down. So why do the bright and intelligent people who win Oscars at the Academy Awards look upward with the palms of their hands together when they thank God or refer to their deceased parents? Maybe we like to hang on to the "myth of up" for reassurance because it is much too frightening to picture ourselves as we really are: hanging on upside down in a no-up-or-down world with our feet glued to the earth by gravity, hurtling outward through space as fast as a rocket. Maybe we need the "myth of up" to get through the week.

References

The references for scientific information are presented first and separately here:

Ferris, Timothy, *Coming of Age in the Milky Way.* New York: William Morrow and Company, 1988. The science of astronomy along with the history of major discoveries. A source for the history of the universe.

Gould, Stephen Jay, *Wonderful Life: The Burgess Shale and the Nature of History.* New York: W.W. Norton, 1989. Although some of the details have been challenged, this account of the Cambrian Explosion of life forms is fascinating reading. The numerous sketches of odd-looking creatures bring to life the fossil findings in the Canadian Rockies northwest of Calgary.

Mack, Katie, *The End of Everything (Astronomically Speaking).* New York: Scribner (Simon & Schuster), 2020. A very recent source on astronomy that confirms theories of the Big Bang and expanding universe. This book becomes an important source in Chapter 7 "The End of the World." The idea of "expansion, not explosion" is on p. 12. The phrase "infinitely dense state" is on p. 32 and "unimaginable tininess" is on p. 38. The quotation "starting at the first billionth..." and ending with the date of 13.8 billion years ago, is on p. 32.

Moche, Dinar L., *Astronomy: A Self-Teaching Guide.* New York: John Wiley & Sons, 2009. A valuable introduction to the findings and methods of astronomy.

Olson, Steve, *Mapping Human History.* New York: Houghton Mifflin, 2002. Excellent source on human origins with the dates and names summarized on p. 19.

Sagan, Carl, *The Dragons of Eden: Speculations on the Evolution of Human Intelligence.* New York: Ballantine Books, 1977.

Sagan, Carl, *Cosmos.* New York: Ballantine Books, 1980. A best-selling classic that brings together the findings of many scientific disciplines to tell the story of the universe. It became the basis for a popular television series.

The references on world religions and myth are listed here:

Agnes, Michael, Editor in Chief, *Webster's New World College Dictionary,* Fourth Edition. New York: Wiley Publishers, 2010. Contains the dictionary definition of myth.

Armstrong, Karen, *The Lost Art of Scripture: Rescuing the Sacred Texts.*

New York: Knopf, 2019. An excellent summary of the Enlightenment is found here with the names of key figures found on pp. 345-412.

Aslan, Reza, *No god but God.* New York: Random House, 2011. The idea of Creation from Blood clots is quoted from the Quran (96: 1-5) on p. 34.

Bhaskarananda, Swami, *The Essentials of Hinduism.* Seattle: Viveka Press, 2002. The discussion of what came before creation is provided here, p. 66, as well as the quotes from the Rig-Veda "Creation Hymn," pp. 171-172. This is also the source of the explanation of *māyā* as comparable to a magician's creation of illusion, pp. 170-171.

Bultmann, Rudolph, *Jesus Christ and Mythology.* London: SCM Press, 1958. Lectures delivered at Yale Divinity School and Vanderbilt University in 1951. The quotation "This method of interpreting the New Testament..." is from p. 18. The quotation "Myths express the knowledge that man..." is from p. 19.

Bultmann, Rudolph, *Kerygma and Myth: A Theological Debate.* New York: Harper & Brothers, 1953. Bultmann's essay on demythologizing is followed by criticisms by colleagues and replies from Bultmann. Quoted phrases are "cosmology of the pre-scientific age" from p. 3, "obsolete view of the world" from p. 3, "in our everyday life" from p. 4, "the real purpose of myth..." from p. 10, and "understanding of existence" from p. 11.

Campbell, Joseph, with Bill Moyers, *The Power of Myth.* New York: Random House, 1988. An edited transcription of the Moyer interviews with Campbell which became the basis of the six-hour PBS television series on mythology. Quotations are "to interpret the mysteries of life" on p. xvii and "metaphors for what lies behind the visible world" on p. xviii.

Chardin, Pierre Teilhard de, *The Phenomenon of Man.* New York: Harper Torchbooks, 1955. An effort to reconcile the views of religion and science.

Collins, John J., *Introduction to the Hebrew Bible.* Minneapolis, Fortress

Press, 2004. The descriptions of the two creation stories are on p. 75ff. (the cosmos) and p. 67ff. (Adam and Eve).

Einstein, Albert, *The World as I see It.* New York: Philosophical Library, 1949. Einstein wrote about his life and discusses religion.

Eliade, Mircea, *The Myth of the Eternal Return, or Cosmos and History.* Princeton: Princeton University Press, 1954. The thesis is that widespread sustainer myths supplement creation myths in ancient cultures.

Flood, Gavin, *An Introduction to Hinduism.* Cambridge: Cambridge University Press, 1996. A comprehensive scholarly work. The creation myth about the dismembered cosmic giant is on p. 48.

Harris, Ian, Consultant Editor, *The Complete Illustrated Encyclopedia of Buddhism: A Comprehensive Guide to Buddhist History, Philosophy, and Practice.* Wigston, England: Hermes House of Annes Press, 2011. The idea that Buddha searched for but could not find a creator god is on p. 36. The concepts of spheres and realms are on p. 40. Eons are described on p. 36.

Lippman, Thomas W. *Understanding Islam.* New York: Penguin Group, 2002. The creation from blood clots is mentioned on p. 37.

Overbye, Dennis, "Neutrinos at Heart of Matter?" Science Times section of *The New York Times,* Tuesday, April 28, 2020. The discussion of matter and neutrinos is drawn from this article on page D1.

Rainey, Lee Diane, *Confucius and Confucianism.* Malden, MA, John Wiley-Blackwell, 2010, Observations about the lack of a creator god in Confucianism are found on p. 62.

Rainey, Lee Diane, *Decoding Dao: Reading the Dao De Jing and the Zhuangzi.* New York: John Wiley & Sons, 2014. Absence of a creator god and the metaphor of the root are found on p. 534.

<utahindians.org/archives/ute/early Peoples. Html> This is the source of the Ute Creation myth.

Waley, Arthur, *The Way and Its Power: A Study of the Tao Te Ching and Its Place in Chinese Thought.* New York: Grove Press, 1958. This is a classic translation with extensive commentary. The quoted passage is from p. 174, designated as Chapter xxv of the *Tao Te Ching.*

Willis, Roy, General Editor, *World Mythology.* New York: Sterling Publishing, also Duncan Baird Publishers, 2006. Paraphrased summaries of creation myths are from brief descriptions provided here, including the Egyptian, p. 38; Native American pp. 222-223; and Japanese, pp.112-113.

3
Human Nature
The Game Between the Devils and the Angels

I live in a small house, a rented bungalow over on Walnut Street, within walking distance of here. This morning my elderly neighbor stopped by to bring me a slice of homemade coffeecake for my breakfast. I don't even know her that well. I guess it was just one of those unexpected acts of kindness. As she left, I had a phone call that turned out to be an obvious scam, and I ended up asking the caller how he could sleep at night spending all day trying to trick innocent people out of their credit card numbers, bank accounts, and email passwords to get at their cash. I didn't raise my voice; I just spoke calmly because I was hoping to get him to think about what he's doing. Now I'm a little confused. Are people basically good or basically bad? Does religion have anything to say about that?

You're asking about the timeless question of human nature: Are we more like the Saint, Mother Teresa, or the Nazi leader, Hitler? Well, that's a little extreme, but I think that's your question. Although we tend to think of religion as being mostly about the ways people think about God and the cosmos, the world's religious traditions have had important things to say about human nature. It's a bit of a mystery, isn't it? Let's begin with something we mentioned last time but didn't discuss.

You may have noticed that I didn't say much about the Adam and Eve story when we were talking about creation. That's because it is part of the creation myth, but is mostly about human nature. It's a good place to start our discussion today. Recall that in the Garden of Eden, Adam and Eve were asked not to eat the fruit of the tree of the Knowledge of Good and Evil, under the threat of death. Neither could they eat from the tree of life, which turns out to be a sustainer of longevity. They could eat from the other trees, just not these. The snake tells Eve "no worries" and assures her that if you eat from that tree, your eyes will be opened, and you will be like God, knowing good and evil. A talking snake? Literally?

Well, Adam and Eve know the instructions and consequences of their actions, but they do it anyway. So, Eve takes some fruit from the tree and gives some to Adam. Their eyes were indeed opened! They became self-conscious not only about being naked, but self-aware as humans.

From our discussion of myth, we understand now how to look for etiologies, the explanations of why things are as they are. Besides explaining self-conscious human shame about nakedness, a more trivial etiology, there is the larger explanation of our freedom to choose and the human tendency to do what we know we shouldn't do. The critical metaphor, however, is the Tree of Knowledge. Is the writer, or the teller of this tale, saying that when humans eat of this tree, they know something that all of the other animals don't know? And in knowing this, do humans become like God? What is it we know?

Naturally there is a lot of disagreement about the symbolism of this tree, but let's suppose that our special knowledge as humans is that we know we are going to die. In addition, we have a sense of time. We hear the clock ticking and we know what's coming. We have a self-awareness that other animals don't have. And even though we know what is right and wrong (knowledge of good and evil), we have trouble doing the right thing because we focus on our own interests and satisfactions first. All of this makes us very anxious in a way that other creatures are not anxious—well, maybe with the exception of those twitchy squirrels we can see out there from my office window.

Modern philosophers call this "existential anxiety," meaning a "pervasive unease about oneself and one's existence." We have a fundamental nervousness about who we are, where we are going, and how long life will last. Some people are very much aware of this anxiety, and others tend to put it out of their mind—a psychologist would say "repress it." Whether in or out of mind, it is always there lurking beneath the surface. Some people don't recognize it until an unusual experience jolts them into identifying it. Because people are free to do what they want, they do odd things to try to deal with it, such as living in a monastery in a state of perpetual silence, becoming a workaholic, or playing golf three days a week to forget everything but improving their score. Do these responses help to manage existential anxiety? Maybe. Maybe not.

The Jewish people had a long history of this kind of anxious disobedience which they eventually called sin, both personal and social. Sin was not only breaking certain rules and laws, but doing what was damaging to other people and displeasing to God. Many of the stories in the rest of the Hebrew scriptures describe this human tendency to do the wrong thing, tale after tale of human nature as disobedience.

Because the Adam and Eve story is cast as a creation myth, it is natural (but mistaken) to think that it was among the first things to be written down by the authors of the Hebrew scriptures, like a novelist would begin "In the beginning..." or "Once upon a time..." Although placed first, in the Book of Genesis, the story actually comes into existence at a relatively late date among the other Jewish writings as a summative description of human nature after Israel's many years of discouraging struggle.

The theme of "existential anxiety" is picked up in the Christian Gospel of Matthew, which contains an extended collection of the teachings of Jesus known as the Sermon on the Mount. The 'sermon" ranges over many topics, but Jesus is portrayed here as having some very important things to say about being anxious:

> "Therefore, I tell you, do not be anxious about your life, what you shall eat or what you shall drink, nor about your body, what you shall put on. Is not life more than food, and the body more than clothing?
>
> Look at the birds of the air: they neither sow nor reap nor gather into barns, and yet your Heavenly Father feeds them. Are you not of more value than they?
>
> And which of you by being anxious can add one cubit to his span of life?
>
> And why are you anxious about clothing? Consider the lilies of the field, how they grow; they neither toil nor spin; yet I tell you, even Solomon in all of his glory was not arrayed like one of these. But if God so clothes the grass of the field, which today is alive and tomorrow is thrown into the oven, will He not much more clothe you, O men of little faith?
>
> Therefore, do not be anxious saying 'What shall we eat?' or 'What shall we wear?"
>
> —Matthew 6: 25-31 (Revised Standard Version)

The teachings of Jesus, not just here but generally, seem so impossible to follow that we wonder if they are worth considering, but we need to remember that Jesus was part of a movement in those times that fostered the apocalyptic belief that the world was coming to an end soon: in one's own lifetime. So, there is an intensity and urgency to what Jesus has to say about almost everything. In these words, he identifies the insecurity (we say existential anxiety) that lies at the root of selfishness, frequently causing us to choose the wrong thing. Is this what we mean by human nature?

Later Christian traditions, even as early as Paul's letters, place a big emphasis on the word *sin* and even make poor Adam responsible (with his original sin) for all of the sin humans have committed ever since the Garden of Eden, taking the myth, it seems, in a way that sounds quite literal. What we gather from the Jewish and Christian traditions is that it is human nature to focus on ourselves and do the wrong thing—to be sinful—because we are anxious about our purpose and destiny. But I'm not sure if I've answered your question about scam callers and the unexpected slice of coffeecake.

You're saying that the Jewish and Christian traditions share common ideas about our insecurity, and to them, it seems like it is human nature to do the wrong thing, which they call sin. I think I understand that, but I still have my question about whether people are basically good or basically bad. As you suggested, there are saints, but also some very evil people in this world.

Let me try again by sharing with you a heated discussion exactly on this point by two followers of Confucius who had differing views of human nature. I mentioned Confucius (551–479 BCE) earlier when we were exploring ideas about God and creation, concluding that Confucius didn't have a lot to add on these topics; but Confucius has many things to say about human nature, and so do his followers.

I mentioned that Confucius lived in the so-called Warring States Period of Chinese history when the existing "empire" had broken into competing petty kingdoms all engaged in a succession of wars with each other. Lying, cheating, murder, and corruption ruled the day in a world that was falling apart. If ever there was an occasion to take a very negative view of human nature, that was the time. Somehow, Confucius remained positive. We can talk later, if you like, about his views of society and government, but let's focus now on his idea of human nature.

Confucius elaborated the idea of filial piety, supporting and respecting one's parents, not only in this life but when they pass away. A son or daughter might disagree with parents, but not disobey. Filial piety is the basis of all family relationships, and the child learns within the family how to behave outside the family, carrying on one's work by doing the utmost with dutifulness and loyalty. There must be honesty and sincerity in all that we think or do. We must know what is right, proper, and moral, and we must have the courage to act on these virtues out in the world. The interesting thing is that Confucius taught that people could actually do these things, achieving exemplary humanity and a serious moral attitude. It is written within our nature to do so. Not everyone agreed.

The most important follower of Confucius was Mencius (371–289 BCE), actually Mengzi, or Master Meng, and his title is Second Sage, meaning second to Confucius. He grew up in a town near to where Confucius taught, and there is a tradition of a direct teaching lineage from Confucius through his son and grandson to Mencius. By the time of Mencius, the ideas of Confucius were under attack from all sides and he needed a strong defender.

Mencius suggested the analogy of sprouts, the beginnings of little plants. Within the mind/heart of human beings, there is a sprout of compassion, shame, dislike, modesty, and a sense of right and wrong. As with young plants, these sprouts need to be nurtured by education and example. We are born with these natural tendencies, and with proper nourishment, they can lead to moral behavior. All people have these sprouts: sages, rulers, and the common people. We have "capacities" but we must concentrate on them to develop them. Human nature tends toward the good.

Another interpreter of Confucius, Xunzi, disagreed strongly with Mencius, taking the position that human nature is basically evil, or at least selfish. Xunzi, or Xun Tzu (310–c.210 BCE) was in his teens when Mencius died, and he had the opportunity to know his work and that of Confucius. He thought of himself as a follower of Confucius; he just had a very different take on his ideas.

Xunzi defines human nature as the part of us produced by nature, the part that is not learned. What we are born with is love of profiting ourselves, and that tendency leads to self-interest, aggression, and greed. Following our natural desires leads to evil. Good comes only through conscious effort. In other words, good is not inborn; it is only acquired through nurture. Natural inclinations toward the bad need to be controlled. Thus, morality is something artificial to be built. When a potter creates a pot, the pot is not coming out of the potter; it is something external to be shaped of clay. Becoming a moral person requires learning and hard work. Now we have two opposing views of human nature, both supposedly Confucian. Does that help or does it make Confucian confusion?

No, the positions are clear and convincing. That's the problem. I don't know which to choose. And I am beginning to wonder: What difference does it make?

If you have raised children, or watched others trying to do so, you've seen a developmental stage with them when they are around two years old sometimes called "the terrible twos." As you watch them and try to shape their behavior, you can view them as sweet toddlers who are sprouting natural goodness, but just need a little help in cultivating things like sharing and self-control. Or you can see them as selfish little monsters who need to be restrained and civilized. It is not easy to decide which approach to take, but it will make a difference, both in your attitude toward them and how you work with them. Teachers face this issue when they work with their students. Do students have a natural curiosity and love of learning that needs to be channeled and encouraged, or are they lazy louts who need a lot of rules and threats, without which they will copy, cheat, and try to get away with as little work as possible? At the office, is it reasonable to trust those with whom you work as basically good people who just need leadership about the organization's mission and guidance in getting there, or is it a dog-eat-dog world where everyone is focused primarily on their own success? Even the highly quantitative discipline of economics must make assumptions about whether people are basically lazy or industrious. What you believe about human nature can matter.

No one can tell you which view to hold; that will depend on your accumulated experience with people. Of course, it may be some of each, where we all have some natural goodness intermixed with natural selfishness. It is as if there is a little game going on within the divided human heart between the devils and the angels, like a tug of war with goodness winning some of the time and badness the other. What we don't want, as we think about human nature, is to be so naïve as to get blindsided by the malicious scammer; and yet we can't become so cynical about people that we don't recognize a natural act of kindness, the neighbor's bringing over a piece of coffeecake.

I like the description of the divided human heart. Maybe it's a little of both. I see now that the way I think about human nature can influence my attitudes and actions. This is fascinating stuff, but I 'm still not sure what to think. Are there other views of human nature from the religious traditions that might be helpful? I'm looking for something practical and modern, maybe without the word "sin."

The Daoist tradition, old as it is, dating from about a century after Confucius, has some very modern sounding ideas, so much so, that you want to ask: How could these ancient Chinese people be so amazingly observant as to sound so modern?

I mentioned earlier the *Dao De Ching* as an important text of Daoism. It contains the suggestion that it is human nature to want the things that others want and that the root of our discontent is a rampant desire to possess more than we need.

No lure is greater than to possess what others want,
No disaster greater than not to be content with what one has,
No presage of evil greater than that men should be wanting to get
more.
Truly: He who has once known contentment that comes simply
through being content, will never again be otherwise than
contented.

Apparently, there were wonderful things to acquire in ancient China—silk, jade, spices—enough that the writer could identify an aspect of human nature that turns needs into wants. Our desire to acquire leads to discontented striving.

The text of the *Dao De Ching* has layers of contributions rather than a single author, but a second piece of Daoist writing appears to be, at least in its central sections, written by an author whose name is used as well for the title, *Zwangzi*. Both works tend toward the poetic and are difficult to understand, spawning many disagreements over translation and interpretation, but if you start searching for a view of human nature and paste together the pieces you find in a book, such as this one here, you get a view from Daoism that comes out something like the following:

We think we know how the world works, when actually we don't. Humans are smart, but maybe not smart enough. Just as we think we know something and start to intervene, that's when we mess up. Oh, we know many things, but mostly it is what the culture has taught us, and a lot of that is wrong. We follow those cultural norms, rather than consider the deeper path of Dao. We act in a calculating way on behalf of the ego to get what we want, when what we need is to be more natural and spontaneous. Not in the sense of self-indulgence as in doing things by whim or impulse, but acting in an effortless way without a plan, letting our actions come spontaneously as a plant grows naturally from a seed. It seems to be in our nature to want to control and manipulate things, forcing them into the artificial products to be acquired. We think that we are the best species ever created when actually we are the "sickest animal." We wonder what the problem is with the world, when we are the problem. We think we are in charge, when actually Dao is in charge. We are the species that fights Dao rather than follows it. Everything in the universe seems to follow Dao, but humans.

What's the book you keep referring to here?

It's Lee Dian Rainey's *Decoding Dao*. Let me read you this summary she has made of passages from *Zwangzi,* an ancient description of everyday life that sounds stunningly modern.

While we sleep, our souls go wandering; when awake, our bodies run around. We become entangled with everything we want.

Every day we use our mind/heart for contention and conflict, that is sometimes deep and sometimes petty. Our little fears make us wobbly; our great fears stun us. Nonetheless, we go off like an arrow being released from a bowstring, absolutely sure we know what is right and wrong, true and false.

If you want a twenty-first century view of human nature, maybe you have just found it in writing from sometime after 312 BCE in the *Dao De Ching* and in the *Zwangzi.*

It hits the mark, doesn't it? All of this running around we do to get things. So much planning. Nothing just happens on its own. We don't even need modern-day examples; we are the example. But now I am wondering if there is one predominant human nature, as I've been searching for, or whether there are many human natures. Maybe no one description fits everyone.

You mean, no universal human nature? Each person is different, so we can't generalize about people, but need to describe each individual as we run into him or her? That leaves things somewhat unpredictable, doesn't it? You don't know what to expect of people, or even of yourself. But maybe you are right. There is a religious tradition that aligns rather closely with what you are suggesting. In the early teachings of Buddha, we find the idea of the impermanent self.

As mentioned earlier, Buddhism grew out of Hinduism and shared some of its beliefs, such as rebirth, but one point where its founder, Siddhartha Gautama (485–410 or 400 BCE) disagreed sharply was with the idea of the self. One of the strong points of Hinduism, one might say, is that it holds the view that the essence of the self, called *ātman,* is identical with *brahman,* the essence of all things. Having this universal self, binds all human beings together. One might say, we are all made of the same stuff. Buddha had a different idea about the self.

Buddha taught that nothing is permanent, including the self. There is no such thing as the constant, unchanging self. Westerners tend to have the view that no matter how much a person changes throughout life, something remains constant—the real me. Buddha taught the impermanence of the self, and that letting go of the self was essential for Enlightenment. An English dictionary suggests that *self* refers to the "identity, character, or essential qualities of a person" and lists two pages of hyphenated words containing *self,* including *self-concept, self-esteem, self-employed,* and *self-realization.* For Buddha, the idea of a permanent self is self-deception—you are kidding yourself—except that there is no self to delude. In Buddhism there is no "permanent, substantial, independent, metaphysical Self."

If we think about this from Buddha's point of view, we could ask: To what extent am I a very different person now than I was as a child in school, as a teen-ager, or before I was married (if married) or became a parent (if a parent)? Some people find it painful to recall how they behaved as adolescents and are eager to erase those years from the record. Others say, I was a completely different person before the children were born. Sometimes in a later stage of life, a rather different personality comes upon an individual after a stroke, during retirement, or at the loss of a loved one, so much so as to make it quite impossible to return to "one's old self." Friends who did not know us when we were young, have no grasp of our former self.

I could definitely forget my teen-age self. Buddha seems to be saying that the older you get, the more selves you accumulate, so it gets harder to say which one is the real you. What does this do to the idea of human nature?

If there is no permanent self even for the individual, just a succession of selves, how can there be a constant human nature? Perhaps the best we can say is that there were points in life when I wasn't very good at doing the right thing, but other times when I was better at it, and still other times when I was actually pretty good. There were times when I was basically good, but at moments or certain points of my life I was a rather terrible person. The famous American poet, Walt Whitman asked in "Song of Myself" the question:

> Do I contradict myself?
> Very well then, I contradict myself,
> (I am large, I contain multitudes.)

Well, maybe we don't contain multitudes, but we may have a constantly changing self, full of contradictions. It may be reassuring to know that the constant in human nature is change, that people grow, change, and undergo fundamental transformations.

And...and...oh, gosh, I hate to bring this up, but where does human sexuality fit into this discussion of human nature?

You mean, not just our gender, but the fact that we have strong sexual drives that don't always fit with what we regard as the rest of our basic nature? I'm afraid that the religious traditions have generally been badly confused about that aspect of human nature, repressing, denying, and disparaging what seems to be a very basic aspect of our being.

It seems like there is an animal nature that invades our human nature, and the religious traditions don't know what to do or say when the animal appears. Put the beast in a cage, look the other way, or run off to a monastery as fast as you can.

Years ago, when I was about to be married, the minister who was counseling us said, "God has played two very bad jokes on mankind; one is death and the other is sex. I thought I understood about death, but I wasn't sure exactly what he meant by sex being a bad joke, but I didn't stop trying to figure it out. Now, years later, I think he was saying something like this: God seems to have created this remarkable being with amazing capabilities for music, art, and literature; with the uncanny ability to do higher mathematics and invent useful technologies; with this incessant spiritual quest to know its purpose and destiny. Then God gives humankind this carnal sex drive that somehow doesn't fit with all the rest. We can hear God laughing at this bad joke he has played on human beings, watching with glee (and sometimes horror) as their sexuality confuses them, produces shame and guilt, and gets them into all manner of trouble, including some very bizarre manias and perversions. Not that God would actually do this; it is just a story offered as a description of the human predicament.

Oh, of course, we should regard this sex drive as a good thing and positive gift, something to integrate joyfully into the rest of our being in a natural way. The Hindus seem to be good at that and possibly the Daoists who follow the Way in nature. But why does human sexuality so often become a source of embarrassment, unease, and Adam-and-Eve-type shame? I may be exaggerating the contradiction here, but I haven't heard of any saints giving instructions on how to have sex and pray at the same time. In other words, for many religious traditions there seems to be a basic incompatibility between our sexuality and spirituality. Perhaps we can say simply that sexuality magnifies the human capacity for goodness and depravity already embedded in human nature, intensifying the conflict between the devils and the angels. Let's just leave it at that.

Maybe human nature just ends up as one of life's unsolved mysteries.

Perhaps it is only "human nature" that we continue to seek ways to describe human nature, so we will keep looking, no doubt. The religions of the world help us explore these questions, providing differing views as well as the suggestion that there is possibly no such thing as a universal human nature. Here is one more attempt to describe human nature. What do you think about it?

Another famous American author is Samuel Clemens, who wrote under the name of Mark Twain. He is often regarded as a profound if somewhat jaded analyst of human nature. He retells the Adam and Eve story with a different twist:

Adam was but human—this explains it all. He did not want

the apple for the apple's sake, he wanted it only because it was forbidden. The mistake was in not forbidding the serpent: then he would have eaten the serpent.

So, Adam would have eaten the snake instead of the apple if it was forbidden? That's certainly disgusting. But I know people like that: complete rebels against authority. My grandpa is like that. And look what happens when you tell little kids they can't do something.

The one thing we can be certain about, Clemens is saying, is that if an action is forbidden, humans will choose to do it. Maybe *that's* the basic principle of human nature. It might work well for a while, until the neighbor brings you another piece of coffeecake out of the goodness of her heart. No one ever told her she couldn't do it...but she did it anyway.

References

Agnes, Michael, Editor in Chief, *Webster's New World College Dictionary.* Cleveland, Ohio: Wiley Publishing, 2010. The definition of self and list of hyphenated self-words are found here.

Bakewell, Sarah, *At the Existentialist Café, Freedom, Being, and Apricot Cocktails.* New York: Other Press, 2016. The quotation defining existential anxiety is on p. 154.

Clemens, Samuel (Mark Twain), "Pudd'nhead Wilson's Calendar," Chapter Two. Cited in Shapiro, Fred R., Editor, *The Yale Book of Quotations.* New Haven: Yale University Press, 2006, #55 on p. 777.

Collins, John J. *Introduction to the Hebrew Bible.* Minneapolis, Fortress Press, 2004. After reviewing the evidence, Collins supports a relative late date for the creation stories, after the captivity in Babylon. See p. 75

Flood, Gavin, *Introduction to Hinduism.* Cambridge: Cambridge University Press, 1996. The relationship of self, *ātman,* and *brahman* is drawn from pp. 84-85.

Harvey, Peter, *An Introduction to Buddhism: Teachings History, and*

Practices, Second Edition. Cambridge: Cambridge University Press, 2013. The description of Buddha's concept of the impermanent self is drawn from pp. 58-59, and the quotation concerning no "permanent, substantial..." is found on p. 59.

Holy Bible, Revised Standard Version. New York: Thomas Nelson & Sons, 1952. Genesis 1-3 and Matthew 6:25-31 are the basis of the discussion. All quotations from the Bible in this book are from the Revised Standard Version. Although a new version (translation) of the Holy Bible, called the New Revised Standard Version (NRSV), was published in 1989, adding to and updating the previous work of the RSV Committee of scholars, I have chosen to quote directly from the older 1952 Revised Standard Version (RSV) because it is likely to have a more familiar sound to those who know that Bible after its being in use for more than 60 years. This is simply the author's preference.

Rainey, Lee Diane, *Confucius & Confucianism: The Essentials.* Malden, MA: Wiley-Blackwell, 2010. A comprehensive study of Confucius and Confucian thought. The date of birth for Confucius is on p.2. The description of the Warring States Period is on p. 5ff. The discussion of Confucian teaching is taken from Chapter 2, pp. 23-32. The position of Mencius on human nature is drawn from pp. 87-93 and the Xunzi rebuttal is on pp. 105-109.

Rainey, Lee Dian, *Decoding Dao: Reading the Dao De Ching and the Zhuangzi.* Malden, MA: Wiley-Blackwell, 2014. Rainey is effective in drawing out the essence of Daoism from the *Dao De Ching* and *Zhuangzi.* Her ideas, restated here, are from pp. 78, 80 and 108-09. The quoted summary of ideas she has provided from *Zhuangzi* is from p. 113.

Waley, Arthur, *The Way and Its Power: A Study of the Tao Te Ching and Its Place in Chinese Thought.* New York: Macmillan, Evergreen Edition, 1958. The quoted passage "No lure is greater..." is from Chapter XLVI, p. 199.

Whitman, Walt, *"Song of Myself,"* line 1324, written in 1855. Cited in Shapiro, Fred R., *The Yale Book of Quotations*. New Haven: Yale University Press, 2006, p. 815.

Ziporyn, Brook, translator, *Zhuangzi: The Essential Writings with Selections from Traditional Commentaries*. Indianapolis, IN: Hackett Publishing, 2009. These are the writings from which an interpretation is made by Lee Dian Rainey in *Decoding Dao*.

4
Social Order
Building Community out of Political Chaos

I have an odd family when it comes to politics. My mother's father, my grandpa, wants the least government possible with no one telling him what to do. He's over eighty now, and he won't even listen to his doctors. My father calls him an anarchist. My mother doesn't agree with her father, but she thinks it is unfair to call grandpa an anarchist just because he doesn't like government regulations. My mom has a sister, my aunt, who rebelled against their father and left home to become a nun. She teaches school and lives in a residence for Sisters.

My father is a professor—he says you probably know who he is—and he comes from a long line of what he calls communitarians. His mother lived as a hippy in a commune during her twenties, the kind where property was held in common and they got their food from a local coop. Her sister, my great aunt, worked in the civil rights movement, but she is retired now and spends her life knitting and watching the news on TV. As for me, I have one older sister who is a communications consultant and is married to a financial planner, and I have a gay, older brother who has been successful with a tech start-up, but he calls himself a progressive.

Yes, I know of your father for his work in the Faculty Senate, but I had no idea that you come from such an interesting family. What happens when you all get together?

Luckily, we don't, at least not very often. We all live in different parts of the country, my brother lives in Canada, and my sister travels a lot. As you might imagine, it's pretty tense when even a few of us are in the same room. But my question is this: Why do people have so many different strongly-held political views? Why is there so much disagreement about the preferred form of government and best kind of leader?

It is a bit strange, isn't it? People appear to have radically different ideas about the social order. Some believe that we prosper best as free individuals, developing our talents and pursuing our own interests without interference. Others believe that we need each other's help, functioning best when we are collaborating and cooperating. Perhaps we have so many strongly-held ideas about government because we have such different views of what people need to be able to live a satisfying life. It reminds me of our discussion of human nature, and the battle of the devils and the angels. Is it in our nature to live life independently, being left alone to survive or thrive through our own ingenuity and hard work, or are we social beings who crave community and recognize that our grandest dreams require significant cooperation? As long as this timeless question goes without a definitive, once-and-for-all answer, there will be disagreements about the social order. And, of course, politics as well. I don't know if this is answering your question or not.

Yes, it is, but it brings up another question. What is this thing you are calling the social order? I remember something from my social studies classes about a social contract.

You may be referring to the English philosopher Thomas Hobbes (1588–1679), who is often misquoted as having a very negative view of human nature, when what he actually meant was that *without society,* "the life of man (is) solitary, poor, nasty, brutish, and short." He saw the importance of making an agreement, a social contract, to structure the life of the community. But there is endless disagreement about what that contract and community should be.

Think about the various levels of community—family, school, business, organizations, city, state or province, nation—and what they all have in common: rules, to begin with, formal policies, and eventually laws. And here is where the conflict comes in: as soon as there are rules, policies, and laws, someone's freedom is restricted. People can no longer do just what they might choose, especially if it hurts someone else or curtails' *their* freedom. How shall we set up the social contract in the fairest and most effective way? That is one of the enduring mysteries of life, although it seems that it shouldn't be so complicated. All of the ancient religious traditions had an approach to this, and they all had their own answers to the timeless questions: What government is best? What laws are most necessary? What type of leader is needed? Let's look at what they had to say. Where would you like to begin?

Tell me about the Ten Commandments. Why are they so important?

My aunt, the nun, says they are the foundation of Western Law.

Yes, some people find them so important that they want to post them in front of the state capitol or county courthouse. At one time they were being sent out to the Boy Scouts to prevent juvenile delinquency. The posting controversies still surface today, and because the Commandments have a religious ring to them, those who object to public postings usually do so because they believe in separation of church and state, which itself is controversial. But are the Ten Commandments the foundation of Western law? Let's think about what they meant to the Hebrews who wrote them.

The question people face if they plan to post or distribute the Ten Commandments is this: Which version of them are you going to use? There are three in the Hebrew Scriptures. The three separate versions include one in Exodus 20, another in Exodus 34, and a third in Deuteronomy 5. Two are similar but not exactly the same: Exodus 20 and Deuteronomy 5. The third, Exodus 34, differs considerably from the other two. Let's try to piece together from them what happens to Moses as he tries to deliver the Ten Commandments to his people. What was the context?

Poor Moses was a reluctant leader to begin with, and he had already freed the Israelites from Egypt and led them through the parted waters of the Red Sea on the trip to the Promised Land. If Judaism has a founder, it is Moses. So, the Israelites are staying at the base of Mt. Sinai somewhere in Arabia. Moses watches what is going on with the people and notices that they could use some order, rules, and structure—what Hobbes, centuries later, called the "social contract." Yahweh, their God, appears to them in an intense storm, scaring them half to death, so that they beg Moses to serve as their intermediary with God. Moses goes up the mountain to get the Commandments from God to be written on stone tablets. From these three accounts, the reader has trouble keeping track of how many times Moses goes up and down that mountain, but it's more than once.

Meanwhile, as Moses is receiving the Ten Commandments, the people down below are acting badly, and with the complicity of Aaron, Moses's own brother, they are making and worshiping a golden calf, and engaging in idolatrous rituals and orgies that appear to have sexual overtones. Of course, God knows what is taking place, and threatens to destroy the Israelites on the spot, but Moses is able to calm Yahweh down. Can you imagine having to get God to settle down?

In any case, Moses goes down the mountain with the tablets and engraved commandments. But when Moses sees the chaos up close, he understands why God is upset, so he throws the tablets down and smashes them. Now he has another problem: broken tablets. So, he climbs back up the mountain with blank tablets in hand, and when he arrives God says he will write the words that were on the first tablets. But these commandments appear to be rather different, not matching well with the versions in the other two stories, especially the commandment about not boiling a kid (young goat) in its mother's milk. In some of the versions it is difficult to tell which commandments to count in order to arrive at ten. In other words, the three stories have their inconsistencies and contradictions.

Let me read to you a version I will edit to skip over the detailed elaborations of some of the commandments, in order to come up with a short list. You tell me what you notice about them.

I am the Lord your God, who brought you out of the land of Egypt,
   out of the house of bondage.
You shall have no other gods before me.
You shall not make yourself a graven image...
You shall not take the name of the Lord your God in vain...
Remember the sabbath day to keep it holy...
Honor your father and mother...
You shall not kill.
You shall not commit adultery.
You shall not steal.
You shall not bear false witness against your neighbor,
You shall not covet your neighbor's house...(and many things in
   it.)
   —Exodus 20: 2-17, with edits

What I notice is that those at the top of the list sound very religious. The only one that sounds like the law is the commandment about false witness. They seem to be rules that govern their relationship with God as well as each other. But I'm bothered by the inconsistencies and contradictions you mentioned. Which version should we follow? First, we have two versions of the creation story; now we have three versions of the Ten Commandments. What's going on here? It sounds like we need to send the Bible to a New York publisher with a skilled copy editor. Why do we have these differences?

Oh, this is just the beginning. We actually have four versions of the life of Jesus in the rather different Gospels of Matthew, Mark, Luke, and John. Maybe this would be a good time to pause to explain how modern scholars study the scriptures, not just the Jewish and Christian scriptures, but *The Analects of Confucius,* the Hindu *Vedas* and *Upanishads,* the *Teachings of Buddha,* the *Dao Te Ching* and *Zhuangzi,* and the holy book of Islam, the *Quran.* It took many years, centuries actually, but scholars are now applying their critical methods in different degrees to all of them. So, let me take a short detour here to explain Biblical scholarship. But stay with me, because this will give you important background information to help you look at any of these scriptures in a more objective way.

As early as 1735 a scholar named Jean Astruc noticed that differing names were used for the divinity in the Hebrew Bible, such as Yahweh and Elohim. That observation set in motion a closer, more careful reading of the text, and scholars began to notice many differences and discrepancies which suggested more than one source was being used in the same narrative. By 1878 a German scholar named Julius Wellhausen proposed four different sources which he named J, E, D, and P for Jahwistic, Elohist, Deuteronomic, and Priestly sources. This was followed by the effort to date these sources and put them in order. This effort to understand sources was aided by Hermann Gunkel, another German scholar, who became interested in the type of story being told (genre) and the social location (*Sitz im Leben*) of the passage in the life of the community from which it came. Others studied how the sources had been redacted (edited) and put together into a running account, often without regard for overlap or discrepancy, perhaps trying to enrich the text with more than one viewpoint. These three branches of Biblical studies were called *source criticism, form criticism,* and *redaction criticism.* Meanwhile the field of archeology developed and was applied to Biblical studies by a scholar named W.F. Albright, providing supporting or contradicting physical evidence for claims about the content of the text.

This scholarly work demonstrated that the books and chapters of the Hebrew and Christian scriptures were very much a human effort drawing on and combining older and newer sources over a long period of time to arrive at an acceptable edited version. It is not surprising, therefore, to find three versions of the Ten Commandments. It is surprising to still find people who want to read all of these stories literally, word for word, and turn somersaults to try to explain obvious contradictions and culturally-conditioned language. As mentioned, these methods are applied today to understanding the texts of the New Testament and the scriptures of other religious traditions as well.

I don't think that was a detour at all. It's interesting to see how scholars do this kind of research in the field of religion. I suppose it makes sense to work around the contradictions to look for the main point. And what is the main point about the Ten Commandments?

Scholars began to see that in the stories of the Ten Commandments we have layers and layers of text, some of it very old, perhaps dating back to legends about Moses in sources from the 10th and 9th centuries BCE with later revisions and editing dating from the 6th century BCE. In addition to the uncountable list of prohibitions, the commandments appear to follow an ancient form of legal agreement, adapted in this case to a covenant between Jahweh and His people. I will be your God and protect you if you will bring about a workable social order and live in this way.

The way to live, not just as individuals but as a society, is set forth in the commandments and what follows them. Naturally, many of the details about slaves, idols, oxen, and kids are particular to the social location (*Sitz im Leben*) of the times. Beyond the three lists of commandments there is also the "Covenant Code" of Exodus 20 and its subsequent chapters spelling out in great detail the ordinances of this society, including a lot of rules about how to treat your slaves, grazing rights, responsibility for an open pit, and uncontrolled fires.

The main point—what you are requesting—is that the relationship with God (Jahweh) involved moral responsibilities in building a social order. The meaning is not in the particular commandments or the details of the code, but in the idea of covenant, that the agreement with God includes building an orderly and just community. That's the main message. And your observation is sound; it's not legal, it's religious. The interesting point to notice as we make the comparison is that most of the religious traditions have profound ideas about bringing order to society through a dedicated leader and a unique community.

I would like to hear about those. I'm guessing that Confucius has some things to say about this.

Yes, let's begin with Confucius, the same Confucius mentioned in our discussion of human nature. He is the place to begin because of his rich ideas about social order and governance. Confucius (551–479 BCE) is the Latin name given for the Chinese *Kong Fuzi, Kong* being the family name, with *Fu* as an honorary and *zi* meaning master or teacher, so we might think of him as Master Kong. Our main source of his teachings is the *Analects of Confucius,* but as we might guess, modern scholarship suggests this is not just a collection of his sayings put together by his students, but another "layered" text compiled over many years. Many myths and legends about his birth and early years have developed, but by sorting through the material, scholars believe they can provide a basic outline of his life and teaching.

His father was a well-known military figure but his parents were not married, his mother perhaps being a concubine, someone just living with his father. In any case, his father left and his mother died young, but Confucius held a certain status among the lower nobility as a scholar/bureaucrat, and we know this from his privilege to become an educated person. For a time, he held a minor post in government, resigned, and became a wandering scholar, traveling to a number of states and earning living expenses from his advice.

Maybe he was the first consultant in the history of civilization?

Now there's a new idea. He was only seeking an influential post in government, but he never got one. He is also described as an avid musician. He was married and had two children, and died a humble man at age 72 with no idea that he would have such influence in the future.

As mentioned earlier, Confucius lived in the midst of China's Warring States period, with a multitude of petty states at war after the relatively stable period of the Zhou dynasty. The noble rulers, besides fighting with each other were corrupt, extravagant, and maybe not too bright. It was natural for Confucius to diagnose the situation and recommend solutions. He believed that government needed to be reformed in drastic ways, and he had many ideas about what was needed.

He taught that leaders need to "set words right," that is, to avoid jargon and buzz words, and euphemisms—what we might call slogans, photo ops, and sound bites—and tell the truth in plain language. Failing to use words right is lying, and one lie leads to another. Some words, such as *mother, father,* or *teacher* carry social expectations to behave in an appropriate way, and this also applies to rulers. If a ruler doesn't behave as a ruler should, he doesn't deserve to be called *ruler*. So, leaders need to speak honestly and perform their roles well.

Confucius also had a surprisingly democratic sounding idea for his time; he believed that government exists for the benefit of the people. Furthermore, government needs the people's trust, and rulers need to build that trust. He was not, however, advocating democracy, but suggesting that even a paternalistic ruler needs to build trust. Leaders need to model virtue as the gentleman and sage.

Societies need order, but laws and punishments tend to teach people to break the laws and avoid punishment. What people really need is a sense of shame, to develop internal control (virtue in the heart), and inner motivation to behave well. They learn this from the family and also from models of virtue; therefore, rulers need to be moral models of the best behavior for the people. In other words, the state needs to be run on moral principles. Leaders must control their self-interest and think of the interest of the people. People will give their support to a state run in this way. At one point, Confucius was offered a job in government—his chance at reform—but turned it down because his values would be compromised too much by that particular ruler.

In the Chinese tradition, the ruler could claim to be "the choice of heaven"—the parallel of divine right of kings comes to mind—but the idea of Heaven is not clear and often appears to be only a justification of power. Although Confucius doesn't say much about God or Heaven, he clearly expresses the idea that a just society requires moral leadership and followers with good intentions.

The flavor of his teachings can be gained quickly be referring to a few passages from the *Analects of Confucius:*

The man of honor thinks of his character, the inferior man of his position.
The man of honor desires justice, the inferior man favor.

Do not do to others what you would not like yourself; then your public life will arouse no ill-will and your private life no resentment.

If a ruler is himself upright, his people will do their duty without orders...

He who speaks without modesty will perform with difficulty.

When those in high position are fond of orderly behavior,
service from the people is easily commanded.

Perhaps Confucius is remembered with such high esteem because he saw the importance of the "social contract" and described this so clearly in moral terms. To Confucius, nothing is more important than a stable society based on moral values. This requires sound leadership.

I love these sayings of Confucius. In the middle of all of the warfare and corruption, he had a gentle voice. What's that other Chinese tradition? Oh, Yes, Daoism. What did they have to say?

Although Daoism grows out of the same Warring States Period of Confucius, approximately one hundred years later, the ideas about social structure and governance are somewhat different. Some have said that the *Dao De Ching* is an anarchist text, but nowhere is there the suggestion that government can be eliminated. We find, instead, many passages that are highly critical of government and its rulers:

While the fields are full of weeds,
And the granaries are empty;
Still they are dressed in fine clothes,
Equipped with swords at their sides,
Stuffed with food and drink,
And with far too much money.
This is called being leading robbers,
And has nothing at all to do with *dao*.

While the conscripted soldiers are off fighting senseless wars, the food supply is threatened, but this doesn't keep the rulers from personal excess. As with Confucianism, the problem is with the ruler, but the solution is a little different. The leader has to guard against "ego-acting," an important Daoist concept meaning acting in one's own interests in a calculating way. The sage-leader needs to be unbiased, without an agenda or ideology, open to all, taking a place not above the people, but below, like a river flowing into a valley. If left to themselves, but encouraged, people will return to a life of simplicity and will rediscover the Way.

In Daoism there is the idea of a previous Golden Age, far back in history, when people followed the *dao* and society worked as it should. People didn't get into wars and valued life.

> There were small states with few people.
> Even though people had the weapons for a platoon,
>   or even a battalion, they did not use them.
> Because they looked at death as a serious thing,
>   they did not move to distant places.

In other words, the solution for the Warring States was to stop the warring and return to the age when people valued human life and could stay at home to enjoy their friends and family. Is it an unrealistic dream, or did people actually live harmoniously in the ancient past by seeking the Way?

I think some of the leaders today could profit from listening to these ancient Chinese sages. But what about Mohammed? What do we know about his life and what he taught? I know that certain countries today speak of Mohammed with great respect and they long for a Golden Age, too.

As I mentioned before, Muhammad (570–632 CE) began his role as Prophet and Messenger of Allah in Mecca but soon migrated through the dessert with a small band of his followers to Yathrib. The *Hijra*, as that migration is known, brought his movement not to a bustling city but a small oasis of villages inhabited chiefly by farmers, and it was there that Muhammad began to design with his followers the type of community they would become. They cut down palm trees, built a small structure that would serve as the first *masjid* (mosque), and started a new society. When a distinctly Muslim calendar was established later, the Year 1 A.H. (After Hijra) was the date of the migration, not Muhammad's birthday, and Yathrib became Medina, "The City of the Prophet." Here the Muslim idea of community and the religion of Muhammad were born.

It is difficult to know for certain what happened there because the traditions were written down years after the Prophet's death, but the history has been pieced together gradually. It appears that Muhammad's group of less than one hundred men, women, and children had to flee Mecca, and when they arrived in their new home, needed to learn how to get along with the Arab tribes and Jewish settlers—producers of dates and wine—who were already living in Yathrib. Muhammad first helped to bring order among the competing tribes by serving as a divinely-inspired arbitrator of disputes. Gradually he became a respected leader, and the number of followers grew, becoming known as the *Ummah*, which can mean *people, nation,* or *community.* Muhammad now had the chance to implement the reforms that had failed in Mecca and shape the ideal community and social order of his dreams.

He reformed the Arab custom of retribution for an injury with an equal injury—an eye for an eye—the common pattern among existing Arab and Jewish tribes. Muhammad eliminated the existing practice of unequal application of the law depending on social status, which had become not exactly an eye for an eye for the privileged, but more like and ear for an eye. He eliminated that privilege and also introduced the concept of forgiveness to reduce the escalation of revenge. He outlawed usury (charging interest on a loan) and instituted the mandatory *zakat*, a tithe or tax to be paid according to one's means and to be distributed among the poor as an act of religious devotion, thus addressing the gap of extreme wealth and poverty. These rather egalitarian ideas sound familiar in our time, but in the context of Medina, they were a revolutionary attempt to build a moral society in the name of Allah.

Apparently, Muhammad was involved in spelling out rules and laws that eventually evolved into the "Constitution of Medina," often acknowledged as the world's first written constitution. Some say it was the first thing that Muhammad did in Medina, but more recent evidence suggests it came about later. The nonaggression pacts and agreements it contains were no doubt Muhammad's work. The Constitution raises an issue that continued in Islam through the centuries to the present: combining both religious and political authority in the ruler, Muhammad. Accustomed as Westerners are to separation of church and state, it is difficult to conceive of a theocracy, a state where religious and political authority are united.

After Muhammad's death, there was no clear successor and extensive conflict developed over control. Eventually, Muhammad's close friend, Abu Baker, emerged as the leader and was given the title Caliph, meaning "the Successor to the Messenger of God." Abu Baker served for two and one-half years and hand-picked the energetic leader Umar as his successor. It was he who built the Islamic empire through military campaigns in which he spread out from Arabia and conquered Syria, Iran, Egypt, Libya, and even Jerusalem. In a very short time, the religion of Muhammad had spread across the middle east becoming the great empire of Islam, a theocracy based on a concept of Universal Brotherhood (equality before Allah), later known as the Golden Era of Islam. The religion was not forced upon the conquered, but many valued the social order it provided and became followers. Over the years, controversy developed over who would become Caliph and what the title really meant, but one of the contributions of early Islam is its effort to construct a moral society within the state.

Do modern examples of a religious state exist? I believe you called it a "theocracy." It seems that the difference today is between democratic and totalitarian states with religious ideas of the state left fairly far behind.

After the Enlightenment, which besides giving us science, provided the ideas for democratic revolutions in the British colonies (America) and in France, the conflict has been between secular democracies and totalitarian regimes. Much is made of the religious roots of Western democracies, but as these countries became more pluralistic within, it was difficult to speak of being rooted in a particular faith. You are asking, though, about current examples of states that truly claim to embody religious principles.

Two come to mind that struggle to find the appropriate way to be a "religious state," and ironically, they are arch-enemies: Israel and Iran. The formation of Israel has a long and interesting history. After the Jews lost their homeland, it was natural to keep alive a hope of return. Zionist ideas about the return to Jerusalem (Zion) go back to the 1850s, and significant settlement on the land in Palestine took place early in the twentieth century. It wasn't an idea that just popped up in 1948 after World War II. Although Israel provides forms of government based on democratic principles, there is also a strong sense that this is a religious state of and for Jewish people. The internal debate about religious identity has practical significance for a sizable non-Jewish population living within Israel, particularly Muslim Palestinians.

Similarly, but also in a very different way, Iran has struggled to express its "religiosity" after the revolution in 1979 that resulted in the overthrow of the last Shah of Iran. Democratic structures were developed, but during the same year a well-educated religious leader from a respected Shi'ite (a branch of Islam) family returned to the country as Ayatollah (religious leader) to usher in a new era and new expression of the Islamic state. Internal tensions still exist over the degree to which the state is or should be "Islamic."

I think we can say that Israel and Iran are the exception, not the rule, but there are other countries where there is some struggle over how to be a "religious" state. India comes to mind with its resurgent Hindu nationalism, and so does Afghanistan with its hope for a theocracy.

Remember that many secular states are home to internal religious communities that often have strong impact on the politics of their country. These religious communities also have a certain social order. Let's pick two examples, Buddhism and Christianity, and explore how they have developed social structures to support their work. In Buddhism, the emphasis was on seeking personal Enlightenment, thus shifting the focus from society to the individual. There appears to be no deliberate effort to build the overall good society within Buddhism, but rather a community apart from society where those within it can work together on the difficult task of pursuing Enlightenment. For this purpose, Buddha and his followers created the *Sanghe,* a community of monks and nuns, devoted to following the path toward Enlightenment. Buddhism can be said to have invented monasticism, in this case not a life of self-denial, but a middle way of communal discipline. In creating the *Sanghe,* Buddhism produced a human institution that has lasted more than 2,400 years. The *Vinaya,* or monastic discipline, provided a special set of rules to shape this ideal community for pursuing Enlightenment. For those who followed the usual path of householders, holding a job and raising children, their best hope (in early Buddhism) was to be reborn into another life where they might be free to join the *Sanghe.*

This does not mean that Buddhism had no concern for life outside the *Sanghe.* An important teaching was compassion for others, and sometimes Buddha is known as the Compassionate Buddha, but there is little discussion of how to build the ideal society or social order, as in Islam, Confucianism and Judaism. The focus is simply elsewhere in Buddhism.

Christianity also had its special community known as the Church, and it developed and spread after the death of Jesus. Christians were persecuted in the Roman Empire so it was not feasible to think of reforming society when their main mission was to survive underground. In Paul's letters to these young churches, he addressed their practical problems of belief and discipleship, and he also developed an important metaphor for what the church is. He called it the Body of Christ. The comparison is intriguing, stressing both diversity and unity, separate functions for the members, yet interdependent and working together, as with the organs of the human body. The Church became a structure within society for the expression of the Christian life, but early Christianity could not afford the luxury of suggesting a new social order or theocracy.

Christians went through difficult persecution during the first few centuries, but eventually with the conversion of Emperor Constantine, persecution was formally stopped by the Edict of Milan in 313 CE and Christianity even became the favored religion. After Constantine's death, Christianity became the established religion late in the fourth century, so we could say that there was a period of time in history when Christianity was a type of theocracy, the Muslim ideal. For the most part, however, the Church has been a religious community—not the Buddhist *Sanghe* to be sure—but a community of the faithful in a variety of expressions, including its own versions of monasticism.

There is another way to think about the Christian interest in the social order, however, and that is in the very early development of the idea of the Kingdom of God, a concept, we might say, that has never gone away. It is found in the teaching of Jesus in the earliest Gospels, Mark and Matthew. They portray Jesus as having the belief that the world will end soon and that a special figure, the Son of Man, (not Jesus himself) will usher in the destruction of the present age and a divine re-creation called "the Kingdom of God." The message of Jesus, therefore, took on urgency. In fact, there is some indication that this new Kingdom of God was already beginning and Jesus was trying to urge his followers through his teachings to implement those ideals in the present. He was not so much trying to build a new society as to alert people to a new world that was soon to come crashing in, ready or not. It was somewhat alarming for people to learn that this Kingdom was especially for the outcasts of society, people with whom Jesus was able to associate quite comfortably. Some would find their fortunes reversed, as Jesus made clear in his teaching that the first would be last and the last first. When the world didn't end, it set off considerable debate in the early Church, but the concept of the Kingdom of God, as a new social order, took on various forms as Christianity developed.

Help me to understand how to interpret what we have been discussing about social order in the ancient religious traditions. What does the comparison of the various religions tell us?

It appears that there is a strong yearning for community in human beings. Although there are surely individuals who prefer the life of the recluse, and others like your grandfather who just don't want people telling them what to do, we appear to have a long history as "social animals," longing for an effective social order and supportive community. Why we have this longing for social order is one of the mysteries of life. What form it should take is the timeless question that lacks a definitive answer. The result is continuous disagreement, not just stressful but harmless family debate, but civil unrest, street demonstrations, violent confrontations, assassinations, conspiracy theories, bombings, and bloody revolutions. By contrast, each of the religious traditions has some kind of hope for effective government and leadership that will bring peace, happiness, and security through social order.

Going as far back as Moses—and we don't know exactly how far back that is—we see the need for order shaped as divine commandments. It was as if the people were tired of their own chaos and wanted Moses to save them from themselves. Yes, Moses, go up that mountain one more time and get the commandments from Yahweh. Give us some laws and structure to end this chaos, but also an agreement that Yahweh cares about our society as we build it. We might call this a divine sanction (support) for social order.

When Confucius traveled around, all he saw was war and corruption. It appeared unwarranted to him, because he thought that human beings as individuals were naturally inclined to good. He was not a revolutionary and appeared to believe that government could be reformed, and he taught that to his followers. His is a simple wisdom: speak the truth, do what your role requires, let government serve the people, and let the people have good intent. Maybe his teaching became so famous and his followers so numerous because his simple ideas were so obvious and rang true.

The Daoists longed for the previous Golden Age, a simpler life, not to go back to, but to bring forward into the present. They knew that the wars had to stop and people needed to once again value human life. Is living by Dao just an ancient utopian dream, they asked, or is it something to put into effect now?

Muhammad and his followers were intent on building a society of order and justice at Medina. He reformed the law of retribution, introduced the idea of forgiveness, and was himself a skillful negotiator and peacemaker. His ideas about caring for the marginalized and redistribution of income have a strong humanitarian tone. Let's put it down in writing, he said and they wrote a Constitution.

The Christian idea of social justice took shape as the coming Kingdom of God. Forget for the moment the common belief of the time that the world was about to end, and picture instead a time of a new beginning. This was a time of great urgency during which one must prepare for life in a new society, a just society, announced by Jesus as especially favoring the marginalized and outcast. This society would be so new and "revolutionary," as to turn the existing social order upside down. We have a popular folk saying "Live each day as if it were your last." We say it, but we have trouble doing it. Jesus meant something like that only he might say *"because* it is your last," not "as if." The new way to live together in the Kingdom of God was already appearing and his teachings are filled with intensity about what would be necessary to live in that new kind of justly ordered society.

Your summary suggests that the concern for social order was quite universal, even though the suggestions for how to build it appear to be rather diverse.

We can't end this discussion of social order without mentioning the Hebrew prophets. They were not soothsayers or fortune-tellers, as they are often portrayed, but dedicated observers of what was taking place all around them during Israel's days of decline and eventual exile to Babylon in 586 BCE. From what the prophets saw, it was not difficult to describe what was going to happen because it was already happening or had happened. (A prophet is someone who speaks for another, in this case Yahweh, whom we met earlier on the mountain with Moses.) You may be familiar with the names of some of the Hebrew prophets: Isaiah, Jeremiah, Micah, Hosea, Amos and others.

The Hebrew prophets repeat over and over how Israel turned away from God, breaking the covenant with Yahweh, thus losing God's favor and ending up in exile. Occasionally, they spell out what has gone wrong with the social order, as in this passage from Jeremiah:

> Do justice and righteousness, and deliver from the hand
> of the oppressor him who has been robbed. And do no wrong
> or violence to the alien, the fatherless, and the widow, nor
> shed innocent blood in this place.
> —Jeremiah 22:3

Isaiah expresses it this way:

> How the faithful city has become a harlot, she that was
> full of justice! ... Your princes are rebels and companions
> of thieves. Everyone loves a bribe and runs after gifts. They
> do not defend the fatherless and the widow's cause does not
> come to them.
> —Isaiah 1:21-23

The prophet Hosea gets even more specific:

> There is no faithfulness or kindness, and no knowledge of
> God in the land; there is swearing, lying, killing, stealing, and
> committing adultery; they break all bounds and murder follows
> murder.

*We have a lot of that going on today. It looks like we have timeless
problems as well as timeless questions.*

A good point. But you know what, in spite of the horrible
circumstances of exile, and the decay of social order that led to that
consequence, the prophets hoped for a better future, when the people
would be restored to their homeland and given another chance to set up
a just society. At that future time:

> Then justice will dwell in the wilderness and righteousness
> abide in the fruitful field. And the effect of righteousness will
> be peace, and result of righteousness, quietness and trust forever.
> —Isaiah 32:16-17

Isaiah's description of peace may be familiar:

> ...and they shall beat their swords into plowshares, and their
> spears into pruning hooks; nation shall not lift up sword
> against nation, neither shall they learn war anymore.
> —Isaiah 2:4

The prophet Isaiah also hoped for an effective ruler who would bring this just society into being. Although the writers of the Gospels took these words and applied them to Jesus, at the time of Isaiah's writing, they simply expressed a hope for a sound leader, someone who did not yet exist.

> For unto us a child is born, to us a son is given; and the
> government will be upon his shoulder, and his name will
> be called Wonderful Counselor, Mighty God, Everlasting Father,
> Prince of Peace.
> —Isaiah 9:6

The prophets lived in desperate times and their longing for a stable and just social order is intense, even though it was always slipping away, beyond the grasp of the people and their rulers. Why should this be? One can almost see the prophet Micah shaking his head in astonishment over something that should be so simple and yet doesn't come to pass:

> He has showed you, O man, what is good; and what does
> the Lord require of you but to do justice, and to love kindness,
> and to walk humbly with your God?
> —Micah 6:8

Centuries later we look around and what do we see? Is it the just society of Micah, that really ought to be quite simple to install, or is it corruption, secret deals, nepotism, harsh treatment of opponents, greed, shameful differences in wealth, unrelieved generational poverty, lies, and hypocrisy?

Sadly, we see a lot of the latter, and continuing chaos. Perhaps this is why there is always a need for reformers.

It is not surprising that Martin Luther King, Jr., in his non-violent movement to bring racial justice to America in the mid-twentieth century would frequently quote the Hebrew prophets, particularly Amos, who wrote: "Let justice roll down like waters, and righteousness like an ever-flowing stream" (Amos 5:24). King knew injustice and chaos, but he also had hope, a dream.

The religious traditions have different things to say about the mysterious human longing for social order, but there is in them a consensus on the need for a good leader, humanitarian concern, brotherhood, compassion, and justice. The timeless question goes unanswered: Why has it proven to be so difficult over the years to build the just social order that so many would like to have?

References

Anderson, Bernard W. *Understanding the Old Testament*. Englewood Cliffs, NJ: Prentice-Hall, 1957. A classic older textbook on the history and content of the Hebrew Scriptures. The definition of a prophet as someone who speaks for another is from p. 184. The idea that prophets focus on the political sphere is from p. 187.

Armstrong, Karen, *The Lost Art of Scripture*. New York: Knopf, 2019. Provides a brief summary of the development of Biblical criticism, pp. 389-392.

Aslan, Reza, *No god but God*. New York: Random House, 2011. Provides background on Muhammad's life and the migration to Yathrib, pp. 51-52. The *Ummah* is described on p.57. Reforms and laws, pp. 59-60. The Constitution is discussed on p. 55. Caliph's title, p. 115. The process of territorial expansion, pp. 114-134. Iran is described as an effort to establish an Islamic state on pp. 191-192.

Brown, Raymond E. *An Introduction to the New Testament*. New Haven: Yale University Press, 1997. The quotation "regulate the relations of Christians..." is on p. 354. Brown cites the major passage where the "body metaphor for the Church is developed as I Corinthians 12:12-31.

Collins, Jon J., *Introduction to the Hebrew Bible*. Minneapolis: Fortress Press, 2004. The history of Biblical scholarship is on pp. 16-20 with a valuable chart on the Chronology of Modern Biblical Scholarship on p. 15. The date of the Babylonian conquest as 586 BCE, is on p.12.

Coogan, Michael, *The Ten Commandments, A Short History of An Ancient Text*. New Haven: Yale University Press, 2014. Provides background for much of the discussion of the Ten Commandments. Issues of posting and distributing are from pp. 1-5. The account of Moses and the three versions draws on Chapter 3 "Which Version of the Commandments," pp. 25-34. Layers of text and dating of the Commandments is discussed on p.37. For the legal agreement and covenant see Chapter 2 "A Covenant with Blood," p. 9 ff.

Diamont, Max I., *Jews, God, and History*. New York: New American Library, 1962. Traces the development if the idea of Zionism and the history of the founding of the state of Israel, pp. 390-411.

Ehrman, Bart D., *The New Testament, A Historical Introduction to the Early Christian Writings*. New York: Oxford University Press, 2016. The Kingdom of God as a continuing idea, see pp. 464-465. Apocalyptic teachings of Jesus and the Kingdom of God, see Chapter 17, "Jesus, the Apocalyptic Prophet," pp.280-285. The Kingdom of God as including outcasts, p.463. Fortunes reversed, p.463. Concept of Kingdom of God continues and develops, p.530.

Gonzales, Juste L. *An Essential Guide to Church History*. Nashville: Abingdon Press, 1996. The Edict of Milan in 313 CE is mentioned on p. 27. Christianity as a state religion late in the fourth century CE, is mentioned on p.33.

Harris, Ian, Consulting Editor, *The Complete Illustrated Encyclopedia of Buddhism*. Wigston, UK: Hermes House of Annes Press, 2011. The monastic community of early Buddhism, pp. 84-85.

Hobbes, Thomas, *Leviathan,* Part I, Chapter 13, dated 1651, found in Fred R. Shapiro, Editor, *The Yale Book of Quotations*. New Haven: Yale University Press, 2006. Quotation on the description of mankind without benefit of society, p. 362.

Lady Hosie, Editor, *The Analects of Confucius*. New York: Oxford

University Press, 1951. First published in the World's Classics in 1937. This translation by William Edward Soothill was first published in 1910. The sayings in the order presented here are from pp. 31, 13, 132, 151, and 159.

Rainey, Lee Dian, *Confucius & Confucianism*. Malden, MA: Wiley-Blackwell, 2010. The essential background information on the early life of Confucius is found on pp. 1-18. His views on government are from pp. 48-54. Choice of Heaven and moral government are concepts from pp. 53-54.

Rainey, Lee Dian, *Decoding Dao*. Malden, MA: Wiley-Blackwell, 2014. Daoism as not anarchistic, p.90. Quotation of *Dao De Ching*, While the fields..." p. 93 in Rainey from Chapter 53 in *Dao De Ching*. The previous Golden Age is described on p. 99 with the quotation "There were small states..." from p. 99 also.

Washington, James Melvin, *A Testament of Hope, The Essential Writings and Speeches, Martin Luther King, Jr.* New York: Harper Collins, 1986. King quotes Amos, "let justice roll down..." in Chapter 11 of his own book *Stride Toward Freedom*. In this anthology, the quote is on p. 481.

5
The Good Life
Stumbling Along the Path to Virtue and Happiness

I think I'm happy, but I'm not sure. I have a job and it is interesting work most of the time, but sometimes I don't know if I'm leading the best life. I come to the end of the day and I'm not sure what was accomplished. I mainly do what is expected of me. I don't have much time for anything else, and I'm beginning to think I didn't really choose this life I am living.

It's like you fell into the life you have and didn't deliberately choose it? Well, you're not alone, so maybe it would be good to talk today about this matter of choosing a good life.

You've probably heard of Henry David Thoreau, the famous American author, who built the little cabin beside Walden Pond, near Concord, Massachusetts. He kept a record of his experiences, and in 1854 published his thoughts in a book called *Walden*. The groups who are working hard to save the environment today love Thoreau because they think of him as a true environmentalist, living close to nature out by that pond. But actually, Thoreau had something rather different on his mind when he went out to Walden Pond.

He looked around at the life of his neighbors and noticed a lot of conformity: people doing what everyone else does without much thought as to why they are doing it. They seemed resigned to routine. Thoreau concluded: "The mass of men live lives of quiet desperation." This may sound a little dramatic, but Thoreau identifies the source of this desperation as a lack of conscious choice, the habit of just going along with what is expected. Thoreau wanted to try out a different kind of life at Walden Pond. Here, in his own words, is his reason for going:

> I went to the woods because I wished to live deliberately,
> to front only the essential facts of life, and see if I could not learn

what it had to teach, and not, when I came to die, discover that I had not lived.

And so, he went to Walden Pond to live a simple life, to see what he could learn from the mink and the muskrats, and to live a life he chose.

That's powerful, especially the part about dying without having lived. I envy him the courage to choose. My problem is that even if I were to set out deliberately to choose a good way to live, I wouldn't know exactly what path to follow. What are some options?

Before we explore the options set forth in the various religious traditions, we should acknowledge that not everyone has the freedom to choose. Some people are born into circumstances—poverty, handicapping conditions, hunger, war, political upheaval—that make it nearly impossible to make *any* choices; thus, having a discussion of the good life seems ludicrous when the goal for them is simply survival. But for those who could live deliberately if they would, it is valuable to explore what those alternatives might be.

Hinduism is an interesting place to begin because Hinduism itself has been characterized as a way of life. Hinduism has no single founder, no creed, and no authority—a religion, it is said, with "fuzzy edges"— but it has a vision of the good life and structure for carrying it out. The structure goes back to the Aryan life of ancient times that gave rise to the *Vedas* (Hindu scriptures) and divides life into stages with differing responsibilities and means of fulfillment. These include the stages of student, householder, retired person and monk (ascetic or hermit).

An Aryan boy would leave his parents to go live in the home of his teacher where he would receive his formal education with an emphasis on developing character. Girls also lived in the house of their teacher and by the fifth century BCE there were many learned women teachers. The *guru* (generic name for teacher in Sanskrit) was a role model and worked without pay. At the end of the student stage, after being bathed in the water of knowledge, young people married and became householders. The householder supports others in the family and this is viewed as a supreme good. Physical love in marriage was a positive thing, intended for enjoyment and mutual satisfaction. Women were to be respected and kept happy.

When a householder becomes wrinkled and with white hair,

responsibilities fulfilled and grandchildren born, it is time to retire and become a forest dweller, along with one's wife if he and she so wish. This is not a time to buy an RV (recreational vehicle) for the grand tour of the country, or even to go camping on the weekends, but to give up one's householder life and establish another, to "renounce fire," which means eating only vegetables, flowers, fruits, and roots, and to transcend culture to be able to focus on spiritual liberation (*moksha*). As if this were not enough for the good life, there is a fourth stage of becoming a hermit, shaving the head to join a monastery or become a wanderer, cutting all ties with family to focus on understanding one's soul as *ātman* (Indwelling Spirit) and one's identity with *brahman (Absolute Reality)*.

One interesting thing about these stages, conceived as they were so long ago, is that they parallel life for humans almost anywhere at any time. The first two stages are familiar, but the last two place greater emphasis on the tasks of old age to be addressed in a serious and (to us) somewhat radical way. The goal is not just to fade away but to become the spiritual person you are capable of becoming. Within the clearly defined stages of early Hinduism, a person does not drift from one stage to the next, but makes a deliberate choice to move into the next stage. Furthermore, there is not just one chance at the good life, but four, and if you are a bit stuck with being a student or householder, it won't last forever. There is change, serious change, in moving from one stage to the next. Thus, in ancient Hinduism life is defined by stages, but living in a certain way within each stage leads to the good life for that stage.

I like that because it provides perspective over a lifetime. It's easy to forget that life won't always continue as it is in the present. Throughout life we have many different opportunities to seek a good life. Where does the Hindu idea of meditation fit it? A lot of my friends are into yoga.

Later Hinduism developed the idea that the good life involves being at one with God. One might say that becoming close to God— sometimes referred to as God-realization—is the goal of Hindu life. How can one get close to brahman, that remote, abstract force behind everything? Keep in mind that brahman is also manifest (comes into form) as Ishvara, the personal god, and thinking of God as having many representations is not a problem in Hinduism, but an advantage. So, the goal of the good life is to be connected personally with Ishvara. There are several ways to go about this and each has implications for how to live.

Yoga is a cherished form of exercise and meditation popular among many in the West today, but the Indian practice of yoga was originally designed to strengthen one's relationship with Ishvara. In fact, the Sanskrit word *yoga* means *yoke*—think of two oxen hooked together by a wooden yoke—and refers to ways of building a connecting link of mental communion with God. They had four different types of yoga.

The Path of Devotion (Bakti yoga) recognizes the capacity for love in human beings, not romance, but true selfless love. In trying to connect with God, it helps to hold in mind human instances of love: the love of a mother for a child, the love of a couple for each other, the child for its parents. The task, while meditating, is to cultivate loving thoughts and attitudes, the serene, serving, friendly, motherly and sweet attitudes, as they are called in Hinduism, to sublimate human love into a means of connecting with God. Whether one gets to God or not, these attitudes and a loving nature are certainly worthy components of the good life.

The Path of Rational Inquiry (Jnāna yoga) recognizes the human need for rational explanations, and its methods encourage the search for the true self. A person might ask: What is not divine in the self? In meditation, one discovers it is not this, and not this...until one finds the divine core of one's being. This meditation has as its goal the discovery that the true self is the divine self (ātman). One might say this is a rational search for one's best self.

The Path of Mental Concentration (Rāja yoga) is practiced to gain mastery over one's mind. Westerners who practice yoga today are familiar with certain aspects of Raja yoga, including yoga postures, breath control, intense mental concentration, and fixing the mind on a specific object. The goal is to have the ego, the I, disappear, and for the mind to be without thought.

I've tried that. I say to myself, okay, mind, 'no thoughts, no thoughts,' and then I realize that I'm still thinking when I'm saying 'no thoughts.'

The task is to control the senses and empty all thought from the mind, and as you point out, it's not easy. The Hindu view is that the mind is a constant collector of experiences, all of which go into a pool of unconscious memories. Freud and Jung made similar observations centuries later. Through meditation, a person can bring these memories up to a conscious level and cleanse them from the mind. Gradually, through meditation, the mind becomes liberated from thoughts and thinking, detached from sensory experience, and absorbed in itself as its own object. That's the goal, anyway.

Along with the mental cleansing comes a release of spiritual energy. Ancient Hindu anatomy conceived of the body as having energy centers called *chakras*. Part of the purpose of yoga postures and controlled breathing is to release dormant spiritual energy from these *chakras*. A later ninth century development of yoga, sometimes referred to as Hatha yoga, stressed the development of the body as well as the mind, drawing on more difficult postures and cultivating inner sound. We might say that the good life includes having a quiet mind and unleashed sources of physical energy.

The Path of Right Action (Karma yoga) adds an additional dimension to the good life by taking a person beyond contemplation to action. It is natural to think of yoga as static, but this branch stresses work, not just any kind of work, but unselfish work, done without attachment to the outcome, that is, without a sense of who is helped or what spiritual progress is being made by the helper. It consists of doing spontaneous good deeds only because they are good.

What is learned through these different types of yoga concerning the good life? Keep in mind that for the Hindu believer, the goal of yoga is to be yoked with Ishvara. The paths to achieving this include useful guidelines, mental attitudes, and practices for achieving the good life: live with a sense of loving relationships, know your true identity, cleanse and calm the mind, and engage in unselfish work.

I like the idea of these guidelines. It appears that living a good life involves many things, not just one. I know that Buddhism stresses meditation, too. Does it have guidelines for a good life?

Buddhism grew out of Hinduism, as noted earlier, and shares some of its traditions, but it became a new religion. Buddha is not a proper name (just as Christ is not the last name of Jesus), but is a title meaning "Awakened One" or "Enlightened One." The original Buddha is Siddhartha Gautama and his personal awakening is the story of a search for the good life. Some might say that he had a good life, because his father was rich, and Gautama threw it away. Although the texts about his birth and early years are often unreliable historically, scholars agree that something dramatic happened to Siddhartha as a young man to change his life. He was from a privileged family, was well educated, and was trained in archery and horsemanship. At sixteen, he won himself a young bride who later gave birth to a son, Rahula. But something happened that set Siddhartha searching.

Siddhartha sometimes traveled by chariot beyond his father's estate, and on successive journeys he encountered an old man withered with age, a person afflicted with disease, and a corpse. The charioteer explained to him that ageing, sickness, and death came to all people. Because Siddhartha had lived a sheltered life, he had never seen such things, and it shocked and disturbed him greatly. He became disillusioned with his own life of ease and his pointless existence. If what he had seen of old age, sickness, and death was what life actually is, then being reborn again into that life was a horrible prospect. He decided to abandon his home and family to search for a better life.

At a Buddhist version of Walden Pond?

There is a parallel, isn't there? Siddhartha went off some distance with his charioteer, stopped, got rid of his fashionable clothes, cut off his hair, and ordered the chariot returned to his father. At around age 29, he had become what we today would call "homeless." A fascinating fictionalized version may be found in Herman Hesse's *Siddhartha,* published first in German in 1922, and although it is full of creative liberties, it pursues the coming-of-age theme of a young man seeking an authentic life.

Siddhartha Gautama sought teachers and wise men, lived a sensuous life for a while, and eventually joined a group of ascetics where he began a discipline of meditation, self-denial, and fasting—only a few drops of bean soup each day—from which he became emaciated and almost died. He concluded that no one could show him enlightenment and that he would need to find it himself. He understood that this path needed to be a "middle way" between self-indulgent pleasures and the ascetic life, both of which he had found unsatisfactory. As he went into deeper experiences of meditation, he thought about the *Dharma* (law) that governs the cycle of death and rebirth.

Siddhartha's ultimate goal was to escape the endless cycles of rebirth, but that's another discussion dealing with the question: What happens after death? Meanwhile, there is the puzzle of how to live the life we have, and Buddha had some things to say about that as well in his teachings. He had some expertise in meditation, and by drawing on the techniques of his Hindu background, he was able to achieve higher and higher levels of transcendence of (going beyond) the self. Meditation is not only the path but the "superhighway to Enlightenment" in Buddhist life, so we need to explore some of the things that came to Buddha *during* meditation that gave him the foundation for his teaching about how to live life.

First of all, to live is to suffer, not only physical suffering, but also the mental suffering that comes from loss. Everything is impermanent and with change comes loss, and with loss, suffering. We need to be realistic about that. Much of our suffering is caused by our own craving, not like a craving for ice cream, but the more general and deeper craving for material things that leads to greed for personal gain. Craving also means selfish desire and attachment, our need to grasp and hang on to things we already have, including our loved ones. Craving, selfish desires, and attachment lead to suffering. So how do we deal with this? Buddha taught that suffering can be relieved through letting go, by detachment, and becoming dispassionate, thereby achieving liberation.

Buddha developed his own outlook and then began to teach what is called the Eightfold Path, two steps for wisdom, three for moral living, and three for meditation. The first step is "Right View," or having the right understanding of what the world is, without illusions. The second is "Right Resolve," serious intention to make a change for a better life. The third is "Right Speech," which is not only telling the truth but avoiding insensitive, angry, and sarcastic remarks and gossip. The fourth is "Right Action," doing no harm to living beings, not killing, but also refraining from anything that can have harmful consequences for others. The fifth, "Right Livelihood," rules out work that hurts others. The sixth, "Right Effort," has to be used (in meditation) to banish harmful states of mind and negative thoughts. The seventh, "Right Mindfulness," involves a constant awareness of mind and body, always holding in check one's wants and cravings. The eighth and last is "Right Concentration," using meditation to calm the mind by concentrating on only one thing at a time.

That's a good list. What kind of life would result from following the Eightfold Path?

The picture one gets is of a person who is realistic about the seriousness of suffering who has, nevertheless, a calm mind and serene manner, eager to contain and relieve suffering, one's own and that of others, wherever possible. For Buddha, relieving suffering is the key to the good life, but a person needs to work at it. At the time, in the earliest years of the development of Buddhism, working at Enlightenment involved entering the *Sanghe,* (the Buddhist monastic community) or assuming the life of a wanderer.

I liked the story of Buddha's own search for the good life, but for me there is a bit too much emphasis on suffering in his teaching. Yes, it's everywhere, but there is more to life than suffering. There also seems to be too much turning away from a normal life in the world. Too little joy. I can't picture anyone in the Sanghe smiling. I'm just not ready for a monastery or the life of a wanderer.

Those are good points. Buddhism has been criticized, somewhat unfairly, as being life-denying, as turning away from this world and society to focus on the individual. Later Buddhism addressed this problem by making it more accessible for the ordinary individual. But that's another story.

Is there a set of teachings or an outlook on the good life that is less complex and more applicable to everyday life?

Confucius (551–479 BCE) is remembered more for his ideas about human nature and social structure, but he also taught that the good society has its foundation in the good person. Remember, he lived in the awful Warring States period of Chinese history when his world was falling apart. His task was to suggest how to fix it. His recommendation was to begin with the life of the individual.

The first step was to revive the notion of filial piety, respect for parents, family, and ancestors. The respect and reverence for one's parents carries over to teachers and elders, with respect for the dead equal to the living. The love and discipline learned first in the family is the foundation of all other relationships in society. For Confucius, the good life begins at home.

Duty and loyalty, initially learned at home, became the important virtues in the workplace and government. Criticism, appropriately framed, is permitted, but ultimately one must put the larger cause above one's own interests. Likewise, honesty and integrity are important virtues in the good life as one tells the truth and only promises what can be delivered. For a sincere person, thinking, saying, and doing are the same thing. Right behavior requires a degree of knowledge and an assessment of what is called for in each situation because rules don't always cover everything. Wisdom involves knowing how to deal with other people. We need to be honest with ourselves about what we do and don't know. These are simple virtues that will lead to a good life, but to act on them requires commitment.

Besides these "inner virtues," Confucius taught compassion for others. Remember the "negative" Golden Rule mentioned earlier, "not doing to others what one does not want done to oneself." The understanding and sympathy underlying that perspective suggest "imagining the other person's situation" and walking "in another person's shoes." The virtues all work together toward a culminating moral attitude of humanity and acknowledgement of one's own humanity linked to the humanity of others. For Confucius, the good life is living with a conscious attitude of humanity. The simple teachings of Confucius may be what you are seeking. There is surely nothing wrong with basing the good life on simple moral virtue born in the family and ending with concern for humanity. We find something very modest and plain about the idea of the good life in the teachings of Confucius.

Yes, I like the simplicity of Confucianism. Recognizing our common humanity makes sense. I'm looking for something to help me find the good life, or at least a better life, in the middle of this rather hectic life I lead, running here and there, without much overall purpose. Maybe I need to cut a few things out of my life.

Daoism, through the writings of the *Dao De Ching,* and *Zhuangzi* suggests that to find the good life we first need to clear away some things that get in the way of living a good life, beginning with our culturally-learned desires. As I mentioned earlier, Daoism tells us that our surrounding culture teaches us to want things, so we set out to get them and put a lot of energy into that. These are not real needs, such as food and sleep, but the culturally-defined, socially-constructed desires that make us want to keep up with the neighbors and grab everything we can for the so-called good life. We learn to be clever and manipulative in order to own and control the things we desire, thus making a chain from socially-constructed values, to desire, to ego-driven actions in order to get what we want. Our need for position, status, and things gets us entangled with "ego-action" to realize our aspirations.

It is not so much that the things we want are bad; it's that we don't know when we've had enough or how to stop. We tend to reach beyond our grasp and engage in precarious behavior. One of the beloved quotes from the *Dao De Ching* is: "One who stands on tip-toe does not stand firm. He who takes the longest steps does not cover the most ground." Daoism seems to be saying: back up from wants to actual needs, slow down, and know when to stop. Turn to the Dao of nature for guidance and develop a more natural life.

Daoism suggests that what we need to do is to replace ego-action with effortless action (referred to as *wu-wei*), so that we can do things in a more natural and spontaneous way, in keeping with Dao. It doesn't mean "doing nothing," but rather getting things done without a "to-do" list, spontaneously as things can be done. The *Dao De Ching* tells us that "Dao never acts and (yet) leaves nothing undone." Effortless action means developing the knack for the job so that it can be done almost automatically. It's the difference between putting together a piece of mail-order furniture with complicated instructions (sometimes quite nerve-wracking and frustrating) and doing something so familiar that you hardly need to think about it, the preferred approach to all activity.

Sometimes we get caught up in the rat race because everyone wants us to do something and we feel we need to oblige. Perhaps we can stand to be a little less in demand; when we are useful, we get used a lot. Maybe we could cultivate being a little useless, like the tall tree still standing in the forest that no one chops down because its lumber is no good. Zhuangzi says, "Everyone knows how to be useful, but nobody knows the usefulness of the useless."

Does this really mean useless or just not quite so self-important? It's easy to become the one who always has the answer. By the way, what's the connection between a good life and a long life?

"Living out one's natural life-span, living a long life and growing old, is one of the highest goals in Daoism." There is only the hint of an after-life in Daoism, so one had better make the most of this life. Unlike Hinduism, with its concept of rebirth and Buddhism with its idea of continuous suffering across many life-times, Daoism finds this present life to be extremely precious. Risking one's life is foolish and bravery is vastly overrated. It is best not to be anxious about either life or death. "When life comes, there is no way to turn it around; when life goes, there is no way to stop it." Daoism seems to be saying that this life is to be enjoyed, and it offers "three treasures" as guidance for the good life: compassion, simplicity, and not having to win. Daoism has the additional concept of Perfected People, who actually live like this with stillness and in harmony with Dao.

I like the stillness part. Isn't it amazing how we continue to run around in circles looking for things to make us happy while the very process of searching makes us anxious? But tell me, how do Christians think about the good life? I know they have especially good people called saints. I'm not planning on being a saint, but I am curious about how saints are able to lead such good lives.

For Christians, the search for the good life is shaped by an understanding of having been redeemed (restored to God's favor), meaning eternal life after death as well as the ability to lead a good life on earth. Some people may take this to mean that the good life is the afterlife, but Christianity also stresses that being forgiven and loved unconditionally leads naturally to a forgiving and loving life now. The good life is not so much the keeping of laws and moral obligations as responding to redemption in like manner, that is, by forgiving and loving others out of thankfulness and joy for God's love. In the New Testament Gospel According to John, Jesus is portrayed as telling his followers when he suspects that he is about to leave them, "A new commandment I give to you, that you love one another; even as I have loved you, that you also love one another (John 13:34). Following the new commandment is done not to earn salvation—that has already happened—but to respond appropriately with love. Thus, the good life in Christianity is expressed through service, not out of a sense of duty, but as a response to salvation.

We remember that the teachings of Jesus took place in a context of belief in the immediate end of the world (apocalypse), and that this gave those teachings a certain impossible urgency that relaxed only as the end of the world didn't come. Few followers, then or now, were prepared to sell all they have and give to the poor, but the Christian ideal based on the joyful response to redemption still involves "giving to the poor" in the sense of the needy, discouraged, and marginalized—"the least of these" as Jesus called them. Many Christians, in varying degrees, find the good life to be a life of service to others. Whether through organized charitable operations, of which there are many, or through individual acts of generosity and kindness in daily life, Christians find the good life through some level of contribution to the greater good of humankind.

And some are so good at this, they become saints?

I almost forgot. You want to know about the saints. Let me explain. Catholic Christianity has a unique way of recognizing those who have lived an especially good life by designating them saints. As we have seen, Daoism has the concept of "Perfected People," and Buddhism has the idea of "Bodhisattva" (enlightened being), one who is following the path to become a true Buddha through compassion and service, but is delaying the cycle of rebirth to help others in this life. Catholic Christianity recognizes that some people go to great lengths to respond to God's love, resulting in truly extraordinary lives of service. The lives of two recent saints, Mother Teresa and Father Damien, provide good examples.

Mother Teresa was born in Albania in 1910. At the age of 18, she began the process to become a nun of the Sisters of Loretto, whom she served for twenty years. When she went by train to an annual retreat for rest and renewal in Darjeeling, India, she received what she would later designate as a "call within a call" to work in the streets of Calcutta as a Missionary of Charity. It was agonizingly difficult work: generating donations of food, attracting volunteer medical services providers, and addressing the misery of the dying. She set up dispensaries and soup kitchens and a place to die (hospice) off the streets. Calcutta had two million destitute people and a consistent flow of refugees from East Pakistan. After ten years, the work she began there expanded across India and eventually all over the globe. At the time of her death, there were 3,842 Missions of Charity with 594 foundations in 120 countries. In 1969 the BBC produced a television series about her. In 1979 she was awarded the Nobel Peace Prize for her compassionate service to the poor. In addition to her daily work and devotion, she wrote and spoke publicly. The simple faith behind her good life is summed up in her own words: "Be a cause of joy to each other. You are precious to Him. He loves you, me, her. He has that delicate love for you."

Father Damien is another Christian saint, a Belgian priest who served the lepers in Molokai Island in what is presently the U.S. State of Hawaii. Leprosy is an infectious disease that produces skin ulcers, scabs and deformities. His father was a poor grain farmer, and as the seventh child, Joseph (Jeff) de Veuster got the leftovers of food and affection. Having been initially rejected for the priesthood because he lacked education and good grades, he persisted, and later as a priest volunteered to be sent to work among the lepers. When he arrived in Molokai in 1864, he built a church, founded a school, and built a reservoir on the windswept peninsula to which the lepers of Hawaii were assigned. Both private and public support for his work were very limited and difficult to obtain. Father Damien, as he was known as a priest, worked among the lepers doing what he could do: bring comfort and a touch of joy to their lives through his attention. But he was essentially managing a large hospice. He made coffins and dug graves for 600 lepers during his years at Molokai. After ten years, he discovered that he also had leprosy. He lived for four more years. In 2009 he was canonized as a saint, an unlikely outcome for an unpromising farm kid who lived deliberately among lepers.

Those are really touching and impressive examples. How did they do this? Are there any Protestant saints? I'm not joking, I just mean I've never heard of any.

The Protestant branches of the Christian Church don't have a formal process for acknowledging saints, but that doesn't mean that they don't have good people who live saintly lives. An interesting candidate for such acclaim is Albert Schweitzer, best known for his philosophy of Reverence for Life and his work as a medical missionary in Gabon, a province of Congo Colony (the colonial designation of the time) in Africa. Schweitzer's life is interesting for its breadth of activity and interests. He first earned his advanced degree in philosophy but also arranged to pass exams in theology so that he could serve a church, following in his father's footsteps as a preacher. He engaged in serious critical studies of the New Testament resulting in the important work, *The Quest for the Historical Jesus,* an early edition appearing in 1906. In his youth he had learned to play the organ and went on to become a famous organist, giving concerts throughout Europe, but he was also a renowned scholar of Bach, writing books on the interpretation of his organ music in French, German, and eventually English. Along the way he learned the mechanics of pipe organs and how to repair them.

Schweitzer lived in Alsace-Lorraine, a disputed area of northern France, often under German control. And although he was German, he became, in his own way, a world citizen. While he was professor at the University in Strasbourg, he arranged for medical studies—a little odd at the time for a professor to also be a student where he taught—to prepare for missionary work as "Jungle Doctor" in Africa. With his studies complete, he had to learn how to raise money to support his mission work and begin to gather up equipment and supplies for shipment to Lambarene, the site of the first hospital he would build.

He also married and had a daughter and grandchildren. With so many interests and travels he probably wasn't the best husband.

His career goes on and on, with years spent in and out of Africa but also with continuing interests in writing, most notably a book on Saint Paul and a three-volume study of "Civilization," in which his philosophy Reverence for Life is spelled out. He also wrote his auto-biography, *Out of my Life and Thought,* on which my comments to you about him are based. I have a paperback copy right here. He said that he worried about his patients at night, but in general he seems very happy in his work and life. Today we would probably diagnose him as hyperactive and medicate him to curtail his sprawling repertoire of interests.

Schweitzer's activities spanned the two world wars in Europe. He was a prisoner of war for a brief time, serving, of course, as the prison doctor. Later in life he received many invitations as a speaker and organist, raising money for the continuing work of the mission in Africa, which had grown into a sizable medical complex, the building of which he had supervised. Then the honorary degrees and awards began to flow in. A special foundation to support his work was established in the United States, The Fellowship of America, "fellowship" referring to those who suffer together in pain.

One might think that such a sophisticated scholar of the Bible might have a rather complex theology, but his philosophy of Reverence for Life is really quite simple. He writes, "I am life which wills to live, in the midst of life which wills to live." Noticing that all living things, not just humans, have this desire to live, "the man who has become a thinking being feels a compulsion to give every will-to-live the same reverence for life he gives his own." The goal then becomes "to preserve life, to promote life, to raise to its highest value life which is capable of development." One then feels responsibility "in an ever-widening sphere for all that lives." Albert Schweitzer's religious philosophy is about as simple as it gets, but with deep responsibility.

How could one person lead so many lives—and so many good lives? Most people would be happy to lead just one of those lives.

He not only worked among the sick and suffering, as did Mother Teresa and Father Damien, but he also had other activities, occupations, hobbies, and projects that made him happy. Schweitzer, with so much intelligence, talent, and energy was far beyond "normal," but he can inspire us wherever we are to be more than we are.

But really, it doesn't seem like any ordinary person can become like these saints. They are truly unique.

It is easy to dismiss the good life of these individuals as being beyond our reach, something not within our meager powers to achieve. Their circumstances were different from ours, we say, and they appear to have some special capability that we don't have. That type of life would simply be too difficult for the ordinary person. We need to remember, however, that these *were* ordinary people, all of humble origins, and that what they did was difficult for them, as it would be for us.

Consider Mother Teresa. Soon after her call, "after a time of feeling intensely close to God, Mother Teresa began to describe an 'interior darkness,' a feeling of distance from God." She told a bishop, "In my soul I feel just terrible pain of loss, of God not wanting me, of God not being God, of God not really existing." The feeling apparently continued until her death. It doesn't sound like a very happy life for Mother Teresa, but look at the better life and dignity in death that she provided for others.

Not every dedicated Christian becomes a saint, but it is not difficult to find people doing "saintly work" all around us, in homes for assisted living, in shelters for the homeless, and countless action centers. Is there something "saintly" about a teacher standing in front of a first-grade class? One wonders sometimes how people have the fortitude to do the work they do, but for them, this is their good life.

I know I will never be a saint, but these stories are truly inspiring me. I think I see a common theme running through all of this linking the good life to making the world a better place. Choosing to make a difference.

Henry David Thoreau made an important point about the deliberate life—choosing the good life—but not all of what happens to us in our life is of our own choosing.

He may have overstated his point?

Yes, or perhaps I did. Maybe we place too much emphasis on *choosing* the good life, when we need to acknowledge also that a portion of our destiny is shaped by *responding* to the things that happen to us. How we respond is also important in shaping our life. We can run, deny, make the best of it, or triumph over it, carrying out a good life within difficult circumstances. In a sense, responding to what happens to us is also a way of choosing the good life, but within given limits.

Perhaps we can conclude that descriptions of the good life found in the world's religious traditions have provided and continue to provide options and inspiration for making *better* lives. Surely, we can be more deliberate in our choices and more positive in our responses to what happens to us. How high we reach—good, better, best—depends upon our outlook, orientation, and motivation. Why some people achieve so little in life and others so much remains a mystery. And how does it happen that people who have been dealt a bad hand—blindness, a genetic condition, a rare disease—find a way to live a good life by making the most of what they have?

References

Bashkarananda, Swami, *The Essentials of Hinduism.* Seattle: Viveka Press, 2002. Refers to Hinduism as a way of life, p.39. Descriptions of life stages are on pp. 32-33. The life of the hermit is described on pp. 36-37. "God-realization" as becoming close to Ishvara, p. 7. Descriptions of four types of Hindu yoga, pp. 115-126, pp. 130-134.

Bunson, Margaret, *Father Damien.* Huntington, IN: Our Sunday Visitor Publishing Division, 1997. The early life of Joseph de Veuster (Father Damien) in Belgium is described on pp. 37 ff.

Creel, H.G., *Chinese Thought from Confucius to Mao Tse-tung.* New York: New American Library/A Mentor Book, 1953. The quotation "One who stands on tip-toe..." is on p. 89.

Flood, Gavin, *An Introduction to Hinduism.* Cambridge: Cambridge University Press, 1996. Describes Hinduism as a religion with "fuzzy edges," p.7. Elaboration of four life stages, pp. 63-64. Discussion of *chakras,* pp. 98-99 and Hatha yoga, pp. 98-99.

Harris, Ian, *The Complete Illustrated Encyclopedia of Buddhism.* Wigston, England: Hermes House of Annes Press, 2011. Summary of Siddhartha's early life, pp.16-19. The "Middle Way," p.21. "Superhighway to Enlightenment," p.41. Suffering, pp. 46-47. The

Eightfold Path, pp.48-49.

Harvey, Peter, *An introduction to Buddhism: Teachings, History and Practices,* Second Edition. Cambridge: Cambridge University Press, 2013. Buddha's title, p. 1. Concept of bodhisattva, p. 112.

Hesse, Herman, *Siddhartha.* New York: Bantam Books, 1951 and 1981. Originally published in German in 1922. The fictional coming-of-age story based on the life of Siddhartha.

Kolodiejchuk, Brian, Compiler and Editor, author of the Introduction, *Mother Teresa, Where There Is Love, There is God.* New York: Random House/Image, 2010. Copyright by The Mother Teresa Center. Early life, p. xii, xiv. Quote "Be a cause of joy..." p. 297. Data on missions and foundations, p. xiv.

Martin, James, SJ, *My Life with the Saints.* Chicago: Loyola Press, 2016. Sources of background on Mother Teresa are from pp.160-167. "Call within a call" quote, p.161. BBC documentary, p. 163. Nobel Peace Prize, p. 164. Canonized, p. 150.

Rainey, Lee Dian, *Decoding Dao, Reading the Dao De Jing and the Zhuanzi,* Malden, MA: Wiley-Blackwell, 2014. Paraphrasing of sources scattered throughout, but especially pp. 79, 83, 103, 76, 79, 85, 118, 146. Quotation of "Dao never acts..." p.77 (I have inserted "yet" for clarity of understanding.) "Everybody knows how to be useful..." p. 118. "Living out one's natural lifespan..." p.83.

Rainey, Lee Dian, *Confucius and Confucianism.* Malden, MA: Wiley-Blackwell, 2010. Chapter 2 Confucius' Teachings I: The Foundation of a Good Person, pp. 23-35 is the source for the summary of Confucian teaching. Negative Golden Rule, p.33. Quote of "Imagining the other person..." p.33. "Walking in another person's shoes..." p.33.

Spink, Kathryn, *Mother Teresa, An Authorized Biography.* New York: Harper One, 2011. Descriptions of work in Calcutta, pp.52-54. Beatification date, 2003, p. 298.
Schweitzer, Albert, *Out of my Life and Thought.* New York: New

American Library, 1949. His autobiography provides the source for the brief description of his life here. The Schweitzer quotations explaining Reverence for Life are on pp. 125-126. Reads like a novel.

Thoreau, Henry David, *Walden*. New York: Bantam Books, 1982. Originally published in 1854. The information about Thoreau's life is paraphrased from the Introduction by Joseph Wood Krutch. The quotation "The mass of men..." is from p. 111 and the quotation "I went to the woods..." is from p. 172 of *Walden*. The quotation "higher laws of nature..." is from Krutch on p. 7 of the Introduction.

6
Suffering and Death
Asking Why and Feeling Worse

*L*ast *week my grandpa—the one who my dad calls an anarchist—*
asked me what I thought would happen to him when he died. I said
that I didn't know. I was embarrassed that I didn't have anything more
than that to say to him. It is as if we are born and left hanging for a
whole lifetime without the answer to one of the most important questions
of all. Why does it have to be such a mystery? Do the religious traditions
provide any useful insights about what happens to us? I assume that
they have ideas about the afterlife.

Not all of them. To some people the question of what happens
to us when we die appears to be very important. Others live most of
their life without thinking about it very much until they grow old, and
then, like your grandpa, they start asking. Young people often think it
won't happen to them, and if it does, it will be a long time in coming.
At certain points in history, salvation involving an afterlife was a major
preoccupation; at other points, not so much. So, a starting point might
be to ask how important the question is.

Confucius appears not to have had a view of an afterlife, just as
he had no expressed concept of creation. For Confucius, Heaven is not
a place; and the afterlife, if there is one, is not a reward for a good
earthly life. In the thought of Confucius, the reward for good deeds is
in the doing. We do good deeds because we should, not for a reward.
When asked about life after death, Confucius is reported to have replied,
"You do not understand life, how can you understand death?" Maybe
the afterlife question was not very important to Confucius. If he was
vague about heaven, he was nevertheless sure that there was no hell or
devil; no need for a supernatural explanation of evil. It was all around
him.

Daoism is also vague about an afterlife, but with hints of

something more. In *Zhwangzi* there is interesting speculation, but no clear affirmation. In observing *Dao,* we see that death is a natural process, as is birth. If we think life is good, the author suggests, we will probably think death is good, too. The dead will like where they are, without regretting their hunger for life. What happens to the body? There will probably be some sort of transformation. Wherever we are sent, they could make us into a "rat's liver or a bug's leg." Maybe your left arm will become a rooster and you will be watching for the dawn. You probably won't go on being human, because you've already had a chance at that.

If the body is transformed, will consciousness continue? Zhwangzi says it will be like falling asleep and waking up suddenly. The waking up part suggests a consciousness of some sort. And maybe when we become fully awake, Zhwangzi suggests, we will realize that in this life we were only dreaming. Here we have a hint of immortality, at least for our consciousness. The Daoist writers emphasize living out a full life-span following Dao, without being overly concerned about death. Maybe our fear of death, they say, is "like being an orphan who does not know the way home."

A modern, more scientific version of death as sleeping might be that when we die, we fall asleep but don't awaken; and because we don't wake up, we aren't aware that we didn't wake up. Death is non-being and without being, there is no awareness, loss, or anguish. That is a rather simple explanation of dying: we just don't wake up.

It sounds to me like "An Atheist's Guide to a Peaceful Death." It's harshly realistic, but I can see how it would be an incentive to place greater value on the life we have now. But non-being? I think I would prefer a paradise.

If it is paradise you are looking for, you might turn to Islam. Paradise is described in the Quran in crisp images of gardens watered by flowing streams where the faithful can recline on soft couches in the shade under palm trees with fruit hanging in clusters overhead. There they will feel neither "scorching heat or biting cold," and "will be adorned with silks and brocades and drink from silver goblets, attended by 'dark-eyed virgins'" and handsome boys. Keeping in mind the landscape of Arabia, one can see why paradise is the oasis in the desert, providing things longed for but often missing in this life. Paradise is for the faithful, observant, and generous Muslim, but there are in the Quran descriptions also of a place where sinners are cast into the Fire, a fate that is anything but Paradise. Images of Paradise often describe what is absent from life, like water and palm trees in a dessert.

Or a warm fire and hot tea on a snowy day. Paradise sounds delightful, but I suppose it's pretty unlikely. Maybe you could tell me more about reincarnation. You mentioned it earlier as something that is important in Hinduism and Buddhism. Is it primarily a description of what happens when we die, or is it part of some larger set of explanations for other mysteries of life, as you like to call them?

Reincarnation, or more accurately, rebirth, is a very old idea, going back into the ancient roots of Hinduism. It does, indeed, as you are suggesting, provide explanations for other human mysteries. It is actually rather good at that. For example, many people die before they have fulfilled their dreams. Perhaps that is why people speak today of having a "bucket list" of things to do before they (pardon the horrible expression) "kick the bucket." Even people who live a long life, still have things they didn't get done. Think then of people who die prematurely from an illness, a natural disaster, or war. Even worse, consider the death of a child. In most lives there is a longing for completion, the hope of fulfilling an unfulfilled desire. In Hinduism, that human longing takes the form of a belief in coming "back to earth, this causing ... rebirth or reincarnation." It gives the individual more time on earth than one lifetime to get everything done.

Consider another question: Why do people enter life at such different levels, with such varying circumstances and opportunities? How can one account for a child prodigy in music, on the one hand, and someone who struggles simply to learn to read. In India, why was one person born into a caste of privilege while another finds it a challenge just to survive? We all have a different start in life—some have a head start—and that's been happening for generations, but no one knows why it should be like that. Hinduism recognizes this and suggests that we had a life (or lives) before this life, giving those who have been here two or three times before, a very different starting point, usually an advantage, from someone who is just now migrating from animal to human existence for the first time. Rebirth helps explain these unequal starting points.

Furthermore, how can one explain the vast differences that often exist between good people whose lives are filled with misfortune, and bad people who prosper and thrive? To understand reincarnation, we also need to grasp the meaning of *karma*, a word that has become popular in the West, that nonetheless deserves some explanation. In Hinduism, every action has consequences: good consequences and bad consequences. The doctrine of *karma* suggests that these consequences accumulate, not only in this life but beyond, going on into future lives. There will be consequences for what we do. They may not appear to be completely fair or justified in this life, so it may take more than one life for things to balance out, but they will. *Karma* is the built-in accounting system for what we do, both good and bad, so it is the goal to add good karma to your life with good deeds and avoid the bad karma that will catch up with you sooner or later. With bad karma, you could wind up as a reptile and have to work your way back up to being human. It is a very tidy system for coping with the injustices we see around us everywhere. It provides a mechanism of delayed but eventual compensation.

Those are interesting examples of how religious traditions try to provide explanations for the unexplained discrepancies in life. Rebirth explains a lot, but leaves behind some puzzles. For example, I'm still confused about what this second or third life looks like. I mean, how do we come back, as a baby or in the prime of our life? Are we like we are now or more of a different person? Would I recognize myself?

You have such interesting questions. It's hard to describe a Hindu position because there are so many manifestations of Hinduism, but one version suggests that a person has two bodies, a gross body, which is the physical body, and the "subtle body of mind, intellect...vital energy," and so forth. When a person dies, the gross body is left on earth, and the subtle body goes to "a different plane of existence." From this plane, or another, the return takes place, but who knows what this new creature will be? One very old Vedic tradition suggests that "different parts of a person go to different places upon death: the eyes go to the sun, the breath (*ā*tman) to the wind, and the essential 'person' to the ancestors." It's odd to think of being divided up like that and recycled through the universe, but it is an effort at explanation. It is doubtful, therefore, that you would recognize yourself, but some Hindus claim that here on earth they can remember aspects of a former self, and that they recognize people they have known before in a previous life.

All in all, Hinduism is comfortable with this rebirth process, but those who believe in rebirth eventually want to be freed from the cycle, arriving at *moksha*, a state of liberation achieved through the gathering of good karma. We have discussed how the various yogis also contribute to this goal. The process of rebirths we have been discussing is called *samsāra* and the ultimate goal of Hinduism is to be free of *samsāra* and to achieve a state of God-realization, as mentioned before as being at one with God. That takes a lot of good karma and probably many hours of yoga.

Buddhism builds on this Hindu idea of *samsāra,* but the effort to be free of continual rebirths is a more intense concern in Buddhism, because of the heightened perception of the amount of suffering that is built into life in this world. The Buddhist view of *samsāra* might be summarized as: "Let me out of here!"

I'm beginning to see why. I was impressed by the description of how Siddhartha, the Buddha, came to discover suffering after leading a sheltered life. I can relate to that. I think society shelters us from suffering, keeping most of it out of view so that someone like myself, only has a vague sort of "drive-by" experience of suffering. I have a neighbor—not the one who brought the coffee cake, but another— whose older sister is dying of cancer. She stops by after her visits to the hospice just to talk. Last week I went with her to visit as a friend and neighbor. It is a really horrible situation. The sister is with stage four cancer and she has just finished her last chemotherapy, what they call "palliative" because it won't cure her but might make her feel better. I wasn't ready for what I saw: a woman under fifty, bald, bedridden, with spasms of pain that even morphine won't curb, so that at times she screams uncontrollably, her eyes rolling back. Frequently, my neighbor comes to talk to me after her visits to her sister, but I don't know what to say to her. Siddhartha had his awakening; now I'm having mine.

With suffering so often hidden from our view, it is shocking, isn't it, when we come face to face with it. Your neighbor probably comes to you because you are a good listener. Siddhartha encountered suffering and he understood it: physical and emotional suffering, the suffering of loss related to change, and the suffering that comes from striving and clinging to things and loved ones. Certainly, there is also much suffering related to disease and physical conditions, and Buddha noticed that these get worse with the approach of old age and death. Are these the exceptions in life, or is this predominately what life is all about, as Buddha perceived?

But why, if there is an all-powerful and loving God, is there so much suffering? Why doesn't such a God prevent or at least alleviate suffering?

Now you have identified one of the oldest mysteries of life and perhaps the most difficult problem in religious thought. It is called the question of theodicy, the 'theological discipline that tries to reconcile the existence of evil with the goodness of God." God is all-loving or all-powerful, but not both; that's the dilemma. One way to address this problem is *not* to think of God as the all-powerful creator. You may recall that when we were discussing creation, we found that Buddha was reluctant to describe a creator God, and it was for this very reason: to avoid making God responsible for suffering. A religion we have not discussed called Zoroastrianism, the religion of ancient Persia, has the dualistic concept of a good God constantly fighting with an evil spirit: light and darkness constantly at war. Atheists would prefer to have no God at all than a God responsible for suffering.

Do some religions find a satisfactory solution to this problem? I remember something about a Biblical character named Job, who experienced a lot of suffering. Although he is known for his patience, he kind of lost control of himself and complained to God about being so miserable. Am I remembering this right?

Yes, you are. That's the key story in the Hebrew scriptures that explores why "the righteous suffer while the wicked prosper." The Book of Job is part of the Wisdom Literature, a late arrival to the Hebrew scriptures, and sometimes one wonders how it made the final cut. The Wisdom Literature also includes the collection of Proverbs, and the book, Ecclesiastes, which suggests that "all is vanity," meaning hopeless and worthless, as "in vain." It is actually a tribute to the redactors (editors) that these out-of-the-mainstream books are included in the Bible.

Job lived in a culture shaped by the philosophy of the Book of Proverbs, which consists mainly of wise sayings, descriptions of the consequences for good and bad actions, not unlike the Hindu and Buddhist idea of *karma*. Here is a sample:

> God scorns the wicked,
> but the upright enjoy his favor.

The house of the wicked will be destroyed,
but the tent of the upright will flourish.
—Proverbs 14: 9, 11

The light of the righteous rejoices,
but the lamp of the wicked will be put out.
—Proverbs 13:9

A worthless person, a wicked man,
goes about with crooked speech,
winks with his eyes,
scrapes with his feet,
points with his fingers,
with perverted heart devises evil,
continually sowing discord;
therefore, calamity will come upon him suddenly;
in a moment he will be broken beyond healing.
—Proverbs 6:12-15

Note the word *therefore*. Certain actions bring sure results, a *quid pro quo* (one thing in return for another) of inevitable consequences. You get what you deserve, they say. It appears that Job's friends believed in this world of certain outcomes for moral (or immoral) behavior delivered in this lifetime. In general, it is sound advice, because bad deeds very often do bring unhappy results. It is good advice except when it is not good advice: when the righteous suffer and the evil ones get off free. Job's friends apparently believed that the maxims of Proverbs always held true.

A character known as The Satan (different from later representations of the Devil), walks the earth as a roving prosecutor to find wrongdoing and test the sincerity of the righteous. Yahweh boasts to Satan that Job is blameless and upright and that there is no one quite like him with regard to good behavior. Satan is not so sure about that, so he strikes a bargain with Jahweh to test Job. Satan asks, "Does Job fear God for nothing?" In other words, aren't people righteous because they believe it brings prosperity and good fortune? There's something in it for them.

Satan may do as he wishes with Job as long as he spares Job's life. For starters, Satan takes away all of Job's property and sees that his ten children die. Job remains patient. Job has no knowledge of what's going on; he's not aware of the bargain with God, as the reader of the story is, but Job is sure there is no reason for his suffering because he is blameless. Then his so-called friends point out that he is not blameless, that there must be a reason why this is happening, and that he needs to admit his sin. Job stands firm because he knows he has not done anything wrong to deserve this. His friends persist. They know from the teaching of Proverbs that the righteous don't suffer. If Job is suffering, therefore, he must be guilty.

Job begins to crack under the pressure and gets very angry with Jahweh. He does not curse God to his face as Satan predicted he would, but he does curse the day he was born. He continues to complain to God, and his friends continue to blame him and defend God. Patient Job grows very impatient in proclaiming his innocence and after a while "he comes across as not only righteous but self-righteous." God has had enough and answers Job from a whirlwind (never face to face) in some of the most beautiful poetry ever written:

> Where were you when I laid the foundation of the earth?
> Tell me, if you have understanding.
> Who determined its measurements—surely you know!
> —Job 38: 4-5

> Have you commanded the morning since your days began,
> and caused the dawn to know its place...
> —Job 38: 12

> Has rain a father,
>   or who has begotten the drops of dew?
> From whose womb did the ice come forth,
>   and who has given birth to the hoarfrost of heaven?
> The waters become hard like stone,
>   and the face of the deep is frozen.
> —Job 38: 28-30

> Shall a faultfinder contend with the Almighty?
> He who argues with God, let him answer it.

—Job 40: 2

Now Job feels even worse. He is humiliated and ashamed. He realizes that he has overstepped. He answers in effect: What can I say? But Yahweh is not finished with him.

Will you even put me in the wrong?
Will you condemn me that you may be justified?
—Job 40: 8

Job repents—we might say apologizes—and the story has a happy ending: his fortunes are restored and his later days are even more prosperous. As for Job's so-called friends, Yahweh lets them know that they are out of order and he has no need for their defense.

What a dramatic story! I feel sorry for Job. And I know now never to get into an argument with God. But did we learn why the righteous suffer?

Not really. We only know that sometimes they do, but we knew that from the beginning. We learn that the teaching of Proverbs doesn't always hold true. We notice that we can often get very bad advice from friends. And as you mentioned, if we get into a shouting match with God, we will certainly lose. We might say that the more-encompassing message is that the universe does not revolve around Job, or us, or even mankind. The question of theodicy, an all-powerful and loving God who tolerates suffering, remains an unsolved mystery.

My neighbor, whose sister is ill, has gone through some of this same type of experience like Job. Her friends blame the sister for lack of exercise and recommend ground up peach pits as a diet cure. On the day of my visit, she kind of lost it and started crying in front of the doctor. She said that she couldn't understand how this could be happening to such a good person as her sister. He gave her a kindly look, full of compassion, and told her, "If it will be any comfort to you, let me say that some things are random and without reason. She simply happens to be the one".

Yes, thank you for sharing the doctor's observation. Maybe that's the modern interpretation of Job. Suffering is often random, not a result of our behavior, not related to anything.

With so many of life's mysteries unresolved, it is only natural, I would think, that people begin to long for a heaven or paradise for some resolution or relief. Tell me about the Christian idea of heaven. Isn't there a hope for eternal life based on a belief in the resurrection of Jesus?

Let me say one more thing about Job. There are sections of the Hebrew scriptures—Isaiah, Ezekiel, Daniel—that suggest another life or the awakening of the dead at the end of the world; but at the time of the writing of Job, there was no clearly developed Jewish idea of life after death. That's why the issue of Job's guilt or innocence is presented so dramatically; it must be resolved in this life, because there is no view of an afterlife or karma and rebirth as in Hinduism. There was no answer beyond this life for the question of innocent suffering, no compensation waiting for Job in heaven.

Yes, Christianity developed a strong concept of the afterlife based on the resurrection. Interestingly, we don't find much about an afterlife in the actual teachings of Jesus; it was the Christian faith that grew up around Jesus and after him that developed that belief. It was not the teachings of Jesus, but the death and presumed resurrection of Jesus that produced the Christian view of eternal life.

The four gospels of Matthew, Mark, Luke, and John differ considerably in their reports of the death and resurrection of Jesus. Mark, the earliest account from 70 CE, the closest in time to the death of Jesus at around age 33, has nothing much to say about the resurrection. (The written account comes 37 years after the event.) Those seeking Jesus at his tomb are told that "he has risen, he is not here," and his friends fled in "trembling and astonishment." That's it for Mark. In the other gospels there are also scenes at the tomb, but no agreement about the people involved, the locality of what took place, or the sequence of events and appearances. There is no detailed explanation of how Jesus arose from the dead in any of the gospels. The support for the idea of the resurrection of Jesus is not in a description of how it happened, but in the many accounts of mystical encounters with Jesus shortly after he died. These include appearances to the disciples, including the new disciple to replace Judas, a special conversation with the "doubting Thomas," an appearance to Mary Magdalene, and the memorable first appearance to Saul (his Jewish name), later known as Paul (his Roman name), on the road to Damascus. These were followed by many other appearances over 40 days. But even within these descriptions there are many contradictions and discrepancies.

I'm remembering a similar situation with the three versions of the Ten Commandments. You told me then that there were four versions of the life of Jesus. But this is an important point in Christianity, this matter of the resurrection. Is there no clear description or agreement about what happened?

Yes, it is very important to Christians, and good for you for remembering that about Moses and the more-or-less Ten Commandments. Maybe I need to take another detour and explain a little about New Testament criticism.

Go ahead. I like these detours and I learn a lot. I'm beginning to understand why it is important to know what we know about the Bible and how we have come to know it.

In addition to the four gospels written in Greek—gospel, *evangelion* in Greek, means the "good news" that Jesus brought—the New Testament provides a collection of letters by Paul, also in Greek, sent to the newly developing churches he had visited or founded, including letters to Galatians, Philippians, Romans and two to Corinthians. These are actually the earliest Christian writings, as early as the fifties of the first century. Scholars know through careful analysis which letters were written by Paul, and they separate these from additional letters attributed to Paul, as well as other letters by those acquainted with the traditions about Jesus, which we are fairly sure were not written by the persons named in the letters. *Attribution* is the word we give to the process of attaching a famous name to a text to give it more authority, and this was a common practice at the time. In fact, there is little assurance that the Gospels were written by people named Matthew, Mark, Luke, and John.

Really? I didn't know this.

There is general agreement that Mark came first at around 70 CE, with Matthew and Luke at 80–90 CE, and John at around 90–100 CE. Considerable time passes after the death of Jesus before a written record is established. One interesting point to notice is that Paul apparently never met Jesus or heard his voice except (allegedly) on the resurrection encounter on the road to Damascus. Paul says nothing about the actual life and teachings of Jesus. Did he assume that everyone knew? Did he know? Before Paul's conversion, he was a persecutor of the earliest Christians. He dropped out of sight for a few years, before he started writing his letters. He apparently needed to establish himself as an apostle (follower of Jesus) or in that line, and he struggled, often with serious contradictions, about how to present Christianity to Jews and non-Jews.

Scholars agree that all of the Gospels are a type of Greco-Roman biography, a different genre from the letters, sometimes called epistles, which also have a common format. One of the interesting things to do with the Gospels is to compare them. When they are placed side by side, it is easy to notice that Mark seems to be first and Matthew and Luke have drawn heavily on Mark, while changing Mark somewhat and using other sources of their own as well. The teachings in Matthew called the "Sermon on the Mount" appear to be drawn from an independent source. The puzzle of how the Gospels do and don't draw on each other is called the "synoptic problem," which means that questions arise when the Gospels are "seen together."

Each of the Gospels comes out of a different community setting and provides its own interpretation of the life of Jesus. Mark, for example, describes Jesus as one of the "sons of God," similar to other divinely inspired teachers and rulers of the time, and suggests that Jesus was the Jewish Messiah, even though everyone around him misunderstood him. They failed to recognize him because he was not a political or military leader, but a messiah who must suffer. Mark's Gospel probably came from a faith community that was enduring persecution and suffering.

Matthew makes a stronger case that Jesus is the hoped-for Jewish messiah and frequently quotes the Hebrew scriptures to show how Jesus is the fulfillment of that hope. The author even goes to the trouble of establishing a genealogy to trace the ancestry of Jesus back to the time of King David, although the genealogy is based on Joseph and appears along with accounts of the Virgin birth. But the Jewish leaders, Matthew relates, reject their own messiah. A unique feature of Matthew's Gospel is the inclusion of many of the teachings of Jesus identified as the "Sermon on the Mount." Matthew tries to explain the relationship of the old Jewish laws to the new teaching, and scholars believe he was writing for or from within a Jewish community and may have been Jewish himself.

The author of Luke also wrote the Acts of the Apostles, still another genre involving a "historical" interpretation of the early church. The Gospel of Luke portrays Jesus in the line of Hebrew prophets. Luke's genealogy goes all the way back to Adam, making Jesus, again through Joseph, the direct descendent of the first man, and of God. But Jesus is rejected as a prophet by his people. And the message of Luke reaches out to the Gentiles (non-Jews), suggesting that Jesus provides salvation to all people, not just Jews. In Luke's Gospel, Jesus is portrayed as having deep concerns, as a prophet would, about the social ills of the day, with special attention to women. The author of Luke is writing for the expanding Christian churches in the non-Jewish world and needs to explain this new religion in a convincing way. Luke attempts to do so, by rooting Jesus in the tradition of the Hebrew prophets.

The Gospel of John stands out from the others as unique, beginning with a Prologue that links Jesus to the Greek idea of Logos, or the "Word" who was with God in the beginning and reenters the world God had made as God's self-revelation. Some stories about Jesus appear only in John, who calls the miracles "signs" of who Jesus is. Whereas Jesus hardly ever talks about himself in the other Gospels, John keeps him busy explaining who he is: "the bread of life," "the light of the world," the "good shepherd," and "the way, the truth, and the life." The Gospel of John, unrelated as it is in many ways to the others, is written for the broader Greek-speaking audience of the Mediterranean world. It has its own sources and is a multi-layered interpretation of Jesus, sometimes portraying him as divine, sometimes as simply human. The early church fathers had strong arguments with each other about his true nature and eventually agreed that he was both divine and human.

I think you can see from our detour, that methods of criticism similar to those used in the Hebrew scriptures have been applied to the New Testament. It is nearly impossible to identify the historical Jesus, a point established by the "Protestant saint," Albert Schweitzer in his book, *The Quest for the Historical Jesus*. What we have before us are layered texts drawing on multiple sources, oral and written, each of which grows out of its own community and faith tradition. We end up with four different interpretations of Jesus—five if we add Paul's letters—and several somewhat conflicting versions of Christianity. Multiple versions of Christianity emerge from the New Testament, not one. All of them are already cast as strong beliefs and are certainly not objective historical statements. Add to this that the world view of the New Testament is pre-scientific and pre-Enlightenment and we realize that we are dealing with stories, legends, metaphors, images, and yes, myth in these accounts. Remember Bultmann's plan for demythologizing? Each of the Gospels is designed to make a statement of belief, so that the accounts we are reading in the New Testament are what the early Christians *believed* about Jesus.

That was a mind-boggling detour, and I needed that background. I can see now why there is so much controversy about Jesus, because there was no agreement in the very beginning. Was he just a great teacher, the Messiah, an outspoken prophet, or the Son of God? Then he was given all of those other names and titles as well. He certainly made a strong impression, so strong it seems, that his followers didn't know quite what to make of him.

Yes, those are very good observations. And now we are ready to get back to the resurrection. The amazing thing is how quickly the movement around Jesus developed, considering especially how he was misunderstood, rejected, and deserted by his disciples in his lifetime. Churches had been established throughout the Mediterranean world within just a few decades. A big explanation for that is the early belief in the resurrection. Christianity spoke to the human mystery of death and also provided a divine figure in human form with whom one might have a mystical identification. That was certainly what Paul wrote about to the young churches. The Jesus movement, as some scholars call it today, took off quickly and became Christianity.

I'm quite puzzled now about what to think about the resurrection of Jesus. Do I need to believe in his resurrection to have a belief in eternal life?

Literally? Some today, and many throughout history, would say you do. They have held that his death and resurrection made ours possible, and you better believe it. Paul elaborates that idea in his letters. The Christian hope of bodily resurrection is clearly inspired by the perceived appearances of Jesus to Paul and other followers. But let's take a step back to gain a broader perspective. It might be fruitless to keep pursuing the question of what to believe about Jesus and his perceived resurrection when the evidence is so shaky. A person can get permanently stuck there, confusing belief in a historical happening with faith in eternal life. It might be best to put those questions about the resurrection of Jesus on hold, or dismiss them altogether, and to ask more directly as we have done with other religious traditions: What does Christianity have to say about the mystery of death and the hope of eternal life? What is its message? Going behind and beyond the myth, what is the belief?

That way I can compare it to, let's say, the Hindu or Buddhist beliefs of samsāra or the Islamic view of Paradise, and decide what to believe or not. I notice that you have a book here on your desk, and reading upside down I see that the title is "Eternal Life."

Yes, it's by Hans Küng, a Catholic scholar who refers to himself as an ecumenical theologian, meaning someone who tries to bring together and unite people of different faith traditions. I referred to another work of his when we were discussing the atheist views of Marx, Freud, Feuerbach, and Nietzsche. Remember those guys? Anyway, Küng delivered a series of lectures on eternal life at the university in Tubingen, Germany, and they were published in this book. I can read for you certain sections where he states things really well. He is aware of the results of New Testament criticism, and he is quite well informed in science. He tries to make modern interpretations of the earliest Christian beliefs about eternal life.

That sounds interesting. I am eager to hear what he has to say. Maybe there will be something I can tell grandpa.

Christians came to believe in what is called the resurrection of the body. This is not the resurrection of the body you have when you die, so there is no reason to panic about being buried or cremated, or to worry about spending eternal life with hip or knee replacements.

Or a colostomy or catheter bag. What a thought.

The concept or image of bodily resurrection is of a life that is like the life we have now, where body and soul (psyche, spirit, mind) are firmly united. As Küng points out here, "When Paul speaks of resurrection, what he means is simply not the Greek idea of immortality, of a soul that has to be freed from the prison of a mortal body." What continues on after death is not a soul but "a living unit of corporeal-mental being." Let me read to you how Küng explains this: "Is it then a *bodily resurrection,* a raising up of man with his body? Yes, and no. No, if we understand 'body' in physiological terms as this actual body, the 'corpse,' the 'remains.' Yes, if 'body' is understood in the New Testament sense as *soma,* not so much physiologically as personally, the same self with its entire history..." Bodily resurrection is the "risen person."

Furthermore, Küng continues, bodily resurrection implies entering into a new and more complete relationship with God. It is not like a drop of water entering the sea "if only because a human being is not a drop of water and God is more than a sea...death is not so much destruction as metamorphosis... 'Life is changed not ended.' it is said in the preface of the Catholic requiem mass."

I like the word "metamorphosis." It reminds me of the larva and butterfly. If mother nature can transform an ugly worm into a beautiful butterfly, maybe there's hope for us. He's saying that we have a metamorphosis that results in a new existence? We continue as a person? But I wonder what this new existence will be like. My mom says that she worries that eternal life could be dreadfully boring.

Küng says that it will not be a return to life in this time and space such as rebirth described in Hinduism. And it's not the continuation of this life in another place "'outside' or 'above' in the 'beyond.'" It will be, Küng writes, in "God's invisible, imperishable, incomprehensible domain. It is not simply an endless 'further': further living, further carrying on, further going on. It is something definitely new: a new human being and new world." It is "a new future wholly different." It won't be boring, because it is not simply more of what we have already. It will not be what Nietzsche called "eternal recurrence." Rather, it will be a "radical transformation into a wholly different, unparalleled, definitive state: eternal life."

But before we become too confident, too sure of our idea of bodily resurrection, Küng reminds us that it is only a hope and not something we can describe very well. He says it so well right here: "The new life remains something for which we can hope, but which is beyond our vision and imagination."

I've never seen someone describe so well something that can't be described. It is a wonderful vision he provides, a great hope. Do you think he is confident about this hope?

Hope is hope, never certainty. But right here in this paragraph he says something that answers your question and reveals his faith. He writes, "I have reasonable confidence that the almighty Creator who calls us from not-being into being can also call us from death into life... that he has the last word as he had the first; that he is the God of the end as well as the God of the beginning."

That's deep. But it has a convincing ring to it. As you have been describing the Christian idea of eternal life, I have had this sense that it would be good for grandpa if he had this belief. It must be reassuring to people who have a confident belief in eternal life. They must be less anxious, less afraid to die, more positive about life.

There is a field of study called the psychology of religion. It began with William James (1842–1910) who studied religious behavior and wrote what became a classic, *The Varieties of Religious Experience,* setting in motion the objective study of religion as it functions in people's lives. For psychologists of religion, the question is not whether a belief is true, but how the belief works for the people who hold it. Does it have an effect on their life? Although one must be careful about sweeping generalizations, in many studies in this field, "there is often a positive correlation between religion and health, especially mental health." It is reasonable to think that some benefit comes from believing that life has meaning, that we have been created for some purpose, and that death is not the end.

The existence of suffering and death remains one of the great mysteries of life, but it is helpful to ask the timeless questions and learn what others have thought. For some people, the questions are important; for others, less so. But in the end, it must surely be better to have thought about suffering and death and reached tentative conclusions about what to believe, than to bury one's head in the sand, ostrich-style, living in denial of life's most fundamental reality: living things suffer and die.

References

Agnes, Michael, Editor in Chief, *Webster's New World College Dictionary.* Cleveland, Ohio: Wiley Publishing, 2010. Definition of the word "theodicy."

Bhaskarananda, Swami, *The Essentials of Hinduism.* Seattle: Viveka Press, 2016. Descriptions of unfulfilled desires and the quotation "back to earth..." are from p. 94. The description of karma is from Chapter IX "The Doctrine of Karma," pp. 79-97 and the discussion of reincarnation is from Chapter XI "The Doctrine of Reincarnation," pp. 91-96. The discussion of two bodies is on pp. 92-93. The quotation "different plane of existence" is on p.93. The terms *moksha* and *samsāra* are on p. 179.

Collins, John J., *Introduction to the Hebrew Bible.* Minneapolis: Fortress

Press, 2004. Identifies the theme of Job as "why the righteous suffer while the wicked prosper," p. 505. The recounting of the story of Job is from the summary on pp. 508-509. The quote "he comes across as..." is on p. 514.

Flood, Gavin, *An Introduction to Hinduism.* Cambridge, UK: Cambridge University Press, 1996. The quotation "different parts of a person..." is from p.86.

Gibb, Hamilton, A.R., *Mohammedanism: A Historical Survey.* New York: New American Library, 1953. A description of Hell is on p. 54.

Harvey, Peter, *An Introduction to Buddhism: Teachings, History, and Practices.* Cambridge UK: Cambridge University Press, 2013. The quote "concern about others' suffering ..." is on p. 266.

Holy Bible, Revised Standard Version. New York: Thomas Nelson & Sons, 1952. All quotations are from this version and are noted by book, chapter, and verse in the text. See the original reference note at the end of Chapter Three for a discussion of RSV and NRSV translations of the Holy Bible.

Küng, Hans, *Eternal Life? Life After Death as a Medical, Philosophical, and Theological Problem.* Garden City, NY: Doubleday & Company, 1984. The quotation "When Paul speaks of resurrection..." is from p. 109. Quote, "Is it then..." p.111. Quote "the risen person" p. 111. Quote "if only because a human being..." p. 111. Quote "God's impossible, imperishable..." p. 113. Quote "new future..." p. 114. Küng on Nietzsche's "the eternal recurrence" p. 65. Quote "the new life remains..." p. 109. Quote "I have reasonable confidence..." p. 114.

Lippman, Thomas W. *Understanding Islam: An Introduction to the Muslim World.* New York: Penguin Group, 2002. The composite description of Paradise is drawn from pp. 59 and 10. The quotations "scorching heat..." and "will be adorned with..." are from p. 59.

Partridge, Christopher, General Editor. *A Brief Introduction to*

Christianity. Minneapolis: Fortress Press, 2018. This is one of a series of brief introductions to various world religions. Part I for each book is the same and consists of chapters on anthropology, sociology, and psychology of religion, among others. The reference here is to Chapter 5, "The Psychology of Religion." It is written by Fraser Watts and is a very brief but informative introduction to this field of study. Mention of William James and his work is on p. 31. The quote "there is often a positive correlation..." is on p. 33.

Rainey, Lee Dian, *Decoding Dao.* Malden, MA: Wiley-Blackwell, 2014. The Daoist perspective on an afterlife is drawn from pp. 142-144. The quote about "rat's liver..." is from p. 143. The quote "like being an orphan..." is on p. 142.

Rainey, Lee Dian, *Confucius & Confucianism.* Malden, MA: Wiley-Blackwell, 2010. The views of Confucius on afterlife are from pp. 58, 62, 66. The quotation "You don't understand life..." is on p. 58.

Stegmann, Ekkehard, and Wolfgang Stegmann, *The Jesus Movement: A Social History of the First Century.* Translated from German by O.C. Dean, Jr. Minneapolis: Fortress Press, 1999. Originally published in Germany in 1995. This social and historical interpretation uses the term "Jesus Movement" to describe the first century of Christianity.

7
The Fate of the World
Extinction, Plague, Atomic War, and Astronomical Disasters

I have a colleague at work who thinks the world is coming to an end, and she thinks it will happen soon. She calls it "Judgment Day." I think she gets her ideas from signs she sees in the Bible. It makes me wonder if other religions have ideas about the end of the world, or if this is only in the Bible.

The idea is not as prominent in other religious traditions, but something like it is there. We can come back to the Bible (hopefully before Judgment Day) to explore where it is exactly that your colleague may be getting her ideas, but first let me try to answer your question about the other religions.

Islam has the idea of a Day of Judgment when Allah will assess the worth of individuals and settle their destinies. Although Muslims believe there is no one superior to the Prophet, one branch of Islam has the concept of messiah, known as the *Mahdi*, the "one who guides divinely" and returns from the form of 'Hidden Imam' (authoritative teacher) "on the Day of Judgment to restore justice on earth." Islam, like other religions, has the sense that something is profoundly wrong with the progress of justice in human history. Many Muslims believe that the whole enterprise will end in a Day of Judgment and restoration.

Hinduism is often portrayed as having a negative view of the present historical world because of its cyclical view of human life as constant rebirth. Life seems to go on and on in the form of many lives, with the focus on the individual's release from the cycle without much concern for the larger meaning of the cycle itself. But the Hindu epics, the *Rāmāyana* and *Mhābhārata,* portray battles between the forces of good and evil" in an ongoing struggle.

Keep in mind that Hinduism not only has a god for creation, Vishnu, but a god for destruction, Shiva. Its complex cosmology is not only characterized by many realms, but also four ages (yugas) which last for thousands of years, some even millions. The present age is one of darkness. Ultimately, "the universe will be destroyed by fire or flood" and then "the process begins again for all eternity." Some say it has no purpose but the play of the gods.

Cyclical and without purpose? The sport of the gods? That's disturbing. Does Buddhism have a judgment day or a belief in a savior who will rescue the world in its last days?

There seem to be no "last days" in Buddhism with its multitude of realms and eons, but there is the concept of Bodhisattvas who stretch across time, reappear, or linger on earth to do good deeds. Some of these figures stood out and something like a cult developed around them. One such figure called Bodhisattva Natha, known as the Protector, was scheduled to reappear as Maitreya, "to be the next Buddha to teach on earth." Naturally, people began to wonder when he would appear, and made claims and predictions about his arrival. The Maitreya Buddha is also known in one of his manifestations as Budai, a tenth century Chan monk who was portrayed as a "pot-bellied, wandering teacher who carried presents to children in his cloth bag (budai)." Images of Budai are often known as the "Laughing Buddha."

A Buddhist version of jolly old Saint Nicholas?

Well, something like that. The main idea is that the Maitreya Buddha, also known as Budai, would usher in the golden age. There seems to be an idea in Buddhism, not that the world will end, but that things will get better. This won't come about with a messiah, but with the appearance of another Buddha.

What about Daoism? Do they have a judgment day or something like it?

Daoism appears not to have the concept of a last judgment or end of the world but of a prior more perfect age and "the idea of devolution, that the world is going downhill from the golden age..." As is often the case with Daoism, the solution is reversed: the inadequacy of the present life will not be resolved at the end of history; it has already been resolved centuries ago, if we would only wake up, notice what is needed, follow Dao, and live a simple life as people did in the golden age.

What is the mystery behind these ideas that the world is going to end and a new age will come?

The reality beyond the myth? Let me try to develop in modern language a description of the mystery we are dealing with here. We'll call it the mystery of meaning.

It is natural to look around at the world, to see the suffering, destruction, and corruption that abound, and ask if it has any meaning or ultimate purpose. We have our life, and no matter what we may believe about how we came to have it, we can't help but wonder if it has purpose or meaning. People find meaning, or invent meaning, in many different ways, gleaning meaning from family, work, or a hobby.

I have that great aunt I told you about whose whole life is bound up in her crafts: knitting, crocheting, quilting, needle-point, and on and on. She's very good at all of these, but really, that's her whole life now.

And that's okay. Perhaps we need to snatch a little meaning wherever we can find it. But I sense in your voice that you might want to get beyond the knitting needles to find some larger purpose and meaning. And that's the timeless question: Does life have any essential meaning?

And not only the meaning of one individual life, but the meaning of life in general?

Yes, now you are asking if the entire human enterprise itself has any meaning. The timeless question goes beyond my life to life itself. This question is often framed by religious thinkers as "the meaning of human history." Is there purpose or substance to the accumulated human effort?

Beyond knitting or golf or cooking gourmet meals? This is getting interesting, but how does it connect with the end of the world?

As the mystery was faced in the religious traditions, particularly in the Bible, which we will get to in a moment, people looked around at the world and what they saw was fairly disturbing. Either things were just going in circles, or slowly winding down, or they couldn't see any progress. They experienced a lot of war and destruction, a lot of misery, violence, and suffering, and more than enough lying, cheating, and corruption to make them deeply discouraged. Sometimes their assessment was: things can't just go on and on like this forever. There has to be a better way leading to a better day. And so, we get the notion that the world as we know it will end, there will be a last judgment about what has been taking place, and a new age where everything will be as it should be.

Now I want to hear about where we find this discussed in the Bible.

In the Hebrew scriptures, it is the Book of Daniel that speaks of "last things" and the "end of the age" in a literary genre known as "apocalyptic," meaning "the time of the end when God will intervene for judgment." It is a judgment of nations as well as individuals, and the final judgment of the dead. The Book of Daniel was the latest book to be written that was accepted into the Hebrew scriptures and is the only apocalyptic book within them although an occasional apocalyptic concern surfaces in the prophets. Written partly in Hebrew and partly Aramaic (with a dash of Greek poetry), Daniel draws its themes from a time after Israel was exiled to Babylon (597 BCE), but the book was written or compiled much later, probably around 164–166 BCE.

The main character is Daniel, who is working in the court for the Babylonian King, Nebuchadnezzar, as an expert interpreter of dreams. The tales of Chapters 1-6 can be thought of as a guidebook for the lifestyle of the exiled: "participate in the life of the Gentile world and be loyal to the king, but realize that your ultimate success depends on your fidelity to your God and his laws." Even though the Book of Daniel may not be well known, its legends are embedded in the popular culture of the Judeo-Christian world: how Daniel's friends Shadrach, Meshach, and Abednego were thrown into the fiery furnace but weren't burnt, how Daniel himself was tossed into a den of lions but was not eaten, and how he alone could "read the writing on the wall" when no one else could, which we recognize today as a shorthand phrase for the ability to predict forthcoming disasters.

The second part, Chapters 7-12, contains Daniel's apocalyptic, nightmare-like visions of beasts, such as a lion with eagle's wings, a bear, a leopard, and an unidentified monster with iron teeth, disguised representations of countries and rulers—maybe Persia, Greece, or Syria? Daniel's view of the end of the world is in the last chapter reference to a resurrection of the dead where "many of those who sleep in the dust of the earth shall awake, some to everlasting life, and some to shame and everlasting contempt." The chapter ends with speculations about when this will actually happen.

As we have seen, apocalyptic ideas continued to develop, so that at the time of Jesus, the writer of the Gospel According to Mark would portray Jesus as preaching the ideas of the end of the world with the Kingdom of God already arriving.

I remember that now. But does the New Testament have apocalyptic books like Daniel?

That would be the Book of Revelation, actually titled The Revelation to John, although we only know enough about the author to be sure that he was not the same person as the writer of the Fourth Gospel, known as the Gospel According to John. The author of Revelation is often called John of Patmos, after an isolated Aegean Sea island used as a prison for banishment, so there is a good chance that Revelation may have been written in prison by an outspoken critic of the Romans, which may explain why he was in prison. He certainly has no affection for the Romans, and he definitely longs for better times.

Apparently, John is known to his readers because he is sending letters to seven churches in Asia Minor (present-day Turkey), giving them specific suggestions about what to do and not do in their churches. Most of the book, Chapters 4-22, is about "John's heavenly vision of the future course of history, down to the end of time." I have here Bart D. Ehrman's *The New Testament, A Historical Introduction to Early Christian Writings,* which provides a concise summary of what happens to John and what he sees in his visions. We'll use it as our celestial travel guide.

John is "taken up into heaven through a window in the sky" where he "beholds the throne of God" surrounded by twenty-four human elders and four angels. "In the hand of the figure on the throne is a scroll sealed with seven seals, which cannot be broken except by one who is worthy." The Lamb appears standing, as if in slaughter (presumably the crucified Christ), and the reading of the scroll begins. "With each broken seal, a major catastrophe strikes the earth: war, famine, death. The sixth seal marks the climax, a disaster of cosmic proportions: the sun turns black, the moon turns red as blood, the stars fall from the sky, and the sky itself disappears." The breaking of the seventh seal is "followed by an entirely new set of seven disasters." Angels with trumpets announce each one, and wild beasts appear "who torture and maim" amidst "widespread calamity and unspeakable suffering." The seventh trumpet announces the beginning of the end, which turns out to be seven more angels, each pouring a bowl of plagues and disasters down upon the earth.

The imagery and symbolism are strong: a red dragon with seven heads and ten horns ready to devour a newborn child, a beast rising out of the sea with haughty and blasphemous words, an angel with a sharp sickle to gather the vintage of the earth for the great winepress of God's wrath, a pale horse whose rider's name is death, hail and fire mixed with blood that burnt up trees and grass, four angels ready to kill one-third of mankind, scorpions, and so forth. And there will be a great final battle with armies assembled at a place called Armageddon.

And who might be responsible for these earthly disasters? An earthly empire with a temporal ruler? All fingers point to Rome. John portrays Rome in a not very well disguised secret as "the whore of Babylon." Did he have anyone in particular in mind as the leader of this mess? Yes: 666. A number? You know how we have Roman numerals composed from letters: V, I, X, C, such as VI for 6. For those who knew how to do the math, 666 turns out to be Caesar Nero. Obviously, things can't go on like this, in this empire under this leader. God won't put up with it. There is too much misery and destruction. God will need to make an end to it and bring in a new age, a new way for the world to be run. That's what John of Patmos is telling us about the end of the world.

I always thought these Biblical ideas about the end of the world were really weird, but maybe John was on to something important. Now I'm thinking about the possible end of the world in our time, and I am wondering if life as we know it really could come to an end. Do you think our species could be wiped out or that the universe could just blow up or something like that?

We can certainly consider those questions from a scientific perspective to see what scholars today are saying about the destruction of life and the end of the universe. There is a secular, modern-day apocalyptic literature that warns us about what could happen—or is happening. Let's call it "the fate of the world." Would you like to explore some of that?

Yes, let's take a look. I'm curious now about how bad things actually are and whether there is any hope.

Well, if you're interested, let's begin with the concept of extinction and examine the possibility that human life itself might become extinct in our age. Elizabeth Kolbert has written a fascinating book called *The Sixth Extinction, An Unnatural History.* I have a copy of it right here if I can find it. Yes, here we are. She reports what scientists have been able to discover about periods in evolutionary history where large numbers of species have become extinct. Species usually go along being at low risk for extinction, but then at rare intervals, high risk comes along; we might say biological boredom followed by panic.

The first extinction occurred 444 million years ago at the end of a geologic period called Ordovician, when for some odd reason the oceans nearly dried up and eighty-five percent of marine species died off. The plants and animals alive today are descendants of those who made it through, because extinction, for those who suffer it, is terminal for the entire species. No more offspring.

The second extinction comes at the end of a period called Permian, and is identified by a "reef gap" when many coral reefs went missing in the geologic record. An ocean disturbance. The third extinction between the Permian and Triassic periods around 252 million years ago was "the biggest of the Big Five, an episode that came scarily close to eliminating multicellular life altogether." It seems to have been triggered by massive climate change, with ocean temperatures rising eighteen degrees producing "hydrogen sulfide, which is poisonous to most other forms of life," killing marine creatures first, then leaking into the air to kill those on land. "By the time it was over, something like ninety percent of all species on earth had been eliminated." A fourth extinction in the late Triassic period appears to be related to ocean acidification.

If people know any of these extinctions, it is usually the fifth that comes to mind, sometimes called the Asteroid Extinction, the one where an asteroid (a small rocky planet) hit the earth leaving a huge crater, discovered in Mexico in the late 1970s. It "caused what may have been the worst day ever on planet earth. By the time the dust—in this case literal as much as figurative—had settled, some three-quarters of all species had been wiped out." The asteroid hit the earth not so much from above but at a low angle from the side and slammed into the Yucatan Peninsula "moving at something like forty-five thousand miles per hour, and, due to its trajectory, North America was particularly hard hit." The event's most famous victims were the dinosaurs, wiped out completely; but three-fourths of bird families went extinct, as well as two-thirds of mammalians. "It took millions of years for life to recover its former level of diversity." So those are the five major extinctions.

But why is this book called "The Sixth Extinction"? When was the...? Oh, oh, Are we in it?

Not only are we in it; we are causing it by our "transformation of the ecological landscape." Some scientists are giving our era a new name: *Anthropocene,* meaning a human-dominated geological epoch. It's not so much that we set about to ruin everything; it's in our nature to be difficult to live with as a species. It is "our restlessness, our creativity, our ability to cooperate to solve problems and complete complicated tasks." It also involves our use of language and storage of information. It's not that we suddenly became this way in the twenty-first century; *homo sapiens* has been dominant for a long, long time.

In a book called *Sapiens, A Brief History of Mankind,* by an Israeli scholar, Yaval Noah Harari, we find this human dominance well-documented. Two striking examples are what happened when *Sapiens* (humans) arrived on the continent of Australia and later in what is now the Americas. Because of its relative isolation, Australia had developed a rich diversity of plant and animal life. When humans first arrived there, some 45,000 years ago, they soon dominated, even the very large marsupial species (like kangaroos). "Within a few thousand years, virtually all of these giants vanished. Of the twenty-four Australian animal species weighing 100 pounds or more, twenty-three became extinct. A large number of smaller species also disappeared."

"The Americas were a great laboratory of evolutionary experimentation, a place where animals and plants unknown in Africa and Asia had evolved and thrived." But not for long. Within 2,000 years of the arrival of *sapiens* "Most of these unique species were gone." Let me read you what Harari says:

> According to current estimates, within that short interval, North America lost thirty-four out it forty-seven genera of large animals. South America lost fifty out of sixty. The sabre-tooth cats, after flourishing for more than 30 million years, disappeared, and so did the giant ground sloths, the oversized lions, native American horses, native American camels, the great rodents and the mammoths. No, there wasn't another asteroid. It was *sapiens*.

So, it isn't just modern industrialized humans that are causing all of this damage. Sapiens has been a serial killer for centuries.

Exactly. But we've also made it worse in modern times. The author of *The Sixth Extinction* refers to a list of large-scale changes drawn up by Nobel Prize winner Paul Crutzen, who gave us the term "Anthropocene" to describe the present age. To paraphrase and summarize, we can say that human activity has "transformed between a third and half of the land surface of the planet," dammed up or diverted most of the rivers, produced more nitrogen (for fertilizer) than nature makes, continues to remove about one-third of the fish from the ocean, and uses more than half of the fresh water. In addition, Kolbert tells us (continuing to draw on Crutzen): "Owing to a combination of fossil fuel combustion and deforestation, the concentration of carbon dioxide in the air has risen by forty percent over the last two centuries, while the concentration of methane, an even more potent greenhouse gas, has more than doubled."

It looks like the world is not a very healthy place for man nor beast right now. How big will this sixth extinction be? Do we have estimates?

There are projections. By 2050, if warming is kept to a minimum, it could be 22 to 31 percent of the species; if warming maximizes, it could be 38 to 52 percent. How many species is that? A headline in the *National Geographic* put it: "By 2050 Warming to Doom a Million Species." And here's the clincher: "By disrupting these systems— cutting down tropical rain forests, altering the composition of the atmosphere, acidifying the oceans, we're putting our own survival in danger." We may become both perpetrator and victim, determining which evolutionary pathways are open for the planet's species while threatening our own.

Humans seem to excel at killing off other species using their special talents and treachery, but what about the little microbes that are killing us off? Are we getting outsmarted by something this small? I'm referring to the pandemic we've been living through, with that awful COVID-19 virus. Can the viruses wipe out the human race?

If we don't do it first ourselves? They can surely threaten and kill large numbers of the human race, spreading as a pandemic, disrupting societies, economies, and individual lives. In the early literatures of the religions, they are often called plagues.

So, epidemics that we call viral infections are the plagues of the ancient world? How long have these plagues been around?

Smallpox is a virus, and scientists estimate that it has been with us since the beginning of agriculture, around 10,000 BCE. One interesting bit of evidence is from the well-preserved Egyptian mummy of Ramses V, who died of a serious illness in 1157 BCE when he was forty. His face and neck show clearly the tell-tale pock marks of smallpox, the scars of skin lesions associated with that plague. Smallpox killed many Native Americans when the settlers brought it with them, and it played a major role in destroying the Aztec empire so that Spain could more easily conquer Mexico. At the time of the American Revolution,

George Washington was sick with it for a month and was left with marks on his face. A planned naval attack on England by France and Spain was averted because their sailors were too sick with smallpox to fight. President Abraham Lincoln contracted smallpox, and when he returned from delivering the "Gettysburg Address," he became sick and was under quarantine at the White House for three weeks. "In 1853, some 80 percent of the native population of Oahu, Hawaii, died when first exposed to smallpox." The virus is estimated to have killed nearly 300 million people in the twentieth century alone, which is "three times more than all the wars in that century." And that's just smallpox. Wait until you learn about Yellow Fever.

Do I have to? No, go ahead. Then I have some questions.

I'll be brief, but some of this is shocking. Yellow Fever, also a virus, is transmitted by a particular mosquito, but it took years to figure that out. "In 1793 Philadelphia was America's capitol..." and our founding fathers "...witnessed the Yellow Fever plague and watched as it shut down the new U.S. government." A few years later, in 1801 when Napoleon had dreams of extending his French empire to the Americas, he sent troops to Santo Domingo, but within a few months 27,000 French soldiers died of Yellow Fever; and that experience convinced Napoleon to sell what territory he had in the new world rather than to expand it, leading to the "Louisiana Purchase" in 1803 by President Jefferson, greatly expanding the territory available for the westward settlement of the United States.

It seems that through much of history these viruses just ran wild. But haven't they been brought under control now?

Yellow Fever was controlled in Cuba in 1901 by attacking the mosquito that carried it, but a successful vaccine was not developed until 1937. Eventually, through groundbreaking scientific research, other vaccines were developed and the major viruses came under control: measles, smallpox, Yellow Fever, poliomyelitis, among many others. More recently we have faced Ebola, SARS, West Nile, and Human Immunodeficiency Virus (HIV). Unfortunately, some nations retain viruses to use in their biowarfare programs. Smallpox has been elevated as a useful "bioterror weapon" because everyone not vaccinated in the last seven years would likely be endangered if exposed. We badly need an international agreement to eliminate smallpox completely, "thus making the virus the first species *purposely* eliminated from the planet."

It is ironic, isn't it, that humans eliminate so many harmless species, but continue to keep smallpox as a pet, playing around with it and dangerously inviting trouble. But tell me, what is a virus exactly and why is it so deadly? And what is this book you keep referring to here?

This is *Viruses, Plagues, & History: Past, Present, and Future* by Michael B.A. Oldstone, a professor of viral immunology. He tells us that "viruses are nothing more than a tiny bit of genetic material—a single kind of nucleic acid...and a coat made of protein molecules." Viruses can enter all "forms of life from plants and animals to bacteria, fungi, and protozoa." I remember being taught about plants and animals as the two major forms of life, but Oldstone says, right here: "Together, viruses, plants, and animals form the three main groups that encompass all living things." Then he explains: "As opposed to plants and animals, viruses lack cell walls and are, therefore, obligatory parasites that depend for replication on the cells they infect."

How do they cause disease? By being directly toxic to the cell and killing it, by altering its function, or by upsetting the host's immune response system, causing it to over react or otherwise malfunction. Viruses can cause acute infections from which the patient can become very sick or die within a few days or they can "persist for months or years, such as the HIV infection that produces AIDS. The so-called flu epidemic between 1918 and 1919, often referred to today, actually killed over 40 million people, "more victims than died in World War I. When one pandemic comes under control, another awaits. We will recover from COVID-19, but that won't be the last.

So, these viruses continue to...well...plague us. I hate to ask, but is there a threat that could wipe out the entire human race suddenly and completely?

One threat that was talked about a lot several years ago is hardly mentioned today; I'm referring to atomic warfare. The so-called "atomic nations" sit on their stockpiles of weapons and try to devise ways to prevent other nations—the so-called rogue states—from joining the nuclear club. But the conversations about arms control and disarmament remain rather abstract, and we tell ourselves that nothing like that could ever happen. But it has already happened.

That's right, the dropping of the atom bombs at the end of World War II. Why did the United States do that?

The United States was getting further involved in the war in

Europe when on December 7, 1941, the Japanese bombed Pearl Harbor, on the island of Oahu, in the Territory of Hawaii. Japanese aggression throughout southeast Asia was widespread and Japan wanted to continue to build its empire without interference from the United States. They didn't really want an all-out war with the United States; they just hoped to neutralize its military capabilities. They thought they could catch the U.S. sleeping (which they did) and destroy its prime naval base and fleet in Hawaii. So, they attacked with six aircraft carriers and four hundred aircraft, sinking many ships and damaging grounded aircraft. They killed more than two thousand service men and wounded more than a thousand others. A coordinated attack on a U.S. base in the Philippine Islands destroyed fleets of B-17 bombers and squadrons of P-40 fighter planes.

Many Americans were reluctant to enter a war, but the sleeping giant had been awakened, war was declared, and bloody fighting continued for three and a half years at a great loss of life in many famous battles to take Midway, Iwo Jima, New Guinea, the Solomon Islands, Guadalcanal, and others. America was slowly winning the war island by island and a difficult decision point came: If the Japanese do not surrender, must we invade Japan to get them to do so? Estimates of war casualties from such an invasion were staggering—between "1.7 and 4 million U.S. casualties including 400,000 to 800,000 killed." The Japanese refused to surrender in the island battles and had a policy of fight to the death. What would this mean for an invasion? A thirteen-point proposal was drafted by the Allies known as the Potsdam Declaration and was presented to the Japanese, who refused to sign it. Meanwhile, the atom bomb was secretly under development. Should it be used?

Couldn't they have just exploded a bomb in a safe place so that the Japanese could see its destructive power, and maybe be inspired to surrender?

A good idea and one that was given serious consideration at the time. But the U.S. didn't know if the demonstration bomb would work and couldn't afford the embarrassment of failure. And even though they wanted the Japanese to think they had a stockpile of a-bombs, in actuality they only had two. If they set off a demonstration bomb (that might fail), then they had only one left to use if the Japanese still did not surrender.

On August 6, 1945, the first ever atomic bomb, code named "Little

Boy," was dropped from 30,700 feet out of a B-29 Superfortress called "Enola Gay," named for the flight commander's mother. An exploding powder set off an atomic chain reaction of uranium above the center of the city of Hiroshima at about 8:30 on a Monday morning. The bright flash, high temperature, tons of force and radiation worked its devastation and destruction. "As a direct result some 60,000 Japanese men, women, and children were killed, and 100,000 injured; and almost the whole of a great seaport, a city of 250,00 people was destroyed by blast or fire." No one knew what had taken place because nothing like this had ever happened before—not from one bomb. Three days later on August 9 a second bomb was dropped on the city of Nagasaki. After that, the Japanese surrendered.

How horrible. I can't imagine the human suffering that resulted to those who survived.

You don't need to imagine it because the effect is fully described in a book by John Hersey titled simply *Hiroshima*. I keep it out here on the top of this small bookcase behind my desk. You know I love books, but this one is so distressing and agonizingly painful that I can't forget it. Nor should I forget; that's why I leave it out.

In May, 1946, approximately nine months after the bomb, *The New Yorker*—the same magazine of that title that we know today—sent the journalist and reporter John Hersey to find out what really happened in Hiroshima. He chose to interview six survivors in depth and piece together their experiences as they remembered them. On August 31, that same year, Hersey's 30,000-word story was published in its entirety in a single issue of that magazine. It was soon published as a book and even read aloud on the BBC radio in England. I won't get into the individual stories of those who were interviewed: the two doctors, a Catholic priest, an office girl, a tailor's widow and her children, and a Protestant clergyman. Instead, I will read you, if I may, some of the more horrifying descriptions that I have marked here in *Hiroshima*. You may stop me at any time.

From every second or third house came the voices of people buried and abandoned, who invariably screamed with formal politeness, '*Tasukate sure!* Help, if you please!

Now not many people walked in the streets, but a great number sat and lay on the pavement, vomited, waited for death, and died.

...twice the heat of the fire forced them into the river.

She and her older sister had been in the salt water of the river for a couple of hours before being rescued. The younger one had huge raw flash burns on her body; the salt water must have been excruciatingly painful to her...(they) borrowed a blanket from someone nearby and wrapped her up, but she shook more and more and said again, "I am so cold," and then she suddenly stopped shivering and was dead.

He reached down and took a woman by the hands, but her skin slipped off in huge, glove-like pieces.

...they were all in the same nightmarish state; their faces were wholly burned, their sockets were hollow, the fluid from their melted eyes had run down their cheeks.

...the twenty-year-old-girl...his former neighbor, who he had seen on the day the bomb exploded, with her dead baby daughter in her arms. She kept the small corpse in her arms for four days.

Stop! I've heard enough. It is completely horrifying. But I know why you are reading it to me. I understand. We must not forget.

After dropping the bomb based on the splitting of the atom (fission) the U.S. and Russia developed the hydrogen bomb, based on the combining (fusion) of two separate atoms, technically referred to as "thermonuclear" weapons, the explosive power of which is measured in megatons (millions) of TNT. A hydrogen bomb is regarded as 1,000 times more powerful than the "Little Boy" dropped on Hiroshima.

I know that different countries have these weapons, but how many of them exist? Do we know?

Agencies watch this as best they can and reporting is required by certain treaties. The Nuclear Weapons States (NWS) are China, Russia, France, United Kingdom, and the U.S. But other countries, as we know, have nuclear weapons as well, including Israel, North Korea, Pakistan, and India. The United States and Russia hold 90 percent of the weapons at 5,800 for the U.S. and 6,375 for Russia. Of these, the U.S. has 1,373 deployed (meaning warheads ready to go on ballistic missiles) and

Russia has 1,326 deployed. If utilized, this would surely be the modern-day Armageddon, the final battle to destroy mankind, don't you think?

I'm sure it would do that. It's unthinkable, but possible. We've been discussing the end of life on this planet, and the scenarios are really awful, but what is known about the fate of the universe?

In the last twenty-five years, physicists and astronomers, more specifically cosmologists, have progressed rapidly in making new observations and developing fresh theories about the beginning and end of the universe. They have given us five theories now about the fate of the world, and these are presented in a new book that just landed on my desk, *The End of Everything (Astrophysically Speaking)*, by Katie Mack. She is an excellent writer, providing clear and sometimes humorous explanations of difficult concepts; but I need to tell you that this material is very difficult, and my summaries won't do justice to her explanations of the five theories. But let me try.

You may remember that we touched on the Big Bang Theory and the expansion of the universe when we discussed creation. What do we mean by expansion? Mack tells us "The universe is expanding: space itself—that is to say the space between things, not the things in it—is getting bigger. This means isolated individual galaxies and groups of galaxies are getting, on average, farther and farther apart." In 1929, astronomer Edwin Hubble was able to establish the concept of the expanding universe through observation of distant galaxies and their movements. We now know that space is "getting bigger in the same way, at the same rate, everywhere." As Katie Mack neatly summarizes it, "The big question, in the long term is: will this expansion continue indefinitely, or will it eventually stop, turn around, and bring absolutely everything crashing together?" She calls this "The Big Crunch," and compares it to throwing a ball up into the air, that eventually stops dead, reverses, and falls back to the ground. Will there be a "transition to a contracting universe"? For now, we don't have evidence that expansion is reversing, and we personally don't have much to worry about, if it were to happen, because the expected date is billions of years away.

But the fact that it could happen raises the question of the ultimate purpose and meaning of life. It complicates the mystery. What are the other theories?

Mack calls the second theory "Heat Death" This is what happens if there is no reversal and everything just keeps expanding. The universe will continue to expand, and there are measurements that suggest that the expansion is at an accelerating rate. "In fact, it has been speeding up for about the last five billion years." Eventually, there will be a slow fade into darkness as the stars burn out and even black holes fade and disappear. Mack calls this "Heat Death," pointing out that *heat* is a "technical physics term meaning not warmth but rather 'disordered motion of particles or energy." Everything will run down and eventually fall apart. As Mack says, "if you leave something alone long enough, it will inevitably decay into disorder." Take a look at my desk, for example.

The lights will go out all over the world, and that includes our star, the sun. How horrible. Do I want to hear the other theories?

Probably not. I will be brief. The third scenario assumes the accelerating expansion of the universe, but something called dark energy—dark because it can't be seen—gets out of balance and starts to "tear the universe apart..." In other words, when some aspect of the universe, such as dark energy, gets out of balance, everything starts to unravel. Mack calls this "The Big Rip." Nothing holds together, not even the atom. When will this happen? Don't hold your breath; it could be 200 billion years.

Not an immediate threat, but another model of the end of the world that casts doubt on meaning, if everything is just going to get ripped apart. These seem to get worse as we go along.

The fourth theory is called "Vacuum Decay." Assume that the universe has a perilous instability built into it. Assume also that among all these things in space, seen and unseen, that some of them could collide. "If this happens anywhere in the cosmos, it creates an unstoppable apocalyptic cascade that nothing in the universe can withstand." In this situation, "the laws of physics, including the ability of particles to exist at all, are contingent upon a balancing act that could be upset at any moment."

Oh, oh. At any moment? This is not billions of years away; this is now. That's different.

Although it is unlikely, it is possible in the immediate future, which I assume makes this theory a little different from the others, wouldn't you say? The final theory, Mack calls "Bounce." Assume that there is more than one universe (as astronomers now assert) and that these universes could bounce off of each other. If that happens, the bounce "has destroyed everything...ended our universe, and created a new Big Bang...with little or no physical remnant of what it once may have held." But then it happens again, and again. This is a cyclical view of destruction and recreation.

This has a Hindu or Buddhist ring to it with their beliefs in ages, eons, cycles, and realms. But tell me, are these theories of doom really science or are they just wild hypotheses?

Doctor Mack puts it this way: "Like everything in science, our understanding of the cosmos is a perpetual work in progress." She is amazed at what has been established in the last few decades and looks forward, with new equipment and technology, to more elaboration of the theories and more empirical evidence to support or challenge them through astronomy. So far, they have shown us that the cosmos is not fixed and static, but ever-changing and dynamic, huge beyond our imagination, pulsating with energy, and quite precarious. What you and I need to note is that the ancient sages from the world's religions weren't completely crazy in thinking about the end of the world.

I'm definitely ready to give them credit for their visions. In fact, their images don't seem outlandish at all compared with what you have just been telling me about the fate of the world. But aren't there some people who look around at certain present-day events and say, "Look here, these are signs of the apocalypse, it's coming, the predictions of the Bible are true.

Yes, indeed, some people look at the Book of Daniel and the Revelation to John in exactly that way, as predictions for our time. A highly-respected New Testament scholar, Raymond Brown, warns against what he calls the misuse of the Book of Revelation, suggesting that this misuse is "based on the misunderstanding that the message is primarily addressed to Christians of our time if they can decode the author's symbols." Brown warns against this not just once, but several times in his scholarly commentary on the Revelation to John. He notes that Revelation "was addressed to the seven churches and its details and historical context pertain to the 1st century rather than the 20th or 21st century." Brown states (in Italics): *The author of Revelation did not know how or when the world will end, and neither does anyone else.* Using the Bible for predictions of any kind is shaky business.

So instead of making predictions, we should be asking: What is the message behind the myth? Let me try to answer for myself this time.

We surely have plenty of myth here with the seven seals and monsters and plagues. Let's just say John is trying to tell us that things are really bad. They are so bad, that there appears to be a flaw in the way the world is set up. Life can't go on like this. Something needs to be done, something drastic. God needs to bring this chapter of human history to a close soon and start over again. As for our time, it's really bad, too. Something like that?

Very good. I couldn't have done better. And now we need to return to our timeless question: Does life have any meaning or is it all hopeless? Not just one individual life, but life in general. The mystery is that we have been given a life, but no set of instructions. We grow to a certain age and ask why we are here, and there is no answer. A few years later we ask whether life itself makes any sense, and there is no clear answer given. Then we look around at the misery and suffering and potential for disaster, and we are no longer innocent; we know there is something inherently wrong with the way things are set up. We wonder if it will go on and on like this.

I remember a literature class where we studied a French writer named Albert Camus, and he said that life is not only pointless but absurd. He wrote a novel about a guy who goes out and murders a total stranger on the beach because he thinks life is absurd.

I believe the novel is called *The Stranger* (*L'Étranger* in French). Camus was part of the underground Resistance Movement at the time of World War II, and he had plenty in his experience to make him think that the world is absurd. Lesser known is his work called *The Plague* (*La Peste* in French), in which he describes the work of the dedicated Doctor Rieux who is engaged in fighting a pandemic spread by rats. But it is not clear exactly what the plague actually is. Is the story a modern-day parable about something much more encompassing than a virus? One of the characters says "But what does that mean—'plague'? Just life, no more than that." So, the plague becomes the symbol of all the evil that human beings must resist, not just plagues, but all the rest we've been discussing and more.

On the final page of the novel, we learn that Doctor Rieux has decided to compile a chronicle of his experiences fighting the plague. He knows that the tale "could not be one of final victory" but "only the record of what had had to be done." Doctor Rieux knows that the fight must continue and that people must "strive their utmost to be healers."

In the face of absurdity (and without God), Camus suggests that we can make an existential choice to be a healer.

So, giving meaning to life is something I have to work out, something I have to think through and choose? A commitment?

Yes, that seems to be the case. It is not a once-and-for-all choice, but a continuing choice we make through our day-to-day choices, but it is a choice. Another French author and philosopher, Jean-Paul Sartre, who lived at the same time as Camus and shared his disbelief in God, suggests that each person must find his or her own meaning, in fact, not just find but create that meaning. In Sartre's own words, "life has no meaning *a priori*... it's up to you to give it meaning." And we have to do that because we have "to exist in the world, to be at work there, to be there in the midst of other people, and to be mortal there." Sartre suggests that we are free to choose, to invent meaning, and suggests that "Man is nothing else but what he makes of himself."

I like that. But the examples you have given about the destructive tendencies of human beings and the fate of the cosmos suggest there is no justification for hope. I can't get those images of Hiroshima out of my head.

No evidence to warrant hope? That may be so, but what is hope based on? Evidence? Statistical probability? We might say that hope is profoundly unreasonable. Hope has a certain "in-spit-of" and "nevertheless" aspect to it. Let's go back to the Revelation to John to see if he had hope. Although John was full of nightmarish pessimism about the reality in which he was living, he had hope that things would get better. Let me find the passage here so I can read it to you. John of Patmos is speaking when he writes:

Then I saw a new heaven and a new earth; for the first heaven and the first earth had passed away, and the sea was no more. And I saw the holy city, new Jerusalem, coming down out of heaven from God, prepared as a bride adorned for her husband; and I heard a great voice from the throne saying, "Behold the dwelling of God with man. He will dwell with them, and they shall be his people, and God himself will be with them; he will wipe away every tear from their eyes, and death shall be no more, neither shall there be mourning or crying or pain any more, for the former things have passed away.

These are the words from a man who has seen just about everything.

This is no naïve optimism from a dreamer, but the words of hope from someone who knows the depth of despair. Let me read you a few more words from Revelation to see if you recognize them.

> The kingdom of this world has become the kingdom of our Lord
> And of his Christ, and he shall reign for ever and ever.

And elsewhere we have these words:

> King of kings and Lord of lords.

Does it ring a bell, or a chorus, or an orchestra?

I think those are the words from Handel's "Messiah." What do we call it—the "Hallelujah Chorus." Yes, it's very familiar now that you mention it.

We seldom realize that it is from the Revelation to John. We tend to think, quite naturally, that George Frederick Handel, the eighteenth-century contemporary of Bach, just dreamed up the words himself, this triumphant message of hope set to music. A respected music historian has written, "It could well be the most popular piece of choral music ever composed." Why? Because we humans need to hear it over and over to restore hope?

The apocalyptic perspective raises the timeless question of meaning in its most extreme and dramatic form. It adds a sense of urgency to the process of choosing, elevating the importance of making deliberate choices, but also raising to a higher level of importance the substance of our choices. With or without hope, the choices we make can actually be better choices if we honestly confront the actual and potential horrors of existence as they really are. Whatever the fate of the world, the meaning we make of it matters.

References

Aslan, Reza, *No god but God.* New York: Random House, 2911. The Islamic idea of a messiah, is on p. 189. The quotations "one who guides divinely" and "on the Day of Judgment..." are from p. 189.

Brown, Raymond E., *An Introduction to the New Testament.* New Haven: Yale University Press, 2010. Brown provides a thorough scholarly analysis of The Revelation to John. The discussion of John and Patmos is on p. 781. Brown's warnings about using Revelation as prediction are frequent. The quotation "based on the misunderstanding..." is from p. 782. The quotations "was addressed to the seven churches..." and "*The author of Revelation...*" are both on p. 810.

Camus, Albert, *The Stranger* (*L'Étranger,* in French). New York: Random House, 1988. Originally published in France in 1942 by Librairie Gillmard. The apostle of the Absurd is the main character Meursault.

Camus, Albert, *The Plague* (*La Peste* in French) New York: Random House, 1991. First published in the United States in 1948. Originally published in France by Librairie Gallimard in 1947. Doctor Rieux is a healer fighting the plague. The quotation "But what does that mean—'plague'?" is from p. 307. The indented quote "nonetheless, he knew..." is from p. 308.

Collins, John J., *Introduction to the Hebrew Bible.* Minneapolis: Fortress Press, 2004. The discussion of the apocalyptic genre is on pp. 563-564. The quotation "the time of the end..." is on pp. 563-564. The quotation "participate in the life..." is on p. 562. The general discussion of the Book of Daniel, the court tales and apocalyptic visions are on pp. 553-571. The date for writing of Daniel is discussed on p. 570.

Drago, Anthony, and Douglas Wellman, *Surviving Hiroshima: A Young Woman's Story.* (no city listed), Virginia: WriteLife Publishing, 2020. This is a recent publication based on extensive notes from the survivor and further research. It is a fine source of information on the war with Japan and dropping of the atomic bombs. The historical descriptions of the bombing of Pearl Harbor and the Philippine Islands are presented briefly on pp. 56-58. The decision dilemma is described on pp. 71-80. Estimates of war casualties are quoted as "1.7 and 4 million..." are on p. 111. The Potsdam Declaration is described on p. 112. The "demonstration" idea is explored on p. 111. The details of dropping the bomb are on pp. 5-11.

Ehrman, Bart D., *The New Testament: A Historical Introduction to the Early Christian Writings,* Sixth Edition. New York: Oxford University Press, 2016. The Revelation to John is discussed in detail in Chapter 30 "Christians and the Cosmos," pp. 529 ff. The quotations "John's heavenly vision..." "taken up into heaven..." "behold the throne..." "In the hand of the figure..." are all from p. 531. The quotation "with each broken seal..." and "followed by a new set of disasters..." are also from p. 531. The decoding of the number 666 is discussed on p. 340.

Flood, Gavin *An Introduction to Hinduism.* Cambridge: Cambridge University Press, 1996. The discussion of Hindu cosmology is on p. 112. The quotations "the universe will be destroyed..." and "the process begins again..." are from p. 113.

Harari, Yuval Noah, *Sapiens: A Brief History of Humankind.* New York: Harper Collins, 2015. The human domination of large-scale species in Australia is described on pp. 63-67. The quotation "Within a few thousand years..." is from p. 63. The description of the effect of Sapiens on the Americas is on pp. 70-72. The quotation "The Americas were a great laboratory..." is from p. 71. The indented quote "According to current estimates...' is from p. 71.

Harris, Ian, Consultant Editor, *The Complete Illustrated Encyclopedia of Buddhism.* Leicestershire, UK: Annes Publishing, 2011. Buddha's past and future lives are discussed in the box on p. 27 along with the Jataka Tales and Bodhisattva Natha as Maitreya.

Harvey, Peter, *An Introduction to Buddhism.* Cambridge: Cambridge University Press, 2013.The discussion of Maitreya "to be the next Buddha to teach..." is on p. 176. The quotation describing Budai as a "pot-bellied wandering teacher..." is from p. 176. "Known as the laughing Buddha..." is on p. 176.

Hersey, John, *Hiroshima.* BN Publishing, 2012. This edition appears to be a reprint from an online publisher with no "home city" listed. The original work by the *New Yorker* reporter, John Hersey, is described in the text. The references are to page numbers in this recent paperback reprint edition. The quotation is from the Publisher's Note, p. v "As a direct result, some 60,000 Japanese..." Mention of the second bomb dropped on Nagasaki is on p. 80. A description of Hersey's assignment from the *New Yorker* is in the Publisher's Note, p. vi, as is the description of participants in the interview study, p. vii. The quotations from Hersey as they appear in order in this text are: pp. 45, 53, 63, 65, 65 (again), 73, and 80.

Holy Bible, Revised Standard Version. New York: Thomas Nelson & Sons, 1952. Summaries of the Book of Daniel are drawn from the text itself, p. 918 ff. The quotation "many of those who sleep..." is from Daniel 12:2,3. Discussions of the Revelation to John are based on the New Testament text, pp. 276 ff. The imagery and symbolism of Revelation are drawn from Chapters 6, 8, 9, 12, 13, and 14. The phrase "whore of Babylon" is Revelation 14:8. The indented quote "Then I saw a new heaven and a new earth..." is Revelation 21:1-4. The quotations that are familiar from Handel's "Messiah" are Revelation 11:15 "The Kingdom of this world..." and Revelation 19:16 "King of kings and Lord of lords."

Kolbert, Elizabeth, *The Sixth Extinction: An Unnatural History.* New York: Henry Holt and Company, 2014. The discussion of species extinction draws on this entire book, but most specifically on the descriptions of the five previous extinctions scattered throughout its pages. The descriptions of periods of low risk and high risk for extinction, including the image of boredom and panic is from p. 16. The first extinction is described on pp. 96-97. The second extinction is mentioned on p. 141 and makes reference to "reef gap." The third extinction is elaborated on pp. 102-103 and the quotation "the biggest of the Big Five..." is from p. 102. The description continues on p. 104 where we find the quotation "hydrogen sulfide..." The quotation "By the time it was over..." is from p. 103. The fifth extinction, known as Asteroid, is described on pp. 71-81, 86-87 and 90-91. The quotation "moving at something like..." is on p. 86. Dinosaurs are discussed on p. 87. The quotation "It took millions of years..." is from p. 88. The sixth extinction is discussed in many ways and in several places, but the more specific are pp. 265-269, 166-168, and p. 3. The quotation "transformation of the ecological landscape..." is from p. 267. The quotation "our restlessness, our creativity..." is from p. 266. The term "Anthropocene" and the paraphrased summary of Paul Crutzen's list of things resulting from human activity is based on p. 108. The quotation "Owing to a combination..." is on p. 108. The data on species extinctions are on p. 167 and the *National Geographic* headline quote is on p. 168. The clincher quote "By disrupting these systems..." is on p. 267.

Mack, Katie, *The End of Everything (Astrophysically Speaking)*. New York: Scribner (Simon & Schuster), 2020. Provides a complete guide to five different ways that the universe might (could) end. Chapter 3 "Big Crunch" is on pp. 51-70. The quotation "the universe is expanding...' is on p. 52. The quotation "In 1929, the astronomer Edwin Hubble..." and "getting bigger in the same way..." and "The big question..." are all on p. 53. The comparison with throwing a ball into the air is on p. 60. The expected date is on p. 62. Chapter 4 "Heat Death" is on pp. 71-104. The quotation "in fact, it has been speeding up..." is on p. 85. Heat as a "technical physics term..." is quoted from p. 90. The quotation "if you leave something alone..." is on p. 91, where I also borrowed the example of the messy desk. Chapter 5 "The Big Rip" is on pp. 105-128. The quotation "to tear the entire universe..." is on p. 112. Chapter 6 "Vacuum Decay" is on pp. 129-155. The quotation "This happens anywhere..." is from p. 144. The quotation "the laws of physics..." is from p. 143. Chapter 7 "Bounce" is on pp. 157-176. The Bounce is referred to as a cyclical view on p. 173. The quotation "Like everything in science..." is on p. 176.

Oldstone, Michael B.A., *Viruses, Plagues & History: Past, Present, and Future*. Oxford: Oxford University Press, 2010. The discussion of smallpox is in Chapter 4 "Smallpox," pp. 53-101. References are as follows: Ramses V, pp. 56-57, Aztec Empire, p. 61, planned attack on England, p. 68, President Lincoln, p. 71, Hawaii, p. 63. The quotation "In 1853 some government..." is on p. 63. Twentieth century deaths of 300 million people, including the quotation "three times more than..." is on p. 53. Yellow Fever is described in Chapter 5 "Yellow Fever," pp. 102-134. The quotation "In 1793 Philadelphia..." is on p. 105

Shutting down the U. S. government is described on p. 106. Napoleon's retreat from North America and the subsequent Louisiana Purchase is on p. 109. Other viruses are addressed in separate chapters, including immunization efforts. Smallpox as a bioterror weapon is discussed on p. 97. . Attempts to ban smallpox are mentioned on p. 92. The description of viruses and the quote "viruses are nothing more than..." are on p. 10. The quotation "Together, viruses, plants, and animals..." is on p. 10. Acute and persistent viruses are explained on p. 18 with the quote "persist for months..." The flu epidemic of 1918 and 1919 is mentioned on p. 8 with the quote "more victims than died..."

Partridge, Christopher, General Editor, *A Brief Introduction to Hinduism*. Minneapolis: Fortress Press, 2018. Chapter 11 "Sacred Writings" by Theodore Gabriel. Discussion of the Hindu Epics is on p. 65.

Partridge, Christopher, General Editor, *A Brief Introduction to Islam*. Minneapolis: Fortress Press, 2018. A section called Rapid Fact Finder has a listing for "Judgment" on p. 118.

Rainey, Lee Diane, *Decoding Dao*. Malden, MA: Wiley Blackwell, 2014. The quotation "the idea of devolution..." is from p. 171.

Sartre, Jean-Paul, *Existentialism and Human Emotions*. New York: Citadel Press, 1985, originally published in English is 1957. The quotation "life has no meaning *a priori*..." is from p. 49. The quotation, "to exist in the world..." is from p. 38. The idea of being free to choose is from p. 28, and the quotation "Man is nothing less..." is from p. 15.

Schonberg, Harold C. *The Lives of the Great Composers*. New York: W.W. Norton & Company, 1981. Handel's "messiah" is discussed on p. 63 and the quotation "It could well be the most popular..." is from p. 63.

Arms Control Association Website www.armscontrol.org>factsheets>factsheets>nuclearweaponswhohaswhat > The source for the stockpile numbers by country.

<time.com>World>Nuclear Weapons> The distinction between the atom bomb and thermonuclear bomb (hydrogen/fusion) is here.

8

Expansion
Growing Bigger and Spreading Out

Last year my boss sent me to Taiwan to meet with one of our tech suppliers there, and I had a chance to visit a big Confucian Temple in Taipei. but at the time, before I had these conversations with you, I didn't know much about world religions or what I was actually seeing. It has been interesting to discuss the ancient traditions of these religions with you, but now I think I'd like to learn how they spread and came to be what they are now. And what are they now?

Yes, a lot has happened through the years as these religions developed and expanded geographically. Actually, one of the most remarkable stories is the development of Confucianism. The growth of Confucianism into a world religion out of a small band of followers of Confucius is its own kind of mystery. The Warring States Period, when Confucius taught, did end finally, and afterword the Han Dynasty (206 BCE–220 CE) spread "both north and south to include much of what we think of as China today." It "lasted for four hundred years and was roughly contemporary with the Roman Empire in the West." Of course, there were other classic Chinese writings besides those of Confucius, many that criticize Confucius, as well as new philosophical ideas, but the teachings of Confucius endured. In fact, "during the Han Dynasty Confucius came to be seen as something more than just an ordinary person who tried to work out solutions to the problems of his time." Stories (myths) about "his miraculous birth and supernatural powers" began to appear.

Other dynasties succeeded the Han, and in the early 600s CE a civil service exam was instituted in China. To pass this exam, students had to know the classic writings of Confucius and the commentaries on his work. This gave an enormous boost to the teachings of Confucius, and the exam system, lasting for centuries up until 1904, ensured that China would be infused with Confucian ideas. Confucius was given many titles through the centuries until 1645 when he was called "Classic Teacher, Accomplished, Illustrious, and Perfect Sage." Oddly enough, he was not called "God" but was worshipped.

The worship of Confucius began when a Han Dynasty emperor venerated (worshipped) him at his tomb. In the 450s CE, the first Confucian temple was established, and soon "any city of respectable size had a temple to Confucius." Through the centuries, images of Confucius were forbidden in these temples to distinguish them from Buddhist and Daoist temples. People worshipped Confucius seeking his help and favor, they prayed to him in the temples, and they lit incense to create a mood of reverence. Celebrations for young people who passed the civil service exam were held in the Confucian temple. Was (is) Confucius a god? Some say yes, acknowledging his supernatural powers by worshipping him and asking his favor; others say that their reverence is simply a way to show respect to the first teacher. Confucianism in its religious forms spread beyond China to Japan, Korea, and Vietnam. And, of course, it was carried to Taiwan.

In more recent times, Confucianism continued to struggle with timeless questions, not only concerning social order and human nature, but with metaphysical questions often in response to Buddhism. Neo-Confucian thought suggests: "There is an eternal, primal, substance that is real and the substance is *qi*." However important *qi* (chee) may be, it is very hard to pin down: maybe it is "air, vital spirit, energy, or ether." Likewise, there emerges a concept of the "Supreme Ultimate" and the idea of "Principles," the forces governing regularities within nature, including human nature.

Naturally, Confucianism suffered under Chinese communist rule, particularly during the Cultural Revolution (1966–1976) when Confucian temples, art, and books were destroyed. But Confucianism had been under attack before that in a movement against Japanese involvement in China called the May 4th Movement, known for the protests of that date in 1915. Confucianism, as sometimes happens, was being blamed for everything. But outside of China, in the second half of the twentieth century, countries with long Confucian traditions began to prosper, including Taiwan. Seeing this and linking it to Confucian values, gave birth to a revival called "New Confucianism." As the foundation of Chinese culture, Confucianism, like the story-book cat, seems to have had nine lives, as it struggled through the ages to provide new answers to timeless questions.

That's why I could visit a Confucian Temple in Taiwan. Interesting. And Buddhism? How did it develop and spread?

As we know, Buddha was born in modern-day Nepal, and Buddhism had its origins in small cities in northern India. But it was "during the reign of the emperor Asoka (268–239 BCE) that Buddhism expanded more widely, reaching most of the Indian sub-continent, and also beyond, thus becoming a 'world religion.'" It was not that Buddhism became the state religion of India; Asoka just made it easier for Buddhism to thrive. As Buddhism became better established, new literatures of interpretation developed and were regarded as containing "authoritative discourses of the Buddha."

A new movement within Buddhism called Māhāyana emerged between 150 BCE and 100 CE (continuing on to the present) that emphasized "compassion, faith, and wisdom" It also emphasized a concept of "Buddha as supremely powerful, omniscient, and omni-present, that is, all-seeing and eternally present to give spiritual help to his devotees." And there could be more devotees with Māhāyana, not only monks, but lay persons, through this broader way to Enlightenment and the spiritual guidance of the Bodhisattvas (embodiments of Buddha). Known sometimes as the "Great Vehicle," as compared to "Lesser Vehicle" or Hinayana Buddhism, Mahayana Buddhism through the next centuries, began to expand into "Central Asia, China, Korea, Japan, Tibet and Mongolia." As it grew it merged with local beliefs and took on new expressions of devotion.

One example of these is the development of Tantric Buddhism, which emerged from the Māhāyana tradition in the seventh century CE in Tibet. Its practices were based on special scriptures called Tantras. Originally thought of as "weavings" symbolizing the unity of mind and body, the Tantras were often cast in a "twilight language" that could only be understood by a lama (guru). The search for Enlightenment continued in Tantric Buddhism, involving esoteric practices, secret languages, and the recitation of sacred words and sounds in mantras.

One practice of Tibetan Buddhism still common today involves the use of mandalas, artistic renderings of circle designs in colored sand or chalk. *Mandala* is the Sanskrit word for circle, and in Tantric practice these sacred cosmic circles are used for meditation. "Devotees visualize themselves crossing the mandala's outer circles, which represent the outer world, and following the path to the internal gateways to approach deity" at the center. We might call it a visual guide to the mystery of finding God, or at least Enlightenment. It is interesting to note that when meditation is over, the mandalas "are destroyed and the sand is swept up and deposited in a river or lake to emphasize the transitory nature of things, an important idea in Buddhism.

So, don't get all attached to your beautiful mandala, right?

Yes, in Buddhism, attachments lead to suffering. But I need to tell you about Zen, another elaboration of Buddhism in China and Japan, one that became better known and admired in the twentieth century in Western countries. Zen (Chan in China) is thought to have been brought to China from India in 520 CE by a priest named Bodhi-dharma. Exactly what he brought and how important it was for him to bring it is not clear. It is well established, however, that "Zen is the product of Chinese soil from the seed of Indian Enlightenment" so that no special "line of transmission need be established to India." Zen drew on local Chinese traditions, including Daoism, and is credited for having "brought Taoism back to life." It seems to assume the world of Dao, stressing growth, movement, and the ever-changing and undefinable Dao, while focusing on the timeless Buddhist question of how to find the most effective path to Enlightenment. That path had become too cumbersome and slow for many Chinese followers of Buddha. A new approach was needed.

Although seated meditation (za-zen) was still important, Zen employed a technique of contemplation using a *koan*, a riddle-like statement with a seemingly unresolvable dilemma. The goal was to find a way through the barrier, eventually coming upon a solution in a sudden flash of insight (Satori). One famous *koan* is this:

A long time ago a man kept a goose in a bottle.
It grew larger and larger until it could not get out
of the bottle anymore; he did not want to break the
bottle, nor did he wish to hurt the goose; how would
you get it out?

Note the dilemma and two unattractive alternatives. So, in the spirit of Zen inquiry, one must continue to meditate on this frustrating challenge, and when the insight comes, there is another *koan* waiting for you to draw you closer to Enlightenment.

I'm sorry to interrupt, but what is the answer to the goose dilemma?

Well, you just need to keep thinking about it to try to get passed the impasse. Try to get to the bottom of the matter. Are we the goose in the bottle with no satisfactory way out? Will we be crushed by our circumstances? Must the goose stop growing and accept the present to keep from breaking the bottle? We can ask a lot of questions and keep seeking alternatives, which is what we usually do—put our mind to work on it, which in Zen is exactly the wrong approach. The master will eventually provide a most unhelpful hint, such as "It will rain at three o'clock today.

What? And what does the rain have to do with the goose in the bottle?

Not much and everything. In a sudden flash of Enlightenment (Satori) we realize that there is no answer to the dilemma and the meaning of the *koan* can't be grasped logically. We need to go walk in the rain, smell the cool air, and stomp in the puddles, because that is the meaning of life, the immediacy and freshness of the rain. We might say, the good life is in the unmediated experience of the rain.

"Zen is sometimes described as 'straightforwardness' or 'going right ahead;' for Zen the task is to move with life without trying to interrupt its flow; it is an immediate awareness of things as they live and move..." What interrupts the flow? Too much thinking, excessive definition and analysis, endless rational interpretation of experience, to the point that the actual experience is lost. A person can miss the good life by thinking about it too much.

Does this mean that we have been wasting our time in these discussions of the mysteries of life? Is it taking us away from the direct experience of life as it is?

Well, that's for you to decide, but a Zen master would probably say 'yes.' But isn't there a difference between excessive analysis and thoughtful exploration? Isn't there a contrast between mindless plodding and enlightened contemplation of life? We don't need to stop thinking completely, but Zen is trying to jar us back from our excesses to the present moment, the experience of living with mind, body, and emotions united. The master wants to make sure we don't miss the quickly-passing flow of life by thinking about it too much.

Before we leave Zen, I want to relate two examples of how it affected the arts in China and Japan. The Chinese developed and then passed to Japan a form of painting that the Japanese call *sumiye*. The artist employs a brush to apply black ink to a rough paper, but the uniqueness of *sumiye* is in the method, which involves considerable Zen meditation and contemplation of the picture followed by a very rapid execution, as if in a sudden burst of creativity (Satori) the artist had to "commit his inspiration to paper while it was still alive..." while "a whirlwind possessed his hand." The picture itself, usually a landscape, is quite simple, like a sketch with as much emphasis on the surrounding space as the actual brushwork, giving the effect of emptiness.

I've seen these paintings. Just the suggestion of a mountain. One or two trees, A tiny little human being. Lots of fog. What does it mean?

It portrays humans in their niche in the larger scheme of nature. Because the painting is executed in a flash of Satori, there is no going back, touching up, or having second thoughts. It is irrevocable, just as Zen portrays the "fleeting, unpredictable, and ungraspable character of life." You get one chance to get it right.

The other development is the *haiku* poem "of just seventeen syllables which drops the subject almost as it takes it up." *Haiku* has that remarkable Zen sense of meditative detachment, where things happen spontaneously in a quick way. The poems establish a mood for contemplation, or are perhaps the result of contemplation, as in these three examples.

> You light the fire;
> I'll show you something nice—
> a great ball of snow.

> On a withered branch
> A crow is perched,
> In the autumn evening.

> Leaves falling,
> Lie on one another;
> The rain beats on the rain.

Haiku poems have a "child's expression of wonder," the immediacy of seeing things as they are without interpretation.

Yes, we had an assignment in the sixth grade to write a haiku poem. I remember it clearly, but I had no idea of where these poems came

*from or their association with Zen Buddhism. This is so fascinating.
You mentioned Daoism earlier. Did it develop and expand through the
centuries as well?*

Critical studies of Daoism today suggest that the *Dao Te Ching*
was not written by one person, and to associate that writing, as many do,
with a single historical figure known as Laozi is a mistake. Nonetheless,
a cult grew up around Laozi, and he was "transformed from the possible
author of a text into a god, representing *dao,* who appears to assist all
people." Various legends grew up around his birth, including the belief
that his mother Lady Li was pregnant with him for 81 years—what a
horrible thought—and that he was born from her armpit, having white
hair (his head, not her armpit) in keeping with one reading of his name
which is 'the old child.'

Daoism evolved, from the philosophical tradition we discussed,
into an organized religion, if one means by religion a movement marked
by priests, scriptures, temples, and sacred ceremonies. The roots of
this transformation are in the two centuries BCE, with the actual
transformation occurring in the first five centuries CE in many interesting
forms. Laozi (or Lao-tzu) was invested with a title and identified "as the
chief deity of religion." Followers, such as Chang Tao-ling and his sons
and grandson organized and spread the new faith. By 420 CE, Central
Orthodox Daoism had become the state religion. An important figure
was Lu Hsiu-ching, who before his death in 477 CE, catalogued the
first canon of Dao "scriptures." But Daoism was already beginning to
develop branches focused on alchemy, magic, and mysticism. We don't
need to explore all of these, but one might be of special interest.

One of the great mysteries of life is how to stay well and promote
longevity, especially if you are not sure about the afterlife. We noted
earlier how classical Daoists valued the idea of living a full life-span.
Consider the host of ideas floating around today regarding how to eat a
healthful diet, stay fit, remain calm, and live a long life, many of these
suggestions reaching far beyond the guidelines of medical science. If
death is a mystery, so is staying alive.

One version of Daoism held that "the human body is a universe
filled with deities, spirits, and monsters." In Shang-ch'ing Daoism, "the
highest and most important deity is called the One. It is the Tao (Dao)
inside us, the undifferentiated primordial vapor that keeps us alive." So,
the key to good health is to keep the One and hold fast to the Dao. But

there are also spirits that protect the five viscera: "heart, liver, spleen, lungs, and kidneys." The goal is to keep these spirits around so the organs can function effectively. And then, there are also monsters in the body that need to be eradicated. A person can also access external sources of energy from the sun, the moon, and the North Star. "Mist, clouds and vapor also contain the essence of the primordial vapor of the Tao." (Dao) Does any of this sound familiar, like the things that people get into today?

Well, I have some health nut colleagues at work who toss around this lingo at lunch almost every day, and they are willing to eat and drink some very weird things to stay healthy. And there I sit, listening skeptically, with my peanut butter and jelly sandwich.

Some parts of Daoism incorporated alchemy, which the dictionary generously defines as "an early form of chemistry" from the Middle Ages, aimed at turning "base metals into gold," while trying "to discover the elixir of perpetual youth." A new solution to the mystery of death. By around 580 CE Daoist alchemists were having second thoughts "about ingesting compounds made from lead, mercury, cinnabar, and sulphates," the reason being that too many of their clients, including some emperors, were dying from elixirs to prolong life. It is a bit ironic to die from an immortality pill, wouldn't you say?

Kind of defeats the purpose, doesn't it? Don't we call those "unintended consequences"?

Indeed. But I can't finish the discussion of the expansion of Daoism without mentioning yin-yang.

Isn't that the symbol with the round circle divided by a curvy line, black on one side and white on the other?

Yes, that's it. And with a small white dot on the black side and a small black dot on the white. "*Yin* and *yang* translated literally mean shade and light. If all things change, it is important to find out, if possible, how they will change, and "divination is a way of seeing the patterns of change... If we understand the underlying nature of change, we will know what has occurred in the past and what will come in the future." It's the timeless question of how to know human destiny.

From here on the yin-yang system gets very complicated with images of hexagrams and broken circles representing celestial realms, a Daoist cosmology where everything is described as either yin or yang. "Thus, yin became associated with stillness, tranquility, softness, flexibility, female, and receptivity; and yang became associated with movement, activity, hardness, strength, male, and initiative." Yin, female, and yang, male, define all things of the world as pairs of opposites: yin is cold, moon, and passive; yang is hot, sun, and active. This system was a new effort to grasp and follow the Dao. One might also think of it as an effort to provide stability and predictability in a world filled with contradiction and ambiguity, that is, a way to control a world of mystery and timeless questions.

It's like trying to make everything fit into a system of opposites, kind of like the Myers-Briggs Personality Inventory: you're either an introvert or extrovert, you're either thinking or feeling, you're either...

Interesting comparison. Hmm. We can look at it as one more attempt to define human nature and make people more predictable. Daoism became popular, and you can see why. In modern times elements of Daoism have been picked up and woven into films, TV shows, and self-help books: the Dao of...this or that. They focus on the superficial aspects of Daoism captured in the simple phrase "go with the flow." Lee Rainey, author of *Decoding Dao,* mentioned earlier, calls this "Dao Lite," the mistaken assumption of taking a part of a text (a simple phrase or image) for the whole (a deep and complex message). She also notes that Daoism in its many forms is alive in the modern world. "If we look at the number of people who belong to Daoist communities, go to Daoist temples, practice Daoist rituals, or who are Daoist monks, nuns, or priests, there are millions and millions of Daoists." They can be found today in China, Taiwan, Korea, Japan, Vietnam, and Hong Kong. And there are also Daoist temples in North America and Europe. Daoism gave birth to *fengshui* (a system of pleasing spatial arrangement), popular forms of martial arts, and the Thai-chi movement patterns. It is hard to distinguish Dao Lite from the original brew, but there are some who would say "that this is Daoism so completely repackaged that it is not Daoism at all." Now you know some Dao Lite answers to timeless questions.

It is amazing what people will do with these religious traditions, some of it good, I suppose, but other things quite warped and twisted around. I'm learning to be aware, or is it beware, of the distortions. What's next? We haven't talked about what happened to Hinduism.

Hinduism, though not called that at the time, had deep roots, as you know, in a civilization in the Indus Valley (in present-day Pakistan) that flourished between 2500 and 1500 BCE. Two thousand years of Aryan culture produced writings in the language of Sanskrit as the Vedas and Upanishads, the foundational scriptures of Hinduism. This is the Hinduism of our earlier discussions.

Hinduism's later development and expansion is difficult to describe because it is so varied, with its many deities, sects, cults, and forms of devotion. There was no common agreed upon core and some say "there had never been an organized Western-style 'religion' called Hinduism." Yet the traditions, in all their variety, spread across the subcontinent of India.

Keep in mind that Buddhism also spread throughout India from north to south and that it remained strong for centuries in northern India. It suffered, however, with the invasion of Muslim Turks beginning in 986 CE, and began to decline in India while growing strong elsewhere. India was then occupied for several centuries by Muslim invaders and occupied again beginning in the eighteenth century by British colonialists who controlled India until 1949. Through all of this—one wonders how—the ancient Hindu traditions survived and grew stronger.

As we have noted with other religions, the timeless questions do reemerge, and the early Indian philosophers continued to struggle to answer questions about human nature, particularly the concept of the self and its relationship to god. A famous Indian philosopher-theologian-saint Shankara (788–820 CE) expounded the belief "that one's true self (Ātmān) is literally identical to Brahman, countering dualist ideas of separation." (Contrast this message of unity of self and absolute reality with the Christian idea of sinner and alienation from god.) The debate about the nature of the self, continued with Rāmānuja (1077–1157 CE), who believed that the self also retained some individual qualities, suggesting both sameness and difference from the Absolute. In any case, the questions about the human self were still alive (against the Buddhist notion of the changeable and unidentifiable self); and the belief that ātman is at one with brahman, the energy that pervades the whole universe, laid the foundation for the principle of non-violence (ahimsā) so important later on for Mohandas Ghandi (1869–1948), India's liberator.

If the self is part of God, then killing people is killing God. I've heard something like this about the Quakers, that they base their pacifism on the divine nature within everyone. But go on with Hinduism.

As people have searched to solve the mystery of human nature, they have also asked the timeless question: Is there a separate "female" nature? Most religions have had male founders, or gods of implied male gender, and in the ancient religious traditions, women have not always fared well, to say the least. But Hinduism has a female God, and as one might suspect, not just one. Within the descriptions of the nature and activities of the Hindu goddess, one senses a drama being played out concerning the true nature of womanhood and the female ideal.

Devī, the Great Goddess, the source of manifestations of the local goddesses, seems to have two natures: the gracious and generous embodiment of maternal qualities, subservient to the divine husband, called goddess of the breast, and the contrasting goddess of malevolent force, who "demands offerings of blood, meat, and alcohol to placate her wrath," called goddess of the tooth. She may be worshipped as a supreme being or the consort (spouse) of a male god.

A vivid myth portrays Devī as the slayer of the buffalo demon (think water buffalo, not bison) in a complicated story with a violent ending. Riding a lion, Devī (also known as Durga) is a beautiful unmarried woman "who possesses all the qualities of love, heroism, laughter, terror, and wonder," but in the end she defeats the buffalo demon, "kicking him with her foot, piercing his chest with her trident and decapitating him with her discus..."

Although the roots of goddess worship are ancient, the myth and accompanying iconography (images) were developed in the sixth to eighth centuries CE. The worship of goddesses continues today, and in a small village in India one may find a temple to a goddess just known in that locality, providing a role model for the worshipper. But which female nature is the model: the gracious and loving wife and mother or the ferocious and powerful leader?

You're asking me? I've known plenty of both types of women, and some who blend both images. I don't think we can say much for sure about a female nature, but it is interesting to see how these conflicting or complementary natures are portrayed in the Hindu goddess. That would be my answer. Have I escaped unharmed?

You seem to know how to walk on eggs without stepping on any. Very diplomatic! One modern day Hindu mystic, Sri Rāmakrishna (1836–1886) was devoted to the goddess Kali, the Mother, and pleaded with her to reveal herself to him. His inner vision of the Goddess and trance-like states became so extreme, that he could no longer carry out his priestly functions at the temple. Odd as it may seem, he married a five-year-old girl, and when she walked the thirty miles to the temple at age seventeen to be with her husband, he was so transformed that he "could not be a husband in a conventional sense." Nevertheless, "she served him in the temple until his death."

But Rāmakrishna came to believe that "all religions are true," and he is famous for this. We might formulate a new timeless question: are religions more similar than different, or are they more different than similar? Building on the Hindu idea of many manifestations of God, Rāmakrishna became the Hindu sage of tolerance. These are his views:

> Many are the names of God and infinite are the forms through which He may be apprehended. In whatever name and whatever form you worship Him, through that you realize Him.

> Indeed, one can reach God if one follows any of the paths with wholehearted devotion.

> Dispute not. As you rest firmly on your own faith and opinion, allow others also the equal liberty to stand by their own faiths and opinions.

In comparing God to an argument about the color of a chameleon, Rāmakrishna says,

> God sometimes assumes different forms. Sometimes He has attributes, sometimes none. One who lives under the tree alone knows that the chameleon has many colors.

Rāmakrishna continued to explore the mystery of how to describe God, but instead of seeking the one true way, he sought to validate many ways.

One of his loyal followers was Swami Vivekānanda (1863–1902), who founded the Vedanta Society in New York in 1895. When he returned to India, he founded the Rāmakrishna Mission, a new monastic order based on an old Hindu idea, *karma yoga,* as the foundation for its programs in education, helping the sick, and social reform. You can see, Mother Teresa was not the only one at work on the streets of India. Swami Vivekānanda is remembered as "the first effective proponent of Hinduism as a world religion."

In spite of being dominated by Muslim and Christian powers for hundreds of years, India continued to develop as a tolerant nation, choosing a secular, religiously-neutral form of democracy, with the vast majority of the people being Hindu. But with the passing of time the ideals of Ghandi and the first prime minister, Jawaharlal Nehru (1889–1964), tolerance became less valued and a new movement of Hindu nationalism emerged. Less tolerant within and with neighboring countries, India might be added to the list of countries struggling to express itself as a religious state.

I appreciate the tolerance of Rāmakrishna. It seems that the religions of Asia each developed in their own way, continuing to seek answers to the timeless questions, but without fighting with each other too much.

There was some conflict, of course, but they managed to produce interesting new developments without destructive internal division. The monotheistic faiths, on the other hand, appear prone to many internal divisions over belief and practice. We can discuss that next time if you wish.

Yes, I need to know about the development of Islam, Judaism, and Christianity.

References

Agnes, Michael, Editor in Chief, *Webster's New World Collegiate Dictionary,* Cleveland, Ohio: Wiley Publishing, 2010. For the definition of alchemy.

Armstrong, Karen, *The Lost Art of Scripture.* New York: Alfred Knopf, 2019. The later development of Hinduism is discussed on pp. 424 ff. The quotation "there had never been an organized... is on p. 423. *Ātman* and *ahimsa* (non-violence) are discussed on pp. 430-431.

Bhaskarananda, Swami, *The Essentials of Hinduism.* Seattle: Viveka

Press, 2016. Quotations of Rāmakrishna's teachings are on pp. 190-92.

Flood, Gavin, *An Introduction to Hinduism.* Cambridge: Cambridge University Press, 1996. A description of the Hindu goddess, Devi "who possesses all the qualities..." along with the quotation "kicking him with her feet... is on p. 176. The description of how the iconography developed in the sixth to eighth centuries is on p. 182. Discussion of Rāmakrishna, his life and early marriage is from pp.256-257. Rāmakrishna's tolerance is described on p. 257. Vivekānanda's founding of Ramakrishnan Mission is from p.258. The quotation "first effective proponent..." is from p.258.

Harris, Ian, Consultant Editor, *The Complete Illustrated Encyclopedia of Buddhism.* Leicestershire, UK: Hermes House, Annes Publishing, 2011. Buddha's birth is discussed on p. 14. The quotation "during the reign of the emperor Asoka..." is on p. 100. The spread of Buddhism under Asoka is described on p. 102. The quotation "authoritative discourses..." is on p. 109. Discussions of Mahayana Buddhism are on p.108. The quotation "Buddha as supremely powerful..." is on p.88. The discussion of Great Vehicle and the Lesser Vehicle is on p. 110. The quote about spreading into "Central Asia, China..." is from p. 88. The description of merging with local beliefs, is on p. 89. Tantric Buddhism is discussed on p. 102. Esoteric practices, are discussed on p. 107. The discussion of the Mandala is based on p. 104. The quotation "Devotees visualize..." is from p. 105. The quotation indicating that mandalas "are destroyed..." is from p. 104.

Harvey, Peter, *An Introduction to Buddhism,* Second Edition. Cambridge: Cambridge University Press, 2013. The discussion of the spread of Buddhism in India is on p. 194.

Rainey, Lee Dian, *Decoding Dao.* Malden, MA: Wiley Blackwell, 2014. The discussion of the authorship of the *Dao Te Ching* and Laozi are based on pp. 30-31. The quotation "transformed from the possible author of a text..." is from p. 206. Birth legends of Laozi are from p. 206. Quotations about "Yin, female, and yang, male..." are from p. 187. Various manifestations of "Dao Lite" are on pp. 220-221. The idea of mistaking a part for the whole, is from p.221. The quotation "If we look at the number of people..." is from p. 219 The quotation "that this is Daoism so completely repackaged..." is from p. 220. The countries where Daoism is found is based on p. 219.

Rainey, Lee Dian, *Confucius and Confucianism*. Malden, MA: Wiley-Blackwell, 2010. Quotations are as follows: on the spread of the Han Dynasty "both north and south..." p. 132 and "...during the Han Dynasty, Confucius came to be seen..." p.140. as well as "...his miraculous birth..." p. 140. Discussion of the civil service exam is based on pp. 148-149. The quotation "any city of respectable size..." is from p. 153. The description of the spread and growth of Confucianism is based on p. 164. The quotation "There is an eternal, primal substance..." is from p. 164, and "air, vital, spirit, energy..." from p. 137. The concepts of "Supreme Ultimate" and "Principle," are from p. 162. The description of the development of Confucianism in modern China and other countries is based on pp. 178, 181, 182, 183.

Suzuki, D.T., *Essays in Zen Buddhism*, First Series. New York: Grove Press, 1949. The general discussion of Zen Buddhism is based on this thorough, older text. The quotations "Zen is the product of Chinese soil..." and no special "line of transmission..." are on p. 169. Discussion of *sumiye* painting and the quote "fleeting, unrepeatable..." is from p. 300.

Partridge, Christopher, General Editor, *A Brief Introduction to Hinduism*. Minneapolis: Fortress Press, 2018. Revised and updated by Tim Dowley. Chapter 9 "A Historical Overview" by Maya Warrier reviews the early Vedic period on p. 54. Chapter 10, "Philosophy" by Tinu Ruparell provides discussion of Shankara and Ramanuja and *atman*, p. 61. Chapter 12 "Beliefs" by Anna King suggests that the goddess is at sometimes the consort of a male god. Chapter 15 "Hinduism in the Modern World" by Theodore Gabriel discusses modern India, pp. 86-87.

Wong, Eva, *Taoism: An Essential Guide*. Boulder, CO: Shambala Publications, 1977. Discussion of growth and development of early Daoism is from p. 31 ff. The quotation "as the chief deity..." is on p. 36. Discussion of staying well and longevity is from pp. 54-55. The quotation "heart, liver, and spleen..." is on p. 55. "Mist, clouds, and vapor..." is on p. 55. The quotation of second thoughts about "ingesting compounds..." is on p. 73. Death from longevity drugs is discussed on p. 73. Discussion of the Yin-Yang symbol, is based on p. 126. The quotations are "Yin and Yang translated literally..." p. 124, "divination is a way of seeing..." p. 124, and "Thus, Yin becomes associated..." p. 16.

Watts, Alan W. *The Way of Zen.* New York: New American Library, 1957. Discussion of *sumiye* painting is on pp. 172 ff. and *haiku* poetry on pp. 179 ff. The quotation "of just seventeen syllables..." is on p. 177. *Haiku* poems presented are from pp. 178 and 179. Portraying them as a "child's expression of wonder," is from p. 178.

Watts, Alan W., *The Spirit of Zen,* Third Edition, London: John Murray, 1958, originally published in 1936. A classic older study of Zen. The description of *koan* is on p. 63, and the quotation of the goose in a bottle *koan* is on p. 62. The suggestion to try to get past the impasse and get to the bottom of the matter is from pp. 65 and 63. The quotation "straightforwardness and going right ahead, for Zen the task..." is found on p. 47. The discussion of *sumiye* painting and quote "commit his inspiration..." is on p. 97.

9
Division
Fighting Over Truth and Goodness

After our last discussion, I've been noticing the number of churches we have in this relatively small town. I think I counted nine, plus a Black congregation, a Jewish synagogue and Jewish temple, and two mosques. It seems like a lot. Why so many?

The technical term for division is *schism.* (It's *siz* or *skiz* with an *m,* so you can take your pick on pronunciation.) It means a split or division over opinion or doctrine. And the new offshoot is sometimes called a *sect.* The monotheistic faiths seem to have a lot of schisms and sects, resulting in many places to worship. Let's take a look at how we got so many.

We'll begin with Islam. As we discussed earlier, the bickering successors to Muhammed—including a close friend, a relative, and a skilled warrior—all brought different qualities of leadership, but with considerable internal strife. Three of the four first leaders were murdered by fellow Muslims. One of them, Ali, a cousin of Muhammad and adopted son, who was married to Muhammad's daughter Fatima, had earned great respect, and for millions of Muslims today in the Shi'ah branch of Islam, "Ali remains the model of Muslim piety, the light that illuminates the straight path to God." For Shi'ah Muslims the key figure of religious interpretation is the *imam,* of whom Ali is regarded as the first. The *imam* as interpreter of the faith is more significant than the caliph as 'secular ruler.' The highest of the *imams* are the "doctors of laws" who make interpretations of Islamic law (Shariah) and the most senior of these are *ayatollahs,* who are still active in Iran with strong influence on governance. The other branch of Islam, the Sunnis, constitute today the Muslim majority of around 85 percent, and they actually developed the body of law known as Shariah. They turn toward the teachings of Muhammad and the first successors for the authoritative Sunnā or 'custom' as the guide for later generations with no need for the office of imam or caliph. Those are the two major divisions within Islam today, Shi'ah and Sunni. Unfortunately, disagreements over the role of Caliph, interpretations of the Quran, and membership in the Ummah "ultimately tore the Muslim community apart, forever shattering any hope of preserving the unity and harmony that Muhammad had envisioned for his followers."

If I remember correctly, Islam expanded across a vast territory that includes the familiar countries of the Middle East, Turkey, North Africa, Southern Spain, and—help me here—where else?

Yes, you might say the northern half of Africa, but also into lands north of India that we know as Afghanistan and Pakistan and east of India to Bangladesh. Sometimes we forget that Islam stretched down through Malaysia, across the vast island country of Indonesia, and up into the Philippines, a very populous region. As Islam spread across these diverse regions, the timeless question of how to put religious principles into the social structure of governance would not go away. It persists still today and continues to divide Islam. In spite of Islam's useful contribution to the discussion of the social order, key issues of national and cross-national structure still go unresolved and divisions remain as many Islamic countries search for new ways to infuse governance with Islamic values.

A few more developments within Islam deserve discussion. One of these is the Muslim dedication to learning about the natural world and physical universe. It began with Ma'mun, the Baghdad Caliph (813–833 CE) who had a dream one night in which he saw the ghost of Aristotle telling him there was no contradiction between religion and reason. Up to that point, followers of Islam believed Allah's creation was unapproachable. But the Caliph gave study the green light by ordering the building of a library—a 'house of wisdom'—to house a collection of all available books in the world.

Like Amazon, maybe with free delivery by camel? Oh, my, that was bad. My bad.

Islamic "science" set about to discover the basic laws of the physical world. And discover they did: the principles of the circulation of the blood, treatment for smallpox, operations with anesthetic, the decimal system, the concept of zero, and the subject of algebra: the mathematics of solving for the unknown. Looking to the sky, they named stars and developed the concepts of zenith (point directly overhead) and nadir (point directly below). They calculated the diameter and circumference of the earth. They made sophisticated travel guides. And let us not forget the development of musical instruments such as lute, guitar, trumpet, horn, and flute. The reasoned study of many fields brought a new understanding of Allah's creation.

"Wherever the West met the East, the West started to learn." This happened, surprisingly, in the Crusades, but more formally in centers of learning in Islamic Spain, specifically in Córdoba. The ancient learning of the Greeks and Romans, lost to Europe, was transmitted through Islamic culture, and, yes, there was subsequently a renaissance of learning in Europe. Muslim learning expanded with Islam. Unfortunately, Muslim scholarship declined after the Mongol invasions of 1258.

I had heard about this transmission of Muslim learning in the Middle Ages, but never knew that they did all of this, especially creating those musical instruments. The Muslims discovered a lot that we take for granted today. I've heard the word "Sufism" in connection with Islam. What is that?

Sufism is hard to define but refers to Islam's broad mystical tradition. It is a movement within Islam (not a sect like Sunni or Shi'ah) of Muslims seeking "intimacy with God through a discipline of spiritual perfection..." and "a heart...purified from the pollution of the world." The Sufis wore "a simple tunic made of wool (*suf*) as a sign of one withdrawing from the world, and pursuing an inward spiritual path to God involving orderly steps under the guidance of a Sufi master." Sufism grew out of a "hodge-podge of influences, but it became a sizable movement of the wandering intentional poor."

As these "wandering dervishes (members of a Sufi order) grew in number, temporary boardinghouses were constructed in high traffic areas" of the cities. Eventually more permanent structures resembling monasteries were provided, and sophisticated schools of mysticism developed. Sufis were not interested in questions of social order, instead, pursuing the life of poverty and simplicity. The goal was "to create one inseparable union between the individual and the divine." That's the aim of mysticism. Although the masters withdrew from society, many followers maintained the everyday responsibilities of work and family. Pursuing systematic efforts toward self-annihilation, the Sufi finds that the principle of love, not belief or the law, is the key to knowledge of God. If you are serious about self-annihilation, you can spin around and around as the earth does on its axis while circling the master, as the earth does the sun, in the Turkish Sufi Order called the "Whirling Dervishes."

Spinning around like that would definitely annihilate me. But would it be correct to identify the Sufi movement as a new Islamic effort to pursue the good life? To find the love of God and express it in the love of others sounds like what the Christian saints are trying to do.

I think you've made a good connection there, both to the good life and to Christianity. We are discovering that many forms of religious expression such as mysticism, meditation, and service to the needy are manifest in many religions, and we begin to notice similarities across differing traditions. Not that all religions are the same, but they sometimes share common interests and practices. For example, in addition to Muslim Sufism, Jewish and Christian forms of mysticism developed across the centuries.

I need to learn more about the development of Judaism. I know some words like "Talmud" and "Yiddish", but I'm not sure what they mean.

We discussed how Christianity grew out of and relied on the Jewish religion, but that Judaism also went its own way and continued to develop as a faith. The Jews suffered under the foreign oppression of various empires and wanted their freedom. One Jewish leader, Judas Maccabeus, even before the Romans, led a temporarily successful uprising against the dominating Syrians in 165 BCE. The Jews marched on to Jerusalem and cleansed and reconsecrated the Temple. This action is remembered and revered in the celebration of Hanukkah still today.

In 40 BCE the Romans gave Herod (73–4 BCE) the title "King of the Jews," and it is not surprising that Jewish hopes for a messiah who would rescue their people grew more fervid at that time. There were several revolts and in one, after some initial success, the Jews experienced "a crushing defeat; Jerusalem was taken, and its Temple destroyed in 70 CE." It is a landmark date for Judaism, because once again the Temple was gone, the priesthood and council were wiped out, and the Jews had no home. Yes, it starts way back then. Already spread about in Babylon, the Jews now dispersed throughout the Mediterranean world, living in what has come to be called *diaspora* (dispersion), often far from the homeland. The amazing thing to consider is that Judaism not only survived, but continued to grow and thrive.

Around the Hellenistic world in which they lived, permeated as it was by the Greek culture coming after Alexander the Great, Jews founded schools, and "*rabbi* (master) became the formal title for teachers." What developed was called 'Rabbinic Judaism,' and it became the dominant faith as other forms died out, including a Christian form of Judaism. Under the Romans, the Jews continued to be persecuted and a new Roman City, Aelia Capitolina, was built upon the ruins of Jerusalem, a humiliating action in what was their Holy Land called Palestine. The conversion of the emperor Constantine to Christianity in 313 CE made life more difficult for the Jews although Judaism was never outlawed. But what was to be their destiny as a people?

The Jews were always interested in learning. They developed interpretations of the scriptures along with collections of law and tradition in the *Mishna* and *Gemara*, which came to be known as Talmud, one version, the Jerusalem Talmud, coming from Jerusalem in the fourth century, and the other, the Babylonian Talmud, perhaps more important, from the seventh and eighth centuries CE. The Talmud contains collections of teachings of the rabbis with their continuing debates over how to interpret the Torah (first five books of the Hebrew scriptures), including opinions on an astounding range of topics and many divergent positions. In addition, poetry was composed, prayer books were compiled, and the text of the Bible (Hebrew scriptures) was fixed and annotated.

As Islam spread, Jews came under Muslim rule, and because they were not treated with hostility, they joined the Muslims in their search for knowledge and enlightened learning. The Jews were granted influential positions in the Spanish Court and developed a strong culture in Spain and Portugal called "Sephardic" Judaism, including their Spanish-Jewish dialect called Ladino.

Moses Maimonides (1135–1204 CE), one of the famous Jewish scholars in Córdoba, Spain, had been studying the ancient Greek philosophers, and while exiled to Egypt, he wrote in Arabic an exploration of the challenges Aristotle's philosophy presented to the Jewish believer, *The Guide for the Perplexed*. He also developed a very clear and simple summation of Jewish belief called 'Thirteen Principles of Faith.' It is an uncomplicated list that includes many of the areas we have discussed—God, creation, life after death—and shows how the Jewish people continued to think about these issues through the centuries.

Although belief was important, Judaism is said to emphasize practice over belief, and maybe that's why it was possible for Maimonides to make a short summary of beliefs like this. In its practice, there are interesting variations, some of which led to division. As with Sufism in Islam, there is a Jewish mystical tradition as well, known as Kabbalah. Remember how God often remains hidden in the Hebrew scriptures? In Kabbalah, God was designated *En Sof,* meaning 'limitless,' but God is also known in ten aspects through mystical insights or 'emanations' that mediate between *En Sof* and the world. The most important guide to mystical practice is the *Zohar*, an exposition of the hidden meaning of the Torah, written in thirteenth century Spain.

So, people who have read about the unknowable God in the old Hebrew scriptures are still seeking, centuries later, some aspect of God they can grasp and understand.

Yes, and experience in their life. Another interesting movement in Judaism called Hasidism developed in Poland in the eighteenth century. It had a dynamic, charismatic leader named Israel ben Eliezer (1700–1760 CE) known as Baal Shem Tov, 'Master of the Good Name."

I've heard better names than that, but continue. This is interesting.

It has been said of Hasidism that "at the core was a passionate devotion to God expressed in ecstatic prayer, singing, and dancing... sustained by Hasidic joy—a genuine religious high."

It sounds better to me than spinning around like a whirling dervish, but it feels like we are a long way from sitting in the lotus position doing yoga with all of that Hasidic singing and dancing.

Yes, a good example of how religions are different. But it is interesting to see all of the things people will do to try to actually experience, not just think about, God.

Then the more rational side of Judaism reasserts itself in the Jewish Enlightenment called *Haskalah.* The leader of this is Moses Mendelsohn (1729–1786 CE), "who emphasized the universal principles of Judaism and translated the Torah into German." He was a strong advocate of separation of church and state. His followers, perhaps even more radical in their pursuit of the Enlightenment, began to reject the Talmud and even traditional ideas of revelation. *Haskalah* eventually led to Reform Judaism.

That's right. Judaism also has its divisions. I've heard of these, but

I don't understand them.

The Talmudic traditions, besides being interesting discussions of belief, contained Talmudic law, full of ancient customs, presumed to be of divine origin. In *American Judaism* by Nathan Glazer, we learn that by the early nineteenth century in Germany, the traditions had become an embarrassment to some, and the need for reform became urgent, especially for those who wished to participate in the mainstream of society. "'Reform' Judaism began as a movement of Jews of high social status who wished to dignify Jewish religious services..." In several important German cities, Glazer tells us, services were conducted in which "prayers were read in German, some were cut, an organ was used, and a preacher delivered sermons in German." The basic Talmudic law was questioned and practices of observance were modified. But "the struggle for Reform was far more successful in America than Germany." An important leader for Reform was the rabbi Isaac Mayer Wise (1819–1900) who also founded in 1875 a school to train American Reform rabbis, Hebrew Union College, in Cincinnati, Ohio. The synagogue in Reform Judaism was called a "temple."

The traditional branch of Judaism known as Orthodox maintained its practices and beliefs both in Europe and the United States, but it struggled against the tendencies of the modern world. A third movement developed called Conservative, but what they wished to conserve was not orthodox Jewish belief and practice, but the concept of Jewish civilization and the Jewish people. Mordecai Kaplan promoted the idea of the Jewish Center (to maintain culture and learning), and his ideas were taken up by students at the Jewish Theological Seminary in New York, who "did not feel strongly about religion but did feel strongly about Jewish people and Jewish culture—about Jewishness."

I know that it is called Conservative, but the ideas sound quite liberal.

I know. The labels get confusing. Meanwhile, in an area of Brooklyn, New York, where three-fourths of the population was Jewish, mostly Orthodox, a group of World War II refugee-survivors from the Hassidic tradition in Europe came to settle in an area known as Williamsburg. They brought their leaders, called *rebbes,* and the movement grew, made converts, attracted more *rebbes,* and established Jewish parochial schools, which spread across the country. The Hassidic Jews try to live a strict Jewish life that is an example to others. Then, of course, there are many Jews who think of themselves as "non-observant" but continue to maintain a Jewish identity.

I remember being impressed by the idea in the Hebrew scriptures that no one shall see God and still live. Does the search for God continue in modern Judaism?

The search for a way to express the mystery of God continued on in the work of a twentieth century existentialist philosopher, Martin Buber, well known for his concepts, I-Thou and I-It. He invented those primary hyphenated words to distinguish types of human relationships. In I-It relationships, other people are treated as things, alongside other things, in an impersonal way, sometimes being used or exploited. In I-Thou relationships, other people are held in high regard and treated in a humane way, and the communication with them often goes deep. In I-Thou relationships the Thou of God can be present and "we are aware of the breath from the eternal Thou; in each Thou we address the eternal Thou."

I-It relationships, which Buber calls 'objective,' are necessary and permit people to organize their life, as with the efficient clerk at the supermarket who gets us through the check-out process quickly. Naturally, the people in line behind would grow anxious and impatient if we try to strike up an I-Thou relationship with the cashier. Buber, however, has touched something important in his philosophy: the tendency toward depersonalization in modern society and the need for authentic human relations, which he sees as marked by a touch of the divine. It is interesting that Buber had to flee Germany during World War II and ultimately ended up as a professor in Israel.

Now that you bring it up, what about anti-Semitism and the Holocaust?

Jewish persecution has deep roots in ancient history, but anti-Semitism occurred throughout the *diaspora* as well, and developed more formally in the tenth century in Europe. Jews as well as Muslims were slaughtered in the Crusades. False rumors about Jews were circulated (we might call them conspiracy theories), blaming them for the Black Death, a plague that killed off one third of the population in Europe in 1348. After expulsion from Spain in 1492 (along with Muslims), Jews scattered throughout Europe, living in the Netherlands, Poland, Lithuania, and Germany. Settling in Germany in the sixteenth century, they developed a second branch of Jewish culture known as

Ashkenazi (distinguished from Sephardic in Spain), and set forth their own German-Jewish dialect called Yiddish. Jews were later forced to live together in enclosed areas of a city called "ghettos." Serious anti-Semitic movements developed in France after the 1880s which led to the distinction of "Aryan" and "Semitic" people, "the direct consequence of which was the Nazi destruction between 1939 and 1945 of six million people in the Holocaust, simply because they were Jewish. European Jewry almost ceased to exist, and one third of world Jewry was killed."

How awful that is. And all because of their religion?

Religion in the broadest sense, not because of their beliefs. Hitler and his followers cared little about religion; it was the Jews as a people he was intent on exterminating. Maybe we should leave this horrible topic. What else would you like to know?

We haven't discussed Christianity yet. How did it expand and develop? How was a religion built up around Jesus?

The first written records of Christianity, as we discovered in our discussion of the Resurrection, presented differing interpretations of Jesus in the four Gospels as well as in the writings of Paul. Remember that modern Biblical scholarship suggests that the "records" we have are not historical accounts, but statements of belief from various "faith communities." Belief spread quickly beyond the local towns and villages where Jesus and the disciples wandered, expanding into the Greek-speaking world of the Mediterranean lands. Although some differences of belief existed in the early churches, as reflected in Paul's letters to them, a more or less consistent message soon developed and spread quickly through vigorous missionary efforts. It was a message of salvation.

Some would call the message myth, and as we discovered in our discussion of Creation, myth is not something false, but an attempt to provide an explanation of a deep mystery. The language of early Christianity is pre-scientific and before the Enlightenment, so that it is full of interpretation, metaphor, story-telling, religious expression, and a degree of exaggeration common at the time to make a point.

Are you saying that the story about Jesus, the account that became the accepted message of Christianity, is myth? I can see how a creation story is myth, but wasn't Jesus an historical figure who actually lived at a particular time?

That's correct, but we don't have the historical record based on what we today consider to be historical fact. We have statements of belief *about* Jesus, and they certainly have the characteristics of myth.

But a lot of Christians will be very upset if you call it myth.

Yes, many indeed. Will they also be unhappy if we use the term *myth* to describe the stories that grew up around Buddha and Confucius? Maybe it is easier to use the word *myth* to describe someone else's religion rather than one's own. But remember, Rudolph Bultmann, a very respected Christian theologian, suggested a need to demythologize the New Testament. He clearly thought the message was cast as myth, or he wouldn't have made such a proposal.

Oh, I'm remembering that name now. Yes, and our job is to get beyond the myth to the message.

In an effort to demythologize the story of Jesus, we might better ask: What would the message of salvation have meant at the time? How was it cast? Why were people eager to believe it? Let me try to provide in modern language a description of the human predicament that lies behind the Christian myth.

The Christian view of human nature that we discussed is that people tend to be anxious about their existence—we used the phrase *existential anxiety*—and they tend to do the wrong thing, the selfish thing. This tendency is inborn and seems to go on generation after generation, thus keeping people alienated from God. What people feel they need is forgiveness for the wrong things they have done, not always intentionally, but with some sense of responsibility that produces guilt. They need some way to prevent doing them again, and a means to draw closer to God. They want to be able to affirm that their individual life is meaningful now and, in spite of their wrong doing, will continue into an afterlife with god—all of which might be called the need for salvation. Keep in mind that this challenge of finding a way to live a meaningful and good life, while drawing close to God, is an enduring mystery that other religions explored and continue to struggle with today. Now let's see what the Christian myth says about salvation in mythological language.

Sandra S. Frankiel in her valuable short book, *Christianity: A Way of Salvation,* expresses the story—she calls it myth—as follows:

God became a human being in order to take on the state of sin, for sin constitutes the fundamental condition since the fall of

Adam and Eve, the first humans according to the Bible. Yet although God-as-Jesus became human, he did not sin; nor (since he was God) did he have any stain of original sin inherited from Adam. Instead, he suffered the punishment—namely death—for the sin of the whole world.

He was resurrected bodily from death, "redeemed" even from the world of the dead. From that time forward it would be possible for human beings also to be freed from the punishment for sin if they repented of sin, believed in Jesus as the Christ, and accepted the offer of salvation.

The message of salvation described here by Frankiel spoke to a timeless question: How is a person ever to live a good life and grow close to God? That question is based on the larger mystery of how to know God.

The message appealed to the earliest believers who spread it systematically as 'good news,' "establishing the new religion throughout the empire, increasingly among non-Jews rather than Jews." The movement started out as small groups of believers meeting in homes on Sunday mornings, with a "deacon" to manage ritual and worship, a "bishop" to oversee the celebration with bread and wine, and with "priests" as the bishop's assistants. The early church was well organized. "By the third century CE there were four centers of power in the church: Jerusalem, Antioch (in Syria), Alexandria (in Egypt) and Rome." It was during those "first three centuries that the literature that eventually became the New Testament was written, copied, and shared among the churches," as they continued to value the Jewish Bible which they began to refer to as the Old Testament.

But what happened to the idea that the world was soon to come to an end? Wasn't Jesus telling people to get ready immediately for the Kingdom of God? And what about the Revelation to John of Patmos?

The world didn't end, so the belief was modified to suggest that Jesus himself would return—the so-called second coming of Christ—and at his return, *that* is when the world would end. During that period between the first appearance and the second coming, people needed to be focused on working out their own salvation with God and building the Kingdom of God. As people waited for the return of Jesus, they believed that the Holy Spirit was present and available to assist them.

So a unified message about salvation developed, and even though the message about Jesus sounds somewhat different from the message set forth by Jesus himself, as portrayed in the earliest Gospels, the idea spread quickly on its own merit.

The message was unified enough for Christianity to expand quickly and widely, but as you might guess, many arguments developed over belief and practice. Christianity was growing in a culture of Greek philosophy, so there was a lot of explaining to do about God, the true nature of Jesus (how he could be truly God and truly man), and the relationship of Jesus to God and the Holy Spirit. What might seem like trivial matters to later generations were subjects of heated debate by the "early church fathers," as they came to be called. Some who were fed up with the debates and wanted to draw closer to God, went off into the desert to live as hermits, most notably an eighteen-year-old Egyptian, the founder of Christian monasticism, who became Saint Anthony. Anthony of Padua (1195–1231 CE) was a different Saint Anthony.

Constantine, the emperor who made it easier for Christians to survive in the empire had moved his capital to Constantinople (today's Istanbul, Turkey) and as the eastern empire grew strong, so did the eastern Church. Meanwhile, in Rome, western Christianity developed a strong hierarchy, including the "patriarch of Rome, who came to be called the pope (i.e., father)." To make a long story shorter, as the power struggle and disagreements over beliefs between east and west grew more intense, the church eventually split into two branches, in a division called The Great Schism. The east became known as Orthodox and the west as Roman Catholic. The two branches of Christianity, which differ in certain areas of belief and practice, have never been reunited.

There is so much development and expansion in Christian church history, I'm not sure what else you might want to explore.

You've described the east-west split. How did the division between Protestant and Catholic develop?

The Roman church, not without its ups and downs, continued to expand and grow very powerful. It developed prosperous monastic orders, forms of mysticism, the magnificent Gothic cathedrals, several famous scholars, and the first universities. It was not until the late Middle Ages, 1100 to 1300, that the doctrine of transubstantiation became official, asserting that through the ritual of the priest, the "bread and wine actually become, in substance, the body and blood of Christ."

The same period also produced the belief in the Immaculate Conception of Mary, proclaiming that she herself (not just her son) was conceived without sin.

As the church grew more powerful, most would agree, it became corrupt. Church leaders such as the Englishman John Wycliff, the Czech John Hus, and the humanist, Erasmus of Rotterdam, saw the need for reform. But the issue that sparked the Protestant Reformation was the sale of indulgences, a way of buying yourself and your relatives out of purgatory (an intermediate punishment stop before heaven) through contributions to the church. It was part of a larger penitential system involving confession, forgiveness (pardon), and penance—doing something positive for one's salvation. The contribution often involved cash gifts that supported the church, monasteries, and universities. In 1517 an Augustinian monk named Martin Luther became the leader of reform in lands we know today as Germany.

Yes, I've heard of Luther, but I don't know much about him. You say he was a monk?

The life of Luther is summarized in this wonderful old tattered paperback I have here called *Here I Stand* by Roland Bainton. Luther was thinking of a religious vocation when on a July day in 1505 a lightning bolt struck and knocked him to the ground. "Struggling to rise, he cried in terror, 'Saint Anne help me.' I will become a monk." He wore the cowl as an Augustinian monk for nineteen years. But instead of finding peace in the church, he developed a "terror of the holy," severely frightened of God's wrath and unable to conceive of anything that would resolve the sinfulness of his whole being. For a man so alienated from God, all the ways of self-help, including the penitential system, were inadequate and alarming. The means to salvation provided by the Church were all useless for him, and, he thought, blasphemous to God. He tried to perform whatever good works he could, but he remained wretched, distressed, and depressed.

Did he have mental health issues?

Today we might label them that way, but what bothered him most were his spiritual health issues. As Bainton tells us, his spiritual advisor at the cloister "tried to bring Luther to see that he was making religion altogether too difficult."

The ideas Luther was developing about salvation as coming only from God's grace (adapting ideas from Paul and Augustine, the founder of his order), put him at odds with a church that by then had developed an elaborate range of ways to achieve one's own salvation, including buying it. Luther had been invited to Rome to help resolve a dispute in the Augustinian Order, and his eyes were opened to what was happening in the Church there, including the construction of the Basilica of St. Peter through payments from indulgences. But he also recognized that the problem wasn't just in Rome; indulgence vendors were busy all around him where he lived in Wittenberg. It was time for reform.

Out of his disillusionment came the famous Ninety-Five Theses, posted on the wall at Castle Church in 1517. Although the propositions were only presented for debate, they caused more controversy than intended, and over the next four years there was considerable challenge and counter-challenge going back and forth between Luther and the Church. The result was that Luther rejected the pope's control over purgatory, the use of indulgences, the merits of the saints (interceding with God), the veneration of relics, monasticism, the infallibility of the office of pope, the authority of Canon Law, the doctrine of transubstantiation, and the seven sacraments, reducing them to two: baptism and the Lord's Supper, the latter regarded as preferable to the mass. It didn't happen overnight, but gradually the authority of the Church was replaced by the authority of scripture (*sola scripture,* in Latin) and "Protestantism subsequently split into churches and sects."

It's interesting how Luther became preoccupied with his own salvation and how the original Christian salvation myth, as you have called it, became corrupted by the Church's offering of these shady deals. It seems that what started out for Luther as reform, ended up as a big conflict within the Church over a lot of beliefs and practices. Now Christianity has Orthodox, Roman Catholic, and Protestant. But there are a lot of Protestant churches, not just one. How did that happen?

As you might expect, Luther was hauled in to the authorities and told that he better recant (change his stand) at a meeting called the Diet of Worms.

That's for the birds. Sorry. I just couldn't resist. What was that?

A Church lawmaking assembly at a German city by that name. But instead of recanting, Luther stuck to his beliefs and actually made things worse, insisting that in matters of religious belief, the Christian must make a personal judgement. This was the foundation of Protestant individualism. Luther had quite a following, so the Church was reluctant to execute him, and he was whisked off to a castle of Frederick, the ruler of Saxony. While Luther was there, he continued to write, including translating the Bible into German, as his friends and supporters went to work developing and expanding his ideas. Now society was in turmoil all around him—about many things, not just religion—and eventually wars broke out.

The urgent need for reform was seen in many places, and other leaders emerged with their own ideas about proper belief and church organization. Think of them not so much as descendants of Luther, but as brothers and cousins springing up spontaneously elsewhere. Once Luther stood up and spoke out, others followed, but they had different things to say. The chief movements with lasting effects were the Reformed Churches associated with Zwingli and Calvin (leading to Presbyterians) the Anabaptists, called by others the "rebaptizers" because they favored adult baptism (leading to Mennonites, Hutterites, Congregationalists, and Baptists), and the Church of England (leading to Episcopalians). Of course, in Germany, the followers of Luther became Lutherans. Associations of like-minded Protestants are called denominations.

To its credit, the Catholic Church recognized the need for internal reform. As one church historian has written: "Partly as a response to the Protestant Reformation, and partly due to its own inner dynamics, the Roman Catholic Church also underwent a renewal which is often called 'counter-reformation,' but which is much more than a mere response to the Protestant Reformation." It included not the elimination of monasticism, but the founding of new monastic orders, including the Society of Jesus (Jesuits), who excelled in teaching and missionary work. The authority of the papacy was strengthened, and doctrine was debated and refined in the Council of Trent which began in 1545 and lasted eighteen years.

That may be the longest meeting in history.

Eventually "Protestantism had deep roots in Germany, England, Scotland, Scandinavia, and the Netherlands." A compromise was reached in France permitting tolerance of Protestants. "In Spain, Italy, Poland, and other countries Protestantism was stamped out by force."

And how did these European Protestant churches jump across the Atlantic Ocean and land in the American colonies? Or am I opening up a can of worms this time?

There were other colonies: Jamestown, Virginia, was established in 1607 before the 1,000 Puritan settlers arrived in Massachusetts Bay in 1630. The Church of England became Virginia's established church. The first Baptist congregation was in Rhode Island, the Quakers settled in (William) "Penn's Woods" in Pennsylvania, Presbyterians from Scotland settled in Maryland along with Catholics, and the Dutch Reformed in New Amsterdam (New York). Outside of the colonies that were later to become the United States, Catholics dominated in French Canada (Quebec) and Spanish Mexico.

Side by side, the Protestant denominations found their way to religious freedom and tolerance as they continued to pursue the timeless questions: What is the right path to salvation, the good life, and the proper relationship of church and state? In the century after the American revolution, representatives of many other denominations settled in the U.S., including Lutherans and Methodists, large numbers of Roman Catholics from Italy and Ireland, as well as members of the Orthodox branch of Christianity from Greece, Turkey, and Russia. Members of other faiths, particularly Jews and later Muslims immigrated as well. New Denominations and movements sprang up spontaneously. The U.S. was open to and alive with religious exploration.

Tell me about some of the different movements outside of the mainstream of the Protestant denominations.

We mentioned the Quakers. Their first leader in England, was George Fox (1624–1691). They believed in the Inner Light of Christ and listened silently in worship for guidance from that light—no sermons, no hymn-singing—and they had a pacifist philosophy against war and strong dedication to a simple life and commitments to social justice that continue today.

Another older group with European origins is the Amish, a strict branch of the Mennonites (also pacifist) going back to the Anabaptists. These groups sought salvation through separation from the sinful world, maintaining a "rural" style of life, and avoiding modern conveniences. They lived in families, but their separation from society has a monastic ring to it. Their salvation was in simplicity.

While we are still in the colonial era, we should remember the Deists, who believed in a deity as the creator of the world, who then gave it over to his rational creatures to exercise their freedom in running it. Their favorite metaphor was of God the watchmaker who made a perfect watch, wound it up, and let it go. Some of the more famous Deists were signers of the Declaration of Independence, Thomas Jefferson and Benjamin Franklin. Jefferson, later to become President, even went so far as to develop his own version of the New Testament, from which "he cut out all of the miracles, the virgin birth and the resurrection, focusing solely on Jesus' teachings."

He demythologized the New Testament, but kept his slaves!

Yes, it's true; he owned slaves. We can discuss slavery in a moment. Another somewhat later deviation from the dominant trend of Evangelical Protestantism, as it came to be called, was the Unitarian Movement. Its founder, William Ellery Channing (1780–1842) laid out the creed (or is it an anti-creed?) of Unitarianism in his distinctive sermon of 1819, in which he "spoke out against traditional beliefs in the Trinity, the deity of Christ, the total depravity of humans, and substitutionary atonement." The Unitarians grew strong in the area around Boston and near Harvard College and had, and continue to have, a strong emphasis on social justice. An old joke asks, fully aware of what Unitarians do not believe, what *do* they believe? And the reply is "the Fatherhood of God, the brotherhood of man, in the neighborhood of Boston." Actually, Unitarians joined with Universalists and spread across the entire country.

Tell me about some of the later movements and experiments that developed in the United States, like the Seventh-Day Adventists and Mormons.

I can do that, but we need to detour briefly to describe a broader movement called the Second Great Awakening. The first Awakening, before the American Revolution, brought a modest revival of interest in Christianity sparked by the revitalized preaching of George Whitfield, a visitor from England, and Jonathan Edwards of New England. The Second Great Awakening, roughly 1795 to 1810, brought "camp meetings, well attended evangelistic gatherings that lasted several days and involved faith healings, singing, dancing and charismatic preaching." The outdoor tent revivals opened up for the common person a new way to experience God directly, stressing access to salvation through conversion and religious awakening. The Great Awakening provided the incentive for splitting churches into even more sects and the development of Holiness churches, emphasizing the building of a holy life; Pentecostal churches, stressing God's presence through the gifts of the Holy Spirit; and Charismatic churches, founded around a dynamic leader and emphasizing the healing of the sick. They stressed post-conversion baptizing, fervent prayer, and (sometimes) speaking in tongues: unintelligible but inspired shouting out. The foundation was laid for some intriguing experiments.

You wanted to know about the origins of the Seventh-Day Adventists. You have probably heard of the season before Christmas called Advent when people anticipate the birth of Jesus. People who anticipate the second birth, or the return of Christ, are called Adventists. These are people who expect the end of the world as John of Patmos did, and who try to set a date for it. Let's discuss the Millerites from whom the Adventists sprang.

William Miller (1782–1849) was a self-educated farmer from New York State. He studied the Bible carefully and concluded that Jesus would return in 1843. His followers, who came to be known as Millerites, were millenarians, meaning a person who believes in a thousand-year age of blessedness beginning with the return of Christ. These are not to be confused with Miller's name or with millennials, a term used for...

...people born in the 1980s or 90s. And I don't think that any millennials are Millerites or millenarians.

You might be surprised. Anyway, people said that Miller was simply putting a date on something that was widely preached, particularly in the revival meetings of the Great Awakening. A great deal of publicity alerted the populace to watch closely as March 21, 1843, approached, but nothing happened. After that, a number of new Adventist movements sprang up anyway, including one under the leadership of Ellen White (1827–1915) that concluded that Christ actually had returned in 1843, but the return was spiritual and not physical. The followers of White also believed in worship on Saturday and became known as Seventh-Day Adventists. They expanded substantially in the twentieth century and are known for their missionary work and hospitals with vegetarian menus.

Another millenarian group is the Jehovah's Witnesses, known for their door-to-door evangelism and belief in a soon-to-arrive Armageddon. They referred to their beliefs as "The Truth" and set the year 1914 for the return of Christ.

And once again were disappointed. These millenarian ideas sound like the Hindu belief in rebirth, but only for Jesus, not the rest of us.

I hadn't thought of it that way. But let me try to describe the Mormons. It's not easy. The founder and first leader of the Mormons was Joseph Smith (1805–1844). He was born into a farming family that moved from New England to upstate New York and his mother was a devout spiritual "seeker" who never found what she was looking for in the traditional churches of her time. Her son Joseph "began to receive visions from heavenly beings in the early 1820s, a few years before the angel Moroni showed him the unique Book of Mormon that detailed God's special dealings with prehistoric settlers in America and long-lost tribes of Israel." Smith published his translation of the Book of Mormon in 1830 and the band of followers grew into a gathering eventually called Latter-Day Saints.

So, son Joseph found—or founded—what his mother had been looking for: a new religion.

Or at least a new interpretation of an old religion because the new movement was based selectively on Jewish and Christian traditions. In mankind's long search for God, along comes a new revelation, something contemporary and current, and that has a strong appeal.

The Mormons began to search for the ideal place to practice this new and controversial faith in peace. For such unusual beliefs, including a belief in polygamy, finding that place involved a long exodus, with stops in Ohio, Illinois, and Missouri. Smith and his brother were actually murdered while in jail for treason by an angry mob in Illinois, and it fell to his successor Brigham Young to "lead the Great Migration to the basin of Salt Lake (1846–1848)." Through extensive missionary work, the Mormon church grew strong in the twentieth century and plays an important role in family and political life, in the State of Utah particularly, but also around the world.

But what is it that Mormons believe? Are they Christians?

They say they are, but many Christians say they aren't. They have many traditional Christian beliefs, but a different understanding of the Trinity, tending to see God and Jesus as unique divine beings and separate from the Holy Spirit, that is, not all three of one essence. They believe that God sent new prophets after the time of Jesus whose hope was to reform the church and return to its origins. But they also have beliefs that appear odd to outsiders: Adam and Eve settled in Missouri after being expelled from the Garden of Eden, the ancient prophets lived in the Americas both before and after Jesus between 2,500 BCE and 400

CE, Jesus also appeared and preached in the Americas, and the Native Americans are descendants of a lost Jewish tribe. One senses with the Mormons an effort to Americanize Christianity, bring it up to date with new revelations, and expand on it in its new land. They had a new way of understanding the mystery of God, and may have made God even more mysterious in the process.

These groups are interesting. Are there others? What am I missing?

Two other prominent movements come to mind. One is Church of Christ, Scientist, the followers sometimes known as Christian Scientists. Founded by Mary Baker Eddy in 1875 and based on her book, *Science and Health.* The central belief is that disease is a mental error and healing works best without medicine. Again, we encounter the mystery of how to stay well and live a long life.

The other is certainly not an American initiative and is known across the world, the Salvation Army. Begun in 1865 in London by William and Catherine Booth, it uses military ranks and a military command structure as an organization. Its followers believe literally all aspects of what we have been calling the salvation myth, in some respects like the holiness churches. But 1.7 million "soldiers" carry out their world-wide work through hostels for the homeless, children's homes, residential addiction centers, hospitals, schools, and food pantries. The good that they do in the world is impressive as they live out the good life through service to others.

That is impressive. These are the people who collect donations in a small bucket at Christmas time by ringing that little bell, right?

Yes, that's the group, and keep in mind also their collections of used furniture and clothing all year round and their thrift stores and charity shops called, "the Sally Ann" in Canada and "Salvos Stores" in Australia.

If I am remembering my American history correctly, it was at about the same time of these movements in the nineteenth century that the institution of slavery was strong in the South and the Abolition Movement had started in the North, eventually leading to the Civil War. How did the conflict over slavery affect Christianity?

Oh, my, I'm glad you asked because that's important. In addition to the natural Protestant tendency toward proliferation of denominations and splitting off of new sects, there was a cross-cutting effect from disagreements about slavery that sawed many of the existing denominations into two parts. Many denominations developed Northern and Southern branches. The Presbyterians were the first to split into "New School" in the North and "Old School" in the South, and although the differences were also about belief and church organization, disagreements about ending slavery had created serious tensions. The two largest denominations by then, Methodists and Baptists, split (internally, not with each other) over the slavery issue in 1844. In 1845 the Southern Baptist Convention was established, a denomination that would grow into the largest of the American Protestant bodies. The churches, which had played a key role in holding American society together were splitting up over "spiraling cultural antagonisms." When the Civil War broke out, "Christianity rapidly became the prop for the efforts of both sides," with special proclamations, fasts, and services of worship, presumably under the same God. "Revivals were common in the camps of both the Blue and the Gray" (military uniform colors for the North and the South).

Meanwhile, separate African-American churches had begun to emerge. Slaves started to catch glimpses of Christianity while still slaves, generating their own forms of worship and songs, most notably the Negro spirituals. Freed slaves participated in and often helped integrate the white denominations where they could, but they understood their outsider status. "In the face of great, sometimes overwhelming odds, African Americans began to establish churches for themselves." These denominations grew after the Civil War and took on names such as African Methodist Episcopal and African Baptist, and they built neighborhood churches and sent missionaries to Africa. And so, still more denominations were created, this time along racial lines as the older denominations maintained their divisions. The issue, of course, was no longer slavery, but an orientation around race.

It seems there is something within the nature of Protestantism that leads to division, reform, separation, and a new sect. Everyone seems to be in search of the one right way.

There is a story told of Roger Williams, the founder of the Rhode Island colony, and an early advocate of religious freedom. "He separated from the main body of Puritans to found his own Baptist Church; then, finding its members were too impure, he eventually separated from them and would worship in company with no one but his wife—and sometimes not her." Protestant individualism can lead away from the good life to a lonely life.

There are so many divisions, splits, and off-shoots in the expansion of Christianity, it seems like Luther unwittingly pushed the Humpty-Dumpty egg off the wall. Have there been any efforts to get back together?

You mean to put Humpty-Dumpty back together again? Yes, it was called the Ecumenical Movement, an effort to promote Christian unity. Several denominational mergers took place in the mid-twentieth century. Earlier, Canadians were able to bring together Methodists, Congregationalists, and Presbyterians to establish the United Church of Canada in 1925. Several ecumenical councils of churches were established and new ecumenical organizations were established, such as the Young Men's and Young Women's Christian Associations (YMCA and YWCA). Protestant and Catholic relations were improved through the Second Vatican Council led by Pope John XXIII in 1962. But as with the case of Humpty-Dumpty, "all of the king's horses and all the king's men" haven't quite put things back together yet—if ever!

Do Catholics have these divisions that we find in Protestantism?

Catholicism has been able to maintain a relatively unified and orderly church through the exercise of authority, both in belief and church structure. It has a strong organization based on geographical jurisdictions, while allowing for many other organizational forms that cut across geography to enhance diversity of thought and action. Without going into all of the definitions and distinctions, we can begin by saying a Holy Order is an association of monks, nuns, or friars living under the same Rule, actually a detailed set of rules governing their individual behavior and life together. Besides monastic orders, there are orders dedicated to teaching, missionary work, and medical service, but there are also other forms of organization called congregations. Orders may be for priests, brothers, nuns, sisters, or friars, some just for men, some for women. Congregations may be focused on a specific need and local to a specific area, international, or worldwide.

Mother Teresa, whom we met while discussing the good life, took her vows as a nun with the Sisters of Loretto, but her mission work in India was done through the international Missionaries of Charity. Father Damien was a member of the monastic Congregation of the Sacred Hearts. Within the Catholic Church, a variety of organizations may sound familiar by their shortened names: Franciscan, Benedictine,

Augustinian, Dominican, and Jesuit; but there are also less familiar orders such as Carmelite, Cistercian, Capuchin, Poor Clares, Sisters of Mercy, Ursulines, Marianists, and many, many others. Thus, Catholicism maintains order while sanctioning diversity within boundaries, and all of these social structures consider themselves to be Catholic.

But there is a dark side to maintaining order by authority in the Catholic Church, particularly in matters of belief, called the Inquisition. With roots as far back as the early thirteenth century, an organization was developed to "make inquiry" into heretical (deviant) beliefs, by conducting investigations in secret, without revealing accusers, confiscating property, and using torture. In 1480, in Spain, the Inquisition was reestablished with a vengeance under the royal authority of Ferdinand and Isabella (the sponsors of Christopher Columbus), and it became a fearful instrument for stamping out dissent or anything that might lead to division. The Spanish model was picked up again in the Catholic Counter-Reformation to make sure there would be no further division. The Inquisition spoils the pretty picture of Catholic diversity within unity.

Wow! Violence and torture to maintain belief and unity? Are there any other divisions I should know about?

By far the most important split in Christianity today, perhaps more significant than Protestant-Catholic-Orthodox differences, is what came to be known as the Fundamentalist-Modernist Controversy. The phrase refers to a conflict at a particular point in time, starting in 1910–1915 with the publication of a widely-circulated set of booklets called *The Fundamentals: A Testimony to Truth.* But the historical controversy continues into the present time as active conflict. With modern Biblical criticism well underway in the early twentieth century, and with the science of evolution more widely acknowledged and accepted, conservative believers in the Christian faith felt under attack, and perceived a need to reestablish their fundamental beliefs. "Together they defended the 'fundamentals,' or basics, of the faith that newer forms of thought had recently called into question, among them assertions that the Bible is the inspired word of God, that Jesus Christ was God in human flesh, was born of a virgin, lived a sinless life, died on the cross for the salvation of men and women, rose from the dead," and...and...

All of this to be taken quite literally, not in the modern sense of myth and metaphor that we have been using in our discussions of

Christianity and the other world religions.

You have just put your finger on the essence of the continuing Fundamentalist-Modernist Controversy: strictly literal interpretations of the basics versus modern interpretations using the findings of science and Biblical scholarship. Some very important church leaders joined the fundamentalists, and the churches, once again, began splitting down the middle, this time dividing over literal and scholarly interpretation.

The controversy seems to be not only about Biblical interpretation, but the role of scholarship in general and science in particular.

Exactly. The fundamentalists feared being attacked, even annihilated, by liberals and secularists, and they withdrew from the mainstream and formed a counter-culture, "creating an enclave of godliness in their own churches, broadcasting stations, publishing houses, schools, universities, and Bible colleges." Scripture had been the basis of Protestant Christianity, and they would cling to Scripture for dear life, using "proof texts" from the Bible to support their positions. "Biblical literalism became central to the fundamentalist mindset..." Fundamentalist controversies have appeared in other religions, particularly Judaism and Islam, and they also continue, as within Christianity. So, we see religious controversy all around us today, extending to issues concerning the uses of scholarship and science, the role of women, and gay marriage.

This is a little depressing. A powerful myth of salvation formed around a humble teacher, and people have been fighting about it ever since, apparently forgetting the essence of the myth in their battle over having their own correct interpretation of truth and goodness.

Yes, it is disappointing, isn't it? At least now you have some sense of how the religions of Asia (Hinduism, Buddhism, Confucianism, and Daoism) developed and expanded over time and how the monotheistic faiths (Judaism, Christianity, and Islam) divided from within. As you point out, it is not always a pretty picture, this portrait of recurring divisions. And now you know why there are so many places to worship in this small town. You can see to what lengths people will go to address the human mysteries, and you can understand why the timeless questions are timeless. People don't just ponder them; they fight over truth and goodness, heatedly and continuously, producing irreconcilable divisions. Do you think this is what the founders intended?

References

Armstrong. Karen, *The Lost Art of Scripture.* New York: Alfred Knopf, 2019. Jefferson's cuts to his version of the New Testament, p. 392. Fundamentalists feeling under attack, p. 401. The quotations are "creating an enclave..." p 401 and "Biblical literalism became..." p. 402.

Aslan, Reza, *No god but God.* New York: Random House, 2011. The successors to Muhammed are discussed in detail in Chapter 5, "The Rightly Guarded Ones," pp. 119 ff. The quotation "Ali remains the model..." is from p. 138. A discussion of Islam and governance is found on pp. 140-141. The description of Sufi beliefs and practices is based on pp. 205, 211, and 215.

Bainton, Roland, *The Reformation of the Sixteenth Century.* Boston: Beacon Press, 1952. Fifth Printing, 1960. Chapter 2, "Luther's Reform," pp. 36-56 provides historical details on what Luther rejected. The quotation "Protestantism subsequently split..." is from p. 50. Luther facing the Diet of Worms is described on p. 61. Luther's activities in Frederick's castle are based on p. 62. The background on other Protestant reformers is drawn from pp. 77-78.

Bainton, Roland H., *Here I Stand: A Life of Matin Luther.* New York: New American Library, 1950.The lightning bolt of awakening is described on p. 15. The quotation "terror of the Holy" is from p. 30. Luther's spiritual struggle is described on pp. 30-34. The quotation "tried to bring Luther to see..." is on p. 43. The famous Ninety-Five Theses are described on p. 60. In the interests of full disclosure, Roland Bainton was my professor at Yale.

Diamont, Max I. *Jews, God and History.* New York: New American Library, 1962. A useful book for general background on many aspects of the development of Judaism. No direct quotations.

Frankiel, Sandra S. *Christianity: A Way of Salvation.* San Francisco: Harper San Francisco, 1985. Reissued by Waveland Press of Long Grove, Illinois, in 2011.The early Christian message and its spread through missionary efforts are described on p. 8. Frankiel refers to "the founding myths of Christianity" on p. 57. The longer indented quote "God became a human being..." is from p. 59 and is Frankiel's summary of the founding myth. The quotation "establishing the new religion throughout..." is from p. 9. Descriptions of church organization and personnel are found on p.11. The quotation "by the third century..." is on p. 11 and "first three centuries..." is on p. 12. The dessert hermit Saint Anthony is mentioned on p.17. The quotation "patriarch of Rome, who came to be called..." is from p. 21. The description of the Catholic and Orthodox split without reunification is on p. 25. Transubstantiation is described on pp. 34, 36. The quotation "bread and wine actually became..." is from pp. 34, 36. Wycliff and Hus are mentioned on p. 39. Indulgences and the penitential system are drawn from p. 41. The story of Roger Williams and his wife is from p.71.

Glazer, Nathan, *American Judaism.* University of Chicago Press, 1957. Embarrassment with the Talmud is described on p. 25. The quotation "'Reform' Judaism began as..." is from p. 27. The quotations are as follows: "Prayers were read in German..." p.28, and "the struggle for reform was..." p. 33. The founding of Hebrew Union College is described on p. 38. The synagogue becomes "temple" is on p. 32. The quotation of how students "did not feel strongly about religion..." is from p. 93. The description of how the Hassidic tradition came to Williamsburg is on pp. 144-145.

Gonzalez, Justo L. *Church History: An Essential Guide.* Nashville: Abingdon Press, 1996. Dates for Reformation and description of Luther, pp. 69 ff. Catholic Counter-Reformation is described on p. 73. The Quotation "Partly as a response..." is from p. 73. The Society of Jesus is described on p. 73 and the Council of Trent on p.74. The description of the spread of the Reformation to European countries is from p. 74. The quote "Protestantism had deep roots..." is from p. 74 as is "In Spain, Italy..."

Herberg, Will, *The Writings of Martin Buber.* New York: Meridian Books, 1956. Describes Buber's I-Thou and I-It terms for human relationships on p. 43. The quotation "we are aware of the breath..." on p. 45 is from Buber's "I and Thou."

Noll, Mark A. *A History of Christianity in the United States and Canada.*

Grand Rapids, MI: William B. Erdman's, 1992. Chapter 2 "The English Reformation and the Puritans," p. 30ff. provides background on the Puritans. The quote "In which all parts of Colonial life..." is from p. 33. The quotations "They believed...", "emphasized the authority...", and "that churches are..." come from pp. 32-33. Puritan contributions are presented on p. 44, 47. "The New England Way" is mentioned on p.42. Background on the other colonies is on pp. 66, 68. Quakers are discussed on pp.65, 67, Amish and Mennonites on p. 396, Unitarians on p. 233,234. The quotation "spoke out against traditional beliefs..." is on p. 234. The First Great Awakening is discussed on p. 91ff. The Second Great Awakening is discussed on pp. 166-190. Holiness churches are described on pp. 378-379, Pentecostal churches on pp. 386-387, and Millerites on p. 193. Mormons are discussed on pp. 195-197. The quotation "began to receive visions..." is from p. 195. The quotation "the Great Migration to..." is on p. 196. The split over slavery in Protestant denominations is described on pp. 316 ff. The phrase "spiraling cultural antagonisms" is from p. 316. The quotation "Christianity rapidly became a prop..." is from p. 318. The quotation "In the face of great, sometimes overwhelming odds..." is found on p. 199. African-American denominations are discussed on p. 204. The Fundamentalist-Modernist Controversy is presented on pp. 381 ff. The quote "Together they defended..." is on p. 381.

Partridge, Christopher, General Editor, *A Brief Introduction to Islam.* Minneapolis: Fortress Press, 2018. Chapter 10 "The Unity and Variety of Islam" by David Kerr provides background on Sunni and Shi'a Islam and on the *imams* and *ayatollahs,* pp. 61-62. Chapter 9 "A Historical Overview" by Montgomery Watt provides information on the spread of Islam to various countries, p. 58. The discussion of Islamic learning is based on Chapter 15, "Science, Art, and Culture" by Lothar Schmalfus, pp. 85-87. The discussion of Sufism is based on Chapter 10 "The Unity and Variety of Islam" by David Kerr, pp. 63-64.

Partridge, Christopher, General Editor, *A Brief Introduction to Judaism.* Minneapolis: Fortress Press, 2018. Chapter 9 "A Historical Overview" by Geoffrey Cowling (revised by Tim Dowley) provides the basis for the discussion of historical development, pp. 54-68. The Quotation "a crushing defeat..." is from p. 58. The quotation "rabbi(master) became the formal title..." is from p. 60. Chapter 10 "Sacred Writings" by Eric Christianson provides background on the Talmud, p. 71. Sephardic Judaism is described on p. 62. Maimonides and the Thirteen Principles are mentioned on p. 63. See p. 65, 66 for Kabbalah and *En Sof* and p. 67 for Baal Shem Tov. The quotation "At the core..." is from p. 67. See p. 67 for Hasidism and p. 68 for Haskalah. The quotation "who emphasized the universal principles..." is from p. 68. For descriptions of anti-Semitism see p. 66. The quote, "the direct consequence of which..." is found on p. 66.

Walker, Williston, *A History of the Christian Church.* New York: Charles Scribner's Sons, 1946. A classic Christian church history text with descriptions of the Inquisition, its roots, p. 254, the Spanish Inquisition under Ferdinand and Isabella, p. 324, and in the Catholic Counter-Reformation, p. 424.

<history. Com/topics/religion/Mormons> provides information on Mormon beliefs about Biblical figures appearing in American history.

<www.salvationarmyusa.org > and en.wikipedia.org/wiki/The_Salvation_Army> provide information on the Salvation Army and its many service activities.

<en.wikipedia.org/wiki/Jehova%27s_Witnesses> provides extensive information on the beliefs and history of Jehovah's Witnesses.

<en.wikipedia.org/wiki/Christian_Science> provides information on Church of Christ, Scientist.

10
Observance
Certainty, Belonging, and Proper Dress

I've enjoyed learning about how the religious traditions expanded and divided, and I have a fairly good grasp now of how they spread to the different countries and distant parts of the world, but I'm not clear about how many followers belong to these religions or which faiths may be growing or declining.

We have available now an interesting study by the Pew Foundation called "The Future of World Religions: Population Growth Projections." Here, let me pull it up on the computer so we can take a look together. The Pew Research Center on Religion and Public Life is the place to turn, by the way, for surveys and statistical reports on religion, and this one is especially interesting because it provides a baseline of populations by religion in 2010 along with projections of likely growth or decline out to the year 2050. Unfortunately, some of the traditions we have discussed, such as Confucianism and Daoism, are not included, perhaps because of their ambiguous status as "religions." But let's draw out from the chart that we have here, the ones that we discussed. Notice that numbers of followers are reported in billions of people.

Religion	2010	2050
Christian	2.17	2.92
Muslim	1.60	2.76
Unaffiliated	1.13	1.23
Hindu	1.03	1.38
Buddhist	.49	.49
Jewish	.01	.02

It is interesting to see Christians as the largest group and also projected to grow in number of affiliates. And the Muslims are next, but appear to be growing faster.

Good observations. Christianity has gained followers in South America, Mexico, and Sub-Sahara Africa. Much of that growth is in evangelical, holiness, pentecostal, and charismatic forms of churches— just an observation. As we glance down below here, we see that four out of 10 Christians will be in Sub-Sahara Africa in 2050. You probably noticed that the actual number of Jewish affiliates is quite small. Recall what happened in the holocaust. It computes to around 12 million, but the numbers are projected to double. In the U.S., Judaism will no longer be the largest non-Christian religion and is projected to be surpassed by Islam. Christians in the U.S. will decline from three-fourths to two-thirds of the population.

I see figures for unaffiliated. I assume that they could be believers, but that they don't think of themselves as committed to observing the practices of a particular faith. Does the report tell us about atheists and agnostics as well?

Let me see. Yes, further down here it lists the number of actual atheists and agnostics world-wide as 450 to 500 million people, around 7% of the population. But in comparison, that is about the same percent of the population as Buddhists. Here, buried deeper in the report itself, is an interesting observation: the growth of religious affiliation does not keep up with general population growth.

Which is another way to say that religious affiliation is in decline.

Yes, you can certainly look at it that way.

But affiliation means belonging in some way, actually observing and practicing the faith, correct?

It does. Observance is different from exploring the ideas of the various religions to help understand, as we have been trying to do, the timeless questions and mysteries of life. You may explore many different ideas as you continue to develop your own set of beliefs and doubts, but these may or may not lead to affiliation with a particular religious faith. Thinking about religions is different from observance.

Which brings me to another question: Why is belonging to a particular religion so important to some people?

That's puzzling, isn't it? I'll offer a hypothesis or two and we can explore them together. Let's begin by considering what appears to be a terrible mismatch between the human desire to know things for certain and the nature of religious explanation. The atheists are right on one point: there is no firm evidence, at least not the kind of observable, empirical evidence that atheists and many others would like to have in order to settle matters of religious belief. As we have explored life's mysteries, we do not find certainty, convincing evidence, and proof. We find myth, etiology, ambiguity, paradox, mysticism, mandalas, *koans,* the poetry of *haiku,* yin-yang, and whirling dervishes. We find belief, but not observable evidence; best guesses, but not proofs; and hope, not certainty. We use words like *sacred, holy, numinous, transcendent,* and *other-worldly.* Those are the words we reach for when we try to talk about the mysteries of life. Into this world of uncertainty marches *homo sapiens.*

Who wants more than anything to have certainty and proof beyond a reasonable doubt? Give us the truth, that's what we say.

People affiliate with a preferred form of one of the organized religions that will take a bit of the mystery out of the mysteries and provide satisfying answers, sometimes rather simple answers, to their troubling timeless questions. It's not easy standing alone with uncertainty, so we join. And when we join, we want confirmation that we are part of the group that has the truth. That's why we are joining this group and not some other. Affiliation confirms that we have it right.

And we humans need to be sure we have it right, because this isn't about what to have for breakfast; this is about G – O – D!

Yes, yes, to get it exactly right, to be certain about God, creation, human nature, social order, and all of the other unsolved mysteries. We humans appear to have that need: to join a group that has the truth. When new members join, they are not only affiliating with the faith; they are seeking reassurance that through belonging they themselves have the truth, the right way. Yes, and the right way sometimes gets turned into the only way, and that's where the trouble starts: the divisions, the religious wars, the genocides.

This is very disturbing. Do you have another hypothesis about religious affiliation?

Yes. In addition to the human need for certainty, there is the need for identity and belonging. We like to think of ourselves as unique individuals, but part of the way we define "I" is in the way we say "we." People have many ways of doing this, for example, by gender, nationality, and race, but also by occupation and avocation (sport or hobby). One of those ways is by religion and it can become very important to some individuals in describing who they are. Children will often ask their parents, "What are we?" They may be trying to discover if there is a religious identity in the family. Being affiliated provides both a sense of identity and belonging. If you don't mind, I need to take another short detour here.

You know I like your detours. Where are we going this time?

Just as the psychology of religion asks how religion functions in an individual's life, sociology of religion describes how religion functions within society. Both disciplines began with the goal of being objective and detached, setting aside judgement about the truth of beliefs in order to ask how those beliefs function. That "methodological agnosticism" is still the general goal, but today it is recognized that a purely descriptive approach is likely to get clouded with biases that are inevitably carried into the study unwittingly. Some consideration is given also to the idea that the objective "outsider" in matters of religion, loses something important that the "insider" (believer) may grasp.

Nonetheless, it is through the lens of sociology that we see that religion, despite many internal divisions, pulls society together. In other words, religion functions to generate cohesion, a kind of social glue. This idea goes back to a French scholar, Emile Durkheim (1858–1917) recognized as the founder of sociology. In France, as the first professor of sociology, he developed a theory of religion in his study, *The Elementary Forms of Religious Life,* and although he was not a believer himself, he saw the value of religion as the social glue. He noticed that the values of a society, including its religious values, are constructed by the members of that society along with pressure to conform to them. Durkheim thought that social cohesion and belonging were ultimately good for the individual.

Thanks for the little detour. I like the hypotheses you use to explain affiliation. The first we could call the human need for certainty and the second we could call the need for belonging and identity. The first seems to tear society apart with more disagreement and division and the second tries to glue it back together with belonging, although society today seems like it is coming unglued. I'm wondering if there is a more obvious explanation of affiliation. Maybe people just need some structure and focus for expressing their beliefs, some type of experience that will help them draw close to what is sacred in their lives.

Thank you for bringing that up. We need to be careful as we provide explanations not to think we can "explain away" something like religious affiliation by reducing it to something else, such as the need for certainty and the desire for belonging and identity. As you are suggesting, people may also affiliate with a particular religion because they genuinely believe in it. Affiliation helps them in their search for the sacred and the holy and provides a connection for them with the transcendent. Some people grow up in a faith tradition, and for them that is the natural way to express their beliefs as they always have from childhood. For others, it is a choice made after puzzling over the mysteries of life. Others choose to become or remain unaffiliated, and their number is not small.

What you may be noticing is that many people, when left on their own, don't have much of an idea about how to express their beliefs. Organized religion gives them structures for observance, such as rituals, sacraments, festivals, pilgrimages, holy buildings, music, art—all of these for experiencing and expressing what they find to be mysterious and sacred in life. Some people need the structure for observance that is provided by affiliation, such as attending weekly services or praying at certain times during the day, and their religious expressions are genuine. Others may prefer to be unaffiliated, remaining at home to express their private faith in solitary observance. Others are unaffiliated because they have no religious beliefs, and would prefer to explore the mysteries of life in secular ways, perhaps through literature, music, or film. Some people prefer to live life without overthinking it.

We might be ready now to look at some examples of religious observance as signs and symbols of affiliation. Will that be of interest?

You know it will be. I think I can do that now without being critical of what may be puzzling practices to me, but important observances to others. We're just trying to understand typical observances in these different religions in a neutral way, right?

We can try. Let's begin with Hinduism. We mentioned earlier the three main gods of Hinduism: Brahmā the creator, Vishnu the preserver, and Shiva the destroyer. In more recent times, in some forms of Hinduism, the three have become five: Vishnu and Shiva, plus Devī, Sūrya, and Ganesha. Devī we remember as a goddess, and Ganesha as the elephant-headed god, while Surya is new to us as a deification of the sun. But most Hindus have a favored, chosen deity and they go into a temple to find the image (icon) of their god. "Many believe that the power of a deity is actually present in the image of the deity." They enter the temple to catch a vision of the god that they believe "brings good fortune, grace, and spiritual merit." They seek "god-realization" through worship and a loving relationship with their deity, as if they are serving an honored guest through offerings of food to the image.

Temples are often built on scenic hills, near lakes, or at the seaside. They can be quite varied, but usually have a dome or spire, an inner chamber (womb), and a hall for worshippers, that accommodates dancing, chanting, or quiet meditation. Hindu temples have no stained-glass windows, in fact, often no windows at all; light is thrown in through a wide front door. Devotees may ring a large metallic bell on their way in or out of the temple.

In temple worship, in a ceremony sometimes called *pūjā,* a Brahman priest purifies himself and worships the image of the deity by bathing and adorning it, feeding it symbolically, and "waving a flaming lamp in a circle around it in a ritual of light," amidst the ringing of bells. Thus, temples became very important in Hinduism and a burst of temple building took place in the eleventh and twelfth centuries (comparable to the period of building Gothic cathedrals in Europe), and many cities in India became "temple cities" with a temple at the hub and as a convenient place to visit. Hindu temples can be very extensive and highly decorated, and the Temple at Angkor Wat in Cambodia is said to be the largest religious monument in the world. Keep in mind, however, that an abbreviated form of worship also takes place before modest shrines in Hindu households.

Because Hinduism had no prohibition of images, but rather depended upon them both in the temple and at home, a rich tradition of sculpture developed with cherished images of the gods in various poses, including the familiar image of gods with two and three sets of arms.

Which might become the god of the multi-tasking, suburban housewife, capable of doing everything if there were only another set of hands.

Some extra help. Or having a good grasp of everything yourself. But, yes, that's the idea. And what better than a god with the head of an elephant to help push through all obstacles. The images are quite effective at representing available power to be drawn on by people in their need.

Hindus believe that God becomes known through various avatars or manifestations (descents into this world) in more familiar human forms, for example, as Krishna, the avatar of Vishnu appearing as a child, as a youth with a flute, and later as a warrior. But God can also take the form of a living saint or guru. Hindu worship expresses a key belief that help is available in many forms. Visual images are very important to all of this.

I remember something about the Hindu belief in the sacred cow. Is that still observed?

Not so much today, but there has been a Hindu tradition of sacred animals that includes cows, monkeys, and even snakes and rats. Although Hindus eat beef (but not rats), they believe that God is present everywhere, which includes all animals and plants, thus cultivating a respect for nature. Some of the scriptures of Vishnu and Shiva recommend a vegetarian diet, but eating the right food is secondary to developing a closeness to god, which we have referred to as God-realization. Perhaps more important than diet are pilgrimages to sacred rivers, such as the Ganges, and sacred towns, of which there are many scattered throughout all of India.

Several Hindu festivals occur throughout the lunar calendar year, each one dedicated to a different god: Krishna, Ganesha, Shiva, and Rāma. There is also a festival of lights, during which people illuminate their homes and exchange gifts. Much observance is local, being oriented to local gods and customs of the neighborhood or town.

We have the expression: think globally, but buy locally. Hindus seem to be creative in finding local outlets for the universal spirit. I've been wondering, are marriages still arranged? I've heard that some are.

Western and Indian (not to be confused with *indie* meaning independent) films set up the dramatic conflict between romantic love and arranged marriages, but arrangement through families is still a common practice in Hinduism. One might say that Hindu marriage is "more a marriage between two families than between two persons." Because there is little "premarital dating or free mixing between young men and women, as in the West, the couple often only see each other a few times." This is an idea that is difficult to accept in a society steeped in romantic love where couples often live together—maybe even have a baby—before getting married. Some evidence exists, however, that "arranged marriages are many times more harmonious and stable than marriages where partners choose each other."

Yes, I have friends with very bad judgment with regard to romantic love. Others tell me that they didn't realize they were marrying the whole family. What diplomat would ever be able to arrange a marriage with my family? One more question about Hinduism: What is that red dot on the Indian woman's forehead?

You must be referring to the bindi, which comes from the Sanskrit *bindu* meaning drop or particle. It has other names in India as well, but it is the dot often worn between the eyebrows on the forehead. Many explanations of its meaning abound. Some say it is a mark of marital status, with red worn by the married woman, black for the young unmarried woman, and white or ash for the widow. You may recall from yoga the idea of energy centers called chakras. That spot is the Sixth Chakra, sometimes thought of as the energy command center that controls concentration. The bindi has also been called the third eye, suggesting that we have two eyes to see the world, but need a third eye to help us focus on God. The dot may also be a symbol of the cosmos or a sign of good fortune. Some believe it will ward off bad luck; others say it is the seat of the inner guru. It has also been identified as a sign of the search for wisdom and god-realization. It is a simple symbol with many meanings. We need to remember that for many Hindu women, the bindi is an observance with religious significance, and that it may be rude to appropriate it thoughtlessly as part of a fashion trend.

Tell me about Jewish observances. I'm sure I have some misunderstandings.

The Jewish Sabbath (Shabbat) is observed from Friday at sunset to Saturday at sunset to commemorate God's rest on the seventh day of creation. Some Jewish families set a special *Seder* meal of foods with symbolic meaning and use special prayers, such as

This is the bread of affliction which our fathers ate in
the land of Egypt.

Let all who are hungry come and eat.

The sabbath is also a remembrance that one's belonging is with an ancient people that extends through the centuries. Certain dietary laws are followed by traditional Jewish believers; others are not observant of these at all. For the traditional, lamb, beef, and chicken are preferred, but pork and shellfish are not. Meat and dairy products must not be served at the same meal. If meat is eaten, there is no butter on bread or milk in coffee. Sometimes, to keep meat and milk separate, the traditional Jewish housewife in "keeping kosher" uses two sets of dishes, one for each. "In kosher hotels, there are two separate kitchens."

In Judaism we have the *Bar-mitzvah* observance, when the thirteen-year-old boy becomes a 'Son of the Commandment' and "reads for the first time from the scroll of the Torah during synagogue service." This signifies that he is a "responsible person," able to fulfill the duties of a Jewish man and eligible to make up a quorum in a community meeting. At age twelve, a Jewish girl is considered *Bat-mitzvah*, 'Daughter of the Commandment.' The ceremonies mark the official belonging of the children to the faith. Belonging is also marked by circumcision, the removal of the penis foreskin on baby boys, at eight days of age, in commemoration of Abraham's covenant with God.

When an observant Jewish man goes out of doors, he covers his head with a round skull cap (*yarmelke*) as a sign of reverence to God "in whose presence all life is lived." It is a simple but profound observance of a central Jewish belief. Different branches of Judaism, particularly Hassidism, may have special dress, such as large hats, or conforming hairstyles and beards, all marking membership and a special identity.

I went to a Jewish wedding once, and at the end, there was some breaking of glass under the groom's feet. What is that?

It is a Jewish observance common at weddings. Some say it is a reminder "that even times of great joy need to be balanced by moments of serious reflection." Others say it is a reminder of the destruction of the temple in Jerusalem, never to be forgotten.

You mentioned Hanukkah earlier. I know there are other Jewish holidays. Where does this fit?

There is a separate Jewish calendar of twelve months. The Jewish festival marking the new year, *Rosh Hashanah*, falls in September on the Western calendar. It is a serious but optimistic observance. "Bread is dipped into honey,—rather than the usual salt—and the following prayer is said: 'May it be your will to renew for us a good and sweet year.'" A morning service the next day includes the sounding of the ram's horn (*shofar*) regularly throughout the service, "literally a wake-up call to the people" based on a passage in the prophet Amos. The Day of Atonement (*Yom Kippur*), ten days into the new year, is perhaps the most serious observance, when Jews examine their past behavior, ask for forgiveness, and turn to face the future with a "renewed commitment to walk the right path."

Three pilgrimage festivals are observed, Passover, Pentecost, and Tabernacles, and other minor festivals, one of which is Hanukkah. Known also as the Festival of Lights, Hanukkah is observed during the Christmas season of Christianity, and perhaps gets more attention than it really deserves as a minor festival. It celebrates the rededication of the Temple in 165 BCE through a famous legend associated with it concerning the "miracle of the oil." In the rededication ceremony they lacked enough oil to keep the temple menorah (eight-branched candelabrum) burning for a day; but it kept burning anyway for eight days. Hence, the eight-day Hanukkah celebration with the lighting of candles.

What about the observances of Buddhists? I'm thinking of a monk in an orange robe in a monastery.

Maybe that's where we start. And the robe wasn't always orange. They used the materials at hand for dying the cloth: red from a special logwood in Tibet; gray in Korea, using charcoal to remind the wearer that the body will become ash; and yellow from turmeric, the spice, to produce the earliest robes in India. Before the monastery, there was the simple life of the wanderer, who possessed only a robe, a cloth belt, a begging bowl, and a water filter to screen out any tiny creatures to be sure they would not be swallowed.

An extreme form of Schweitzer's reverence for life, I must say.

It was exactly that. The wanderers did eventually build monasteries, and the complex often included a library and temple. The types of observance grew and the landscape was dotted with stupas.

What's a stupa?

Buddhist observance begins with the stupa, a small bell-shaped dome built upon a square base to house a relic, usually an alleged bone or tooth of Buddha, or something from a Boddhisattva. Picture the inverted bell with a handle that the musical bell-ringer uses, only much larger. The stupa has a *chattra,* a spire-like vertical axis at the top (the handle), usually a stylized parasol, representing the dome of the sky and shade provided by the Buddha as protection from "craving, lust, and vices."

So those pictures we see of people in Japan walking with an open umbrella when it isn't raining, aren't just seeking shade from the summer sun.

Well, they are that, but the parasol has this deeper significance of protection in Buddhism and you will find it in many forms on top of the stupa. The stupa was built bigger and more complicated with several stories. Often the stupa had a temple built around it, and some were brightly painted inside. In the earliest times, Buddhist monks lived in caves dug deep into the hillsides, and many of these sites have been found and excavated both in India and China. One cave in India includes an enclosed temple-like structure, 121 by 43 feet, with a stupa, pillars, roof, and many decorations, all carved from the stone *inside* the cave. One site of these numerous caves is the Bimiyan Valley in present-day Afghanistan, and besides numerous caves, large-scale Buddha figures— we will discuss these in a moment—were found there carved from stone. Some of these figures, existing for more than 1,500 years were destroyed by the Taliban in 2001.

In China and Japan, the stupa was called a pagoda. Westerners have been fascinated with pagodas—Louis XIV built one on the grounds of the Palace of Versailles—but for Buddhists, the stupa is a sacred means of expressing reverence and respect for the Buddha. Sometimes Buddhists walk in a circle around a stupa because being close to a stupa is to be close to Buddha. A Buddhist might carry around a small wooden replica of a stupa as an object of devotion.

Buddhist art is filled with special symbols as an aid to observance. We've mentioned the parasol, but there are also two golden fish facing each other, representing salvation through Enlightenment; the conch shell for hearing the voice of Buddha and his teaching; and footsteps, a symbol of the constant presence of Buddha. Most important of all is the lotus, a beautiful, fragrant flower blooming on the surface of what is often a murky lake, symbolizing the ability of the mind to transcend human desires through Buddha's teachings. The central figure in a Buddhist painting may be seated on an enlarged lotus blossom, or may be holding a lotus bloom in one hand and a jewel in the other, the jewel representing how Enlightenment cuts through ignorance. And we must not forget the charming sound of a distant bell, recalling us to the task of achieving Enlightenment.

Buddhism seems to be filled with reminders of the need to keep searching for Enlightenment. The images and symbols bring to mind Buddha, but also appear to provide a means for focusing on the task.

This is especially true of the sculptures of Buddha. Images of the Buddha were first employed in the stupa and temple or just outside. At first the statues used a formula of eight common postures, for example, cross-legged in meditation or with one hand raised to represent teaching. Some have a "protuberance on the crown of the statue's head, often prominent enough to represent a halo or spire," identifying the original Siddhartha. Statues of Buddha often have elongated ears, a sign of nobility and wisdom. Gradually, artists created "colossal Buddha figures" to represent his great achievements and supernatural powers. Thailand has the longest reclining Buddha at 151 feet, with a seated Buddha in China at 233 feet. The sculpted images are important in remembrance and as a point of focus, but also as a calming aid in meditation and the search for Enlightenment. Usually, a Buddha image has a very serene expression with a calming effect, but if things get too serious, you can gaze at a laughing Buddha.

Surely a person doesn't have to join a monastery to be a Buddhist. I know that many still do, but can't an ordinary person with a job and a family be a Buddhist?

As a Buddhist monk and scholar, Walpole Rahula, writing in *What the Buddha Taught,* tells us that it is a sad misconception to think that every Buddhist must become a monk in a monastery and that it is a big mistake to think "Buddhism is so lofty and sublime a system that it cannot be practiced by ordinary men and women in this workaday world of ours..." People may withdraw periodically from the world to spend time in meditation or go on a 'retreat' to improve the mind and character. But, Rahula tells us, "...if a man lives all his life in solitude... this is surely not in keeping with Buddha's teaching which is based on love, compassion, and service to others" As we have noted before, "Theravada is a monastic tradition, Mahayana is not."

Are there ceremonies and religious occasions for this ordinary, everyday Buddhist?

Followers may visit temples and monasteries and offer flowers, light lamps, and burn incense, but not so much as worship as a way of paying respect to the memory of the Master who showed the path. These observances, though not essential, can be helpful in continuing along the right path toward a good life.

I can't seem to get out of my mind this image of a Buddhist monk setting himself on fire as a protest against some horrible political regime.

Many of the countries to which Buddhism spread have had political upheavals, including Tibet (invasion by China), Vietnam (war), and Cambodia (massacre). Although Buddhist temples were often destroyed and libraries gutted, Buddhism not only survived but kept up a witness to its basic values. In 1989 the International Network of Engaged Buddhists was formed to stress the importance of "creating a better world now." In spite of its focus on personal Enlightenment, Buddhism has a strong concern for social justice, including its advocacy of non-violence in the search for peace. To a modern-day Buddhist, observance is also action for justice, even to the point of giving one's life in fiery self-immolation.

Do Daoist observances exist?

It is difficult to describe distinctive Daoist observances because Daoism, Confucianism, and Buddhism went through a period of synthesis during the Ch'ing Dynasty (1644–1911 CE) in which there was a significant mixing of ideas and observances among them. Daoism also broke into various sects and systems, so that it is hard to say which best represents Daoism. Many are still practicing today. Perhaps in thinking of Daoism we should note that practices sometimes become separated from their "religious" origins. An ardent practitioner of martial arts or of t'ai chi ch'uan, that popular "set of slow-moving exercises for cultivating health and circulating internal energy," may have little sense of belonging to or identifying with Daoism at all. Yes, t'ai chi was developed by a famous Daoist of the Ming Dynasty (1366–1644) in China, but not many who take classes for it today know or care about its religious origins.

So, we need to be careful about making assumptions about affiliation as we notice certain practices and customs that may or may not be actual religious observances. Tell me more about the daily observance of prayer in Islam. Then I want to know about Ramadan and the practice of women wearing a veil.

The minaret is the name given to the slender tower associated with the mosque from which comes the call to prayer from the *muezzin,* or prayer leader. The five times for prayer are dawn, midday, mid-afternoon, sunset, and night. It is a distinctive observance of Islam and its purpose is to remind everyone of their dependence on Allah. Remember that "Islam means 'submission to God.'" The ritual of prayer, called *salat,* is designed to demonstrate this submission, and on Fridays it is a communal act, inside or in front of the mosque. Everyone, all over the world, wherever a Muslim may be, faces toward the Ka'ba in Mecca (present-day Saudi Arabia). Women and men assemble separately in rows but pray in a single body, reciting prescribed words from the Quran, while "standing, bowing, rising, sitting, turning east and west, and falling prostrate, all repeated in cycles," in prayerful acts of submission.

Unlike Hinduism and Buddhism, Islam does not employ images to assist the believer in observance, but instead prohibits representation of God or Muhammad. One may find very large and beautiful mosques, such as the Blue Mosque in Istanbul, Turkey, but they are without images of Muhammad, or anyone else, for that matter. On the other hand, Muslims have crafted very fine and intricate designs in stonework and tile; and religious buildings, including the minaret, are often covered in beautiful non-representational designs. The mystery of Allah is not expressed in human form, but there seems to be no limit to the imagination of geometric forms and abstractions.

Ramadan is a month-long celebration during one of the months of the Muslim lunar calendar called Ramadan. It's association with the Western calendar varies. Ramadan is the month, Muslims believe, when the Quran was first revealed to Muhammad. During the month of Ramadan, "no one may eat, drink, or have sexual intercourse from sunup to sundown," and the observance is "a reminder of the suffering and poverty of those among them who go without food throughout the year." A month of fasting may sound like a grim observance, but there are also celebrations at sundown to break the fast, and the final night celebration, *Eid al-Fitr,* is the most widely celebrated holiday in the Muslim world. It is a time of serious self-examination and reflection, taken very seriously by most Muslims.

The other important observance is the *Hajj,* a pilgrimage to Mecca conducted annually (except during a pandemic) and to be undertaken by the devout Muslim at least once in a lifetime. Although a person may visit several nearby sacred sites on the *Hajj,* the central event is moving around the *Ka'ba* in a clockwise circle with thousands of other Muslims. The *Ka'ba is* a large black cube with no architectural significance or intrinsic sanctity. In fact, it has been torn down and rebuilt several times. It houses nothing special and is not a temple. Remember, however, that all Muslims from around the world face toward it during prayer. It is, therefore, the geographic and spiritual center of Islam, the hub of the wheel, around which Muslims revolve at *Hajj.*

Pilgrims shed their personal clothing and put on plain garments that signify a state of purity. The men wear two seamless white cloths, "shave their heads and trim their beards and nails; the women clip a few locks of hair." "In the sanctified state, when every pilgrim is identically dressed, there is no longer any rank, or class, or status; there is no gender and no ethnic or racial identity: there is no identity whatsoever, save as Muslims." We might say, that as a religious experience of belonging and identity, the *Hajj* is difficult to surpass.

If you don't like being jostled around in crowds, it may be out of your comfort zone, but I can see how for a Muslim pilgrim, it is the ultimate experience of belonging. What about the veils?

I nearly forgot. It is such an issue in some countries today! Wearing the veil or *hijab* (the *birqa* provides head to toe coverage), was actually banned in several European countries. Some said the veil was a wonderful symbol of the modern Muslim woman's freedom from Western cultural dominance (liberation from the Parisian fashionista?), while others viewed "the veiled Muslim woman as the sheltered and docile sexual property of her husband..." Both views are "misleading and simpleminded," writes Reza Aslan in *No god but God.* He provides the fascinating, if ironic, account of how the practice may have started.

There is no universal expectation for wearing a veil expressed in the Quran, he tells us. The tradition of seclusion and veiling—*hijab* emphasizes both—apparently grew up around Muhammad's nine wives at Medina. The quarters where Muhammad lived also included the community mosque and an open courtyard where visitors were often encamped, so it became a busy place with people "constantly coming in and out of the compound at all hours of the day." Some rules were needed to separate and protect Muhammad's wives. Through Arab contacts with Syria and Iran, it was known that the veil and seclusion were signs of social status for women who did not need to work in the fields. Borrowing this tradition, Muhammad was able to shelter his wives from the peering eyes of visitors through *hijab.* During his lifetime, no other women in the *Ummah* (community) wore veils. Exactly when and how the practice became more widely adopted is hard to say, but it was likely many generations after Muhamad's death. Today, when *hijab* is observed by a Muslim woman, it may be as a symbol of piety or a sign of modesty and privacy before unrelated males.

It is difficult to understand how so much intense controversy can swirl around a piece of clothing. I guess it's not the veil, but what the veil symbolizes about belonging and identity that generates the intense feeling. Do we find signs and symbols like this in Christianity?

Before we leave the veil, I need to mention that the observance of the veil also exists, or at least did exist, in certain places in Catholic Christianity. Women who came to the Church to witness the mass were expected to cover their head and face with a veil, black for a widow or older woman, and white for virgin girls. It was shameful to come to mass or confession without a veil. I'm sure you can see the irony in Christian objections to the *hijab*.

To answer your question, yes, we find symbolism in Christianity in the crucifix or sign of the cross. A crucifix (an image of Jesus on the cross) may appear on a wall in a Catholic school, hospital, or private home. A cross may be worn as a necklace or earing as a sign of belonging. Some Catholics make the sign of the cross by moving the right hand from the forehead down and from the left side to the right in front of the chest. The sign of the cross is sometimes accompanied by a prayer asking for protection or with a moment of thanksgiving at the end of a safe journey. It is often incorporated into worship inside the church or before or after saying the rosary. Catholics also sometimes genuflect, which is to bend the knee to the ground, or toward the ground, while facing the altar inside a church where there is also a cross.

I'm thinking about how people of other faiths look at Christians, like outsiders looking in, just as Christians look at the customs of other religions as outsiders. I guess it depends on your perspective—the shoes you are walking in—to understand religious observance. What would you say are the most important observances of Christianity?

Even though there are many different branches of Christianity, there is some agreement on observance. Let's begin with the Last Supper. Christians, as we discussed, began to meet in homes and shared a common meal called the *agape* (love) feast. But the common meal faded away after one hundred fifty years and what remained was the remembrance of Jesus through the ritual celebration of the bread and wine, reenacting the last meal he had with the disciples. It grew in importance until the "Lords, Supper, Communion, or Eucharist was the distinctive event of Christian worship."

In the Catholic (Latin) tradition, the Eucharist, which means thanksgiving, became the central liturgical rite of the mass. Spoken, chanted, or later set to music, the mass has several parts: *Kyrie, Gloria,*

Credo, Sanctus, and Agnus Dei. The concluding words of the last section "*Ite, miss est*" meaning "Go, it is the dismissal" gives the mass its name. It has come to imply "Go on your mission." Pope Gregory I (540–604 CE) established the text of the Mass, which has remained unchanged. (The musical form of Gregorian chant also took its name from him.) Protestants, as an alternative, celebrate the Lord's Supper in various ways as a remembrance, but they tend to stress preaching and hymn singing in their worship services more than the periodic observance of the Lord's Supper, sometimes referred to as communion, in which small portions of bread are served with grape juice, symbolic of wine.

As we have seen, baptism was celebrated in various ways by Protestants, infant and adult, as an initiation rite or as a sign of conversion. It is a ceremony of belonging to the Church as a community. Christians also attend a church service on Sunday, "making the first day of the week holy in place of the seventh," and they observe certain holy days and a cycle of festivals throughout the calendar year. In some of these celebrations, pagan (non-Christian) and Christian elements combine. Christmas, as the celebration of the birth of Christ, was established as December 25th in the fourth or fifth century CE. The season doesn't end with New Years, but officially with Epiphany on January 6, which celebrates the recognition of the Christ by the three wise men. The Orthodox churches, on the other hand, have established January 6 as Christmas Day.

What is that celebration in Canada on the day after Christmas, called Boxing Day?

It has nothing to do with the sport of boxing and very little to do with Christmas except for the spirit of giving. It follows a British custom of the wealthy giving gifts to the servants in small boxes on the day after Christmas.

The day after? Small boxes? Most American kids hope for a present so big it won't fit in a box.

Let's move on to Easter, but before we do, I need to say a word about the physical church structures that evolved as counterparts to the temples, stupas, and synagogues of other faiths. From the original meetings of Christians in homes, there developed elaborate services of worship that required the right place for observance. These became the sturdy, castle-like, Romanesque churches of the Middle Ages followed by the thinner, taller structures of the late Middle Ages that came to be known as Gothic. Some truly magnificent structures were built at great expense over many years. They had a cruciform (shape of a cross) floor plan with soaring pillars joined by distinctive pointed arches and high ceilings over an open central nave. They were highly decorated with sculpture and stained-glass windows, and when the Protestant movements emerged, naturally they protested against the style of the Catholic churches as well, insisting on much simpler structures. But, of course, they couldn't agree, so today you may find very simple churches with plain interiors, churches in the "gothic revival" style that follow the manner of the old cathedrals, or "store front" churches that may look more like a Walmart than a church, at least on the outside. If you go into any of these churches on Easter week, you will find special services commemorating the last days of the life of Jesus.

The Easter celebration actually starts forty days before Easter with the beginning of a period called Lent (an Old English word for the season of spring). Shrove Tuesday, the Day before Ash Wednesday, the official beginning of Lent, has become in many countries a carnival day, in some places known as Mardi Gras (French for Fat Tuesday), but the period of Lent was initially intended as a time of "self-reflection, repentance, and abstinence." Lent, as a period for giving up something you enjoy, is generally less observed by Protestants than Catholics. The culmination in the "Holy Week" of Easter, involves special services of remembrance of events in the life of Jesus: on Palm Sunday (arrival in Jerusalem), Maundy Thursday (final meal), Good Friday (crucifixion), and Easter (resurrection). The observances of Holy Week often tend to cut across divisions and unify the vast differences that have developed in Christianity. Easter, in case you are interested, is dated as falling on the "first Sunday after the first full moon following the spring equinox, and it coincides in many northern latitudes with the beginning of spring, echoing at another level the gift of newness of life."

I always wondered why the date changes every year.

What else would you like to explore as practices of observance in Christianity?

I've never understood about confession and the use of a rosary in the Catholic Church.

In the sixth century, Irish monks introduced the idea of the sinner having the opportunity to enjoy a private audience (secret meeting) with a priest to confess sins and receive instructions for "making amends in the person's relationship to God." The "correction" usually involved saying a certain number of prescribed prayers, not just once but repeated several times. That presents problems: keeping track of how many prayers have been said (out loud or in the mind) while focusing on the true meaning of the prayer. The rosary helps to address that problem.

A rosary is a string of beads—crystal, wood, pearl, or plastic—with a shield and cross at one end. The beads can be of many shapes and sizes and are arranged in a special way to help with counting. The word *rosary* comes from the Latin and means garland of roses, a flower symbolizing the Virgin Mary. It facilitates a way of praying by focusing on Mary, who it is believed in Catholic Christianity, can intercede for (work on behalf of) individuals by offering prayers to God through her Son, Jesus, thus mediating between the believer and the holiness of God. The interesting thing about the beads is that they go back to the eleventh and twelfth centuries in the West, possibly growing out of the practice of carrying a few stones in one's pocket for counting prayers. The term *bead* may derive from an old Saxon word *bede* meaning prayer.

Even more interesting is the finding that other religious traditions have used beads or something similar for counting prayers. There is actually an Anglican or Episcopal (Protestant) rosary organized by four sets of seven beads called *weeks*. Buddhist and Hindu traditions have beads called *mala*, consisting of 108 human passions to be overcome to reach Enlightenment. A *mala* can also be used to help count the repetition of a *mantra* such as "Om Mani Padme Hum" which translates to "Hail the jewel of the Lotus," the jewel symbolizing full Enlightenment.

In prayer observances we have widespread use of beads across faiths, but with particular meaning attached by that faith, giving the user a concrete approach to a particular mystery, how to be close to God. Religious observances can look similar and yet have very different meanings.

This discussion of observance is making me think about non-religious observance. I mean, you don't need to be religious to celebrate a birthday. A lot of activities that have nothing to do with religion have rituals, rules to observe, and even special clothing.

Yes, that's true. We make a party for that special day (a festival) with a cake (special food) we light candles (to count the years) and we sing a song (hymn). The celebration varies by region, language, and culture, but the elements of ritual are there, are they not?

And Halloween. People put a pile of pumpkins on their front porch, decorate the shrubbery with polyester cobwebs, pump up inflatable ghosts, set out rows of plastic skulls, and place faux, foam tombstones on the lawn. Then they go begging to their neighbor's house, demanding a treat, with their children dressed up in weird costumes. What's that all about?

It can be an observance of All Saints Eve, but for most it's not. Most of the symbols have lost their meaning. It's a secular festival of fun for kids.

And sporting events—football, basketball, hockey—they're full of rituals, rules to be observed, and special clothing.

And when we view secular observances in that way, religious observances don't seem so odd.

In fact, secular observances can appear to be just as odd, or even more so.

Which makes us wonder, what is it about humans that we have this need for observance, ritual, and proper form?

Oh, gosh. I think you just invented another timeless question. You know, at first, I thought of these observances as weird and superstitious, and in some respects, I guess they can be thought of in that way. But now I am a little envious of people who appear to enjoy and feel at home in their religious observances without questioning them much.

Observance is a humble, often quite simple, attempt to express a person's particular religious view of one or more of the mysteries. If we think back to our very first discussion about God, we spoke of God as "something more," in and beyond the universe, as the sacred, or the encounter with the holy. We also said that God remains essentially unknowable: the ultimate mystery. As religions developed, they provided a seemingly endless creation of buildings, symbols, festivals, pilgrimages, recitations, prayers, rituals, ceremonies, and, yes, even dress, for believers to express their beliefs.

And there you have it. Lots of timeless questions and not very many answers. But that's about all I have to share with you for now.

As usual, you have given me a lot to ponder. I'm so glad I came to talk to you. I learned more than I ever expected. Maybe this is enough for now, so let me say thank you, but I am going to miss our meetings.

And I will miss them as well. But let me suggest one more meeting. Perhaps you can help me with a project that I have had in mind for quite some time now. I have been trying to imagine what the founders of these various religious traditions would have to say to each other if they all met together, let's say for breakfast at an outdoor café. You know a lot about the founders and their traditions now, and I'm sure you will have creative ideas about what they might discuss at such a gathering and how they might act. I'd love to hear your questions about what you would like to learn from their conversation. Besides, you have a great sense of humor. It would be an opportunity to let your imagination run wild.

Well, I'm flattered at your invitation, but don't you think we could get into a lot of trouble imagining such a thing? These founders, each in a different way, are respected, even worshiped, by their followers, some of whom, I am sure, will be deeply offended by the audacity of a project like this.

I'm sure you are right. That is a risk I would be taking, especially if I write down this imagined dialogue or publish it. It will be quite unlike what I have written previously.

Write it down? Publish it? That could be even more risky. But to tell the truth, I have been wondering about that same question. What would the religious leaders say about the things their followers have done to them through the ages? You've set me to thinking about that. Let me see here, you're assuming a setting free of the limitations of space and time, where the founders can come out of their own era, their own culture, even their language, and somehow converse with each other about...well, the timeless questions, I guess.

Yes, that's it exactly, like the fiction genre of "magical realism." We just have to imagine that the founders have the power to overcome those obstacles so that they can engage in some serious talk, and perhaps some not-so-serious small-talk, in a realistic setting. I'm only asking if you will join me for some brain-storming about this idea.

Where? Here in your office?

No. It's warm enough outside now to meet at the Moulin Bistro over on Main Street. It will be a good outdoor setting to put us in the mood for generating creative ideas about what the founders would say if they were chatting informally with each other in a small café in modern times.

This is crazy, but...yes, I'm in.

References

Aslan, Reza, *No god but God*. New York: Random House, 2011. Times for prayer are listed on p. 148 as well as the quotation "standing, bowing..." Ramadan is presented on p. 150. The quotations "no one may eat..." and "a reminder of the suffering..." are also on p. 150. The quotation "men shave their beards..." is on p. 151. The *Ka'ba* and clothing for the pilgrimage are described on p.150. The quotation "In the sanctified state..." is on pp. 151-152. The veil and its origins are presented on pp. 73-74. Quotations 'the veiled Muslim women..." and "misleading and simple-minded" are on p. 74. The veil for Muhammad's wives is mentioned on p. 65 with the quotation "constantly coming in..." Veiling and seclusion are described as *hijab,* on pp. 65-66. The idea that no other women wore veils is on p. 66.

Bhaskarananda, Swami, *The Essentials of Hinduism*. Seattle: Viveka Press, 2016. The discussion of Hindu marriage is based on pp. 40 ff. The quotations "more a marriage between..." "premarital dating or free mixing..." "arranged marriages are many times..." are all from p. 41. The description of Hindu temples is based on Chapter VII "Temples," on pp. 151-157.

<Brittanica.com/topic/mass-Christian-religious-service> provides the history and explanation of the name of the mass as well as the names of its parts.

Ciosek, Jessica, "The meaning of Rosary Beads" was found on <everydayhealth.com/healthyliving/meaning-rosary-beads> and provides detailed background on the history and use of rosary beads in the Catholic Church as well as descriptions of the use of beads in other religions, including Buddhism and Islam.

Flood, Gavin. *An Introduction to Hinduism*. Cambridge: Cambridge University Press, 1996. *Surya* is identified as sun god, p. 47 and p. 113.

Frankiel, Sandra S. *Christianity, A Way of Salvation*. Long Grove, IL: Waveland Press, 2011. The mixing of Christian and pagan festivals is mentioned as well as the dates for Christmas on p. 78. Describes Lent and Holy Week along with Easter, p. 79. The quotation that describes the dating of Easter "first Sunday after..." is on p. 80. The origins of Confession and the quotation "making amends..." is on p. 86.

Harris, Ian, Consultant Editor, *The Complete Illustrated Encyclopedia of Buddhism.* Wigston, Leicestershire, UK: Annes Publishing, Hermes House, 2011. The belt, begging bowl, and filter are described on pp.134 along with the different colors of robes. Stupas are presented on pp. 28-29. The parasol is presented as protection from "craving, lust, and other vices" on p.134. Pagodas are described on pp.146-147. The symbolism of golden fish, conch shell, footsteps, lotus, and jewel are explained on pp.134-135. Buddha statues and formulaic poses are presented on p. 39. The quotation "Protuberances on the crown..." is from p. 39. The longest and tallest Buddha statues are identified on p. 39. Caves and carved stone figures are described on p. 98, 99.

Partridge, Christopher, General Editor. *A Brief Introduction to Buddhism.* Minneapolis: Fortress Press, 2018. Chapter 9 "A Historical Overview" by Paul Williams makes the distinction "Theravada is a monastic..." on p. 55. Chapter 13 "Buddhism in the Modern World by Elizabeth J. Harris describes the fate of Buddhism in selected countries on pp. 83-84. The Network of Engaged Buddhists and quotation "creating a better world now," is from pp. 87.

Partridge, Christopher, General Editor. *A Brief Introduction to Christianity.* Minneapolis: Fortress Press, 2018. Chapter 13 "Worship and Festivals" by Colin Buchanan provides background on the *agape* meal and Eucharist on p. 82. The quotation "Lord's Supper, Communion..." is from p. 82. Baptism is discussed on p. 83. The quotation "Making the first day of the week..." is from p. 83.

Partridge, Christopher, General Editor. *A Brief Introduction to Hinduism.* Minneapolis: Fortress Press, 2018. Chapter 12 "Beliefs" by Anna S. King provides discussion of five gods, p. 68. Chosen deity is mentioned on p. 70. The quotations "Many believe that the power..." and "brings good fortune..." are from p. 70. Avatars and manifestations of gods are discussed on p. 70. Chapter 13 "Worship and Festivals" by Maya Warrier describes temple worship and contains the quotation "waving a flaming lamp..." on p. 75. Sacred animals are discussed on p. 79. Sacred rivers and towns, p. 77. Hindu festivals are mentioned on p. 79.

Partridge, Christopher, *A Brief Introduction to Islam.* Minneapolis: Fortress Press, 2018. Chapter 13 "Worship and Festivals" by David Kerr summarizes ritual prayers on pp. 76-78. The quotation "Islam means submission..." is from p. 75. The description of communal prayer is on p. 78.

Partridge, Christopher, General Editor, *A Brief Introduction to Judaism.* Minneapolis: Fortress Press, 2018. Part I, Chapter 4 "The Sociology of Religion" by Malcolm Hamilton provides historical and general background. The term "methodological agnosticism" is on p. 28. A discussion of insider and outsider on p. 20. Discussions of Durkheim are on pp. 29-30. Chapter 13 "Worship and Festivals" by Liz Ramsey provides background for the Jewish Sabbath and the quotation of the prayer "This is the bread..." p. 90. Circumcision is explained in the Glossary, p.128. A description of festivals and the prayer "May it be your will..." are on p. 90. The quotation "literally a wake-up call..." is from p. 90. The Day of Atonement and Hanukkah are presented on pp. 91-92. Chapter 12 "Family and Society" by David Hardy provides background on food and the quotes "Kosher hotels..." and "two sets of dishes..." The description of *yarmelka* and the quotation "in whose presence..." is from p. 83. The discussion of Bar-Mitzvah and Bat-Mitzvah is on p. 82. The explanation of breaking glass at weddings and the quotation "that even in times of great joy..." is on p. 86.

Pew Research Center, "Future of World Religions: Population Growth Projections, 2010–2050" is found at www.pewforum.org The discussion of affiliates and growth in world religions is based on this report. There is much more of interest in the report than is discussed here, but these are some of the highlights.

Rahula, Walpole, *What the Buddha Taught.* New York: Grove Press, 1959. The quotation "Buddhism is so lofty..." is from p. 76 and supports the point that Buddhism is practiced by ordinary men and women, not just monks. The quotation "if a man lives all his life..." is from p. 76. A summary of observances is on p. 81.

Walker, Williston, *A History of the Christian Church.* New York: Charles

Scribner's Sons, 1946. Descriptions of the Inquisition are found in this old classic on p. 254, 324, and 424.

Wong, Eva, *Taoism, An Essential Guide*. Boulder. CO: Shambala Publications, 1997. The synthesis of Daoism with other faiths is mentioned on p. 88. Daoist systems are described on p. 95. Originator of Thai-chi-ch'uan is mentioned on p. 89.

Founder's Day at the New Life Café

It is a small café, reminiscent of the outdoor cafes of Paris with their striped awnings, clusters of sidewalk tables and chairs, and evenly-spaced sycamore trees thriving on the edge of a busy street. It could be anywhere—Toronto, Chicago, Jeddah, Mumbai, Sydney, Shanghai, or Johannesburg—but it has an unearthly ambiance, fitting for the unusual gathering to be assembled on this particular morning. No one knows the purpose of the meeting or why it has been called for this time or place, but because they have received formal invitations from Sri Rāmakrishna, the nineteenth century Hindu saint, whom they all know as the prophet of the harmony of religions, they make it a priority to attend and set about to do whatever is needed to get there on time.

But why is it called Founders Day and what is this New Life Café? They can't remember a time ever before when they were all brought together in one place for a face-to-face meeting, and they are eagerly anticipating this occasion, being certain that there will be lively and serious discussion. Such a meeting has been a life-time dream of Rāmakrishna, but he can't remember which lifetime.

But now Rāmakrishna is nervous. He has invited to breakfast the founders of several major world religions, but he knows that Hinduism has no founder, as most religions do, and he worries about being a non-founder among founders. He feels uncomfortable about representing Hinduism, because it is so vast and unorganized, and besides, he is from a completely different era. He decides that he must focus on his role as convener and moderator, speaking of his tradition only when it seems appropriate to do so. He wants to hear what the others have to say to the questions he has prepared. He hopes they won't waste time discussing paradoxes and ambiguities today. He takes a deep breath and lets it out slowly to try to calm down.

He has arrived early at the New Life Café to remind the owner and two young women servers of the very, very important religious leaders who will soon arrive. They exchange indifferent glances, shrug, and go back inside to the kitchen. Now he wonders if those who were invited will actually show up, coming from so many different countries and realms, such different centuries and eons, and speaking that Babel of languages. He assumes they will have the power, perhaps with the assistance of Ganesha, to overcome those obstacles. He hopes the Founders won't get into quarrels as their followers often did.

Now he regrets that he wrote "Informal Dress" on each invitation and worries about how he will recognize the guests when they arrive—if they arrive. He checks his digital watch nervously and wonders if they are all on the same time or if they even have time zones. Here comes an older gentleman now, striding along toward the café, wearing blue jeans and a short-sleeve t-shirt. As the man advances, Rāmakrishna notices a person of advanced years who nonetheless appears to be quite chipper and alert.

"Ah, yes, the New Life Café," he says, glancing at the sign near the entry. "This must be the place." He looks at Rāmakrishna and smiles. "I'm Moses."

"My pleasure. You're looking well and in such good shape."

"Maybe from carrying those stone tablets up and down that mountain so many times." He grins and tugs at his long white beard. "And you must be Rāmakrishna, our host. But you also represent one of the oldest of the great religious traditions going back even before Abraham and Isaac."

"Well, yes, the British called it Hinduism. I'm a little nervous because I'm not of the same stature as the others of you who are founders, but..."

Moses shakes an outstretched finger back and forth as he whispers, "Most of us didn't know we were founding anything."

Several others are walking toward the café, all of them dressed in sneakers, blue jeans, and t-shirts, what appears to be the unspoken code for "informal dress" anywhere in the universe. They are chatting like they already know each other; which Rāmakrishna realizes would certainly be possible and probably not accidental. One by one, the new arrivals come up to Rāmakrishna, sensing that he must be the one who sent them their invitation.

A tired, gray-haired old man who looks like he has walked many miles or kilometers or whatever it is he walks, is introducing himself humbly, with a slight bow, as Confucius. Next to him, a handsome brown-skinned man with dark hair and flashing black eyes says he is Muhammad. A relatively younger man with long hair comes up to shake hands, and Rāmakrishna observes what appear to be scars on his hands and wrists. "You must be Jesus."

"I am." He rubs his hands together. "I never completely recovered from what they did to me."

Rāmakrishna senses a double meaning in what Jesus has just said and notices that his eyes are not really blue.

A short man with long ears and a round tummy swelling the front of his t-shirt is laughing among the others before he comes up to Rāmakrishna, who greets him, "You must be Buddha."

"Yes, one of many who make that claim, but I'm actually Siddhartha Gotama."

"The original, genuine Buddha. I love the statues they made of you in all of those different poses. You seem unchanged."

"Oh, but I am. Nothing is permanent, you know."

A shy, slightly-built wisp of a gentleman makes his way forward like a leaf blown in on the wind. He introduces himself as Zhuangzi. "I'm also known as Zhuang Zhou, and you can call me Joe if you prefer." Then he says, "You must know, of course, that no one can tell who wrote the *Dao De Ching*, certainly not the old master Laozi, and I suspect you have invited me to represent Daoism because I have been identified as the author of the first part of the book with my name, Zhuangzi, as the title." He speaks softly with the sound of a bubbling stream, but Rāmakrishna is not sure he is understanding what Joe is saying. "I didn't intend to found anything and I probably won't have much to say because when I speak only a few people seem to get it. Does that make any sense?"

Before sitting down, the guests chat informally, renewing old acquaintance by asking about family, as people often do. Rāmakrishna circulates, listening in anxiously, not sure how that's going to go. He hears Buddha asking Confucius about his children.

"Yes, fine thank you. Much better than before. I had one son and one daughter, but I wasn't a very good father, traveling around so much as I did and being preoccupied with my many students. And what about you—do I remember a son?"

"Yes. His name is Rahula," Buddha replies. "I married very young at sixteen, and he was born before my awakening. My situation is somewhat like yours; I left home for what has been called 'the wider benefit of humanity.' Perhaps it was also for the narrower benefit of my family as well."

"But you lived into old age?" Confucius asks.

"I did. I don't remember exactly how old I was, being in the mental state of Enlightenment, but they say I was around eighty."

"Yes, I was fortunate with so many wars, to live to seventy-two. If I recall correctly, someone asked you about your cause of death, and you answered, 'birth.' Were you joking?"

"No. It was not about the cause of *my* death; I was trying to explain that the alternative to rebirth is Nirvāna. But without Nirvāna, you will be born again, and when you are born again, of course, you will die again. Therefore..."

"I've never been very good at thinking about such matters, Confucius adds, looking perplexed.

Rāmakrishna hears Jesus asking Muhammad about his family and he's worried about how that conversation is going to turn out.

"I know that you had a very happy marriage with your first wife, but her name escapes me," Jesus says.

"Khadija," Muhammad replies. "Yes, she was fifteen years older than I, well established, and a wealthy merchant. I was an orphan, you know, raised by my uncle, whose caravan I tended. So, it changed my life when I married Khadija."

"But then she passed away, and you were left..."

"I lived a monogamous life with her for twenty-five years, but, yes, alas, she passed away too soon."

"And there were other wives?" Jesus asks.

"Yes, in Medina. I actually married nine women in ten years there, but they were primarily political unions to build links within the community and beyond." Muhammad seems perfectly comfortable talking to Jesus about this, so it is not to change the subject when he asks, "And what about you? Your life was so short, you hardly had a chance at romance."

"It's true," Jesus replies with a look of regret. "Crucified at thirty-three. There was a band of women followers, not exactly like the disciples, but devoted, and I got to know some of them quite well."

"There has been some speculation..." Mohammad probes gently.

"About Mary from Magdala? A fine friend who followed me to the end. Perhaps the speculation you are referring to comes from that Broadway musical where they tried to make me into some kind of superstar. No, I had too many other things on my mind for romance. I was trying to..."

Rāmakrishna is encouraging the group to sit down at the comfortable arrangement of four, square tables, which the manager has covered with a large white tablecloth on which he has placed a small bouquet of flowers. It accommodates the six guests, two to a side, with a single space for himself at one side as moderator. Yes, face-to-face, the meeting he has always wanted. He checks his shirt pocket for the file card with the list of questions he has compiled. As the guests are seated, there is a moment of awkward silence, when no one quite knows what to say, soon broken by the approach of the servers, who come flouncing up, dressed in short skirts, checked aprons, and t-shirts with 'New Life' printed across the back. One is blond, the other with red hair, but both have the same Miss Universe smiles, making it hard to tell them apart.

"Hi, I'm Christy and this is Sarah, and we're going to be your servers today." Christy continues, "Can we start you off with a round of Bloody Marys?"

Eyes dart back and forth and around the table in a moment of stunned silence. It's not just the alcohol, but the name of the drink.

Moses, seated next to Jesus, suspects he is thinking that this refers to his mother Mary and wants to tell him that those drinks are actually named for Queen Mary I, who died a martyr trying to reestablish the Catholic Church in England. But every one remains silent.

Then the server Christy says, "Maybe you just need some more time."

"Time?" Buddha remarks. "Oh, we have plenty of time."

Rāmakrishna needs to rescue the moment and asks the servers if they have something without alcohol. "Maybe some tea? Darjeeling?"

Zhaunzi says, "I'm fine with water," and others quickly join in a chorus of "Water's fine."

As they wait for the water, Rāmakrishna calls the manager over to the table to negotiate the menu. Hoping to avoid another embarrassing moment, this time over the choice of food—it's hard to tell who is forbidden to eat what—he asks the manager to bring trays of fruits and vegetables, cheese boards, olives and pickles, and assorted breads and rolls. Let each nibble on what he prefers, which, when he stops to think of it, is also what he believes about religious harmony. Rāmakrishna thinks he should welcome them and thank them for coming, which he does, and observes, "You all seem well acquainted." They nod to each other and smile.

"Yes, but we've never met as a group," Muhammad says, "and it is good of you to bring us together. I'm looking forward to some serious discussion of what is going on and to getting some ideas about what happened." Others nod their agreement.

Rāmakrishna begins, "Of course, we can let the conversation drift where it will, but I thought I might start off with a question or two." He pulls the card from his pocket. "I'm curious about what you think about your followers. More specifically, how do you feel about what your followers thought of you?"

There is no awkward silence this time. The guests lean forward, each ready to speak. Confucius, like a shy bashful student, raises his hand, so Rāmakrishna calls on him.

"To tell the truth, I have been completely flabbergasted. Do you all have that word?" They nod. "I could not possibly imagine a movement growing out of my simple teachings. My followers could not even agree on what I was saying, and I had many critics. Then someone started to worship me. Did I say worship? And they started building temples for that purpose." Confucius was usually quite soft-spoken, but suddenly he has become extremely agitated, as if he has been bottling up these feelings for centuries. "I certainly never planned to be the founder of anything."

"Here, here," others chime in.

Buddha speaks next. "I was happy to have followers who were interested in learning what I had discovered about the relief of suffering. My awakening was painful, and after some experimentation in which I nearly died, I found what I thought was a middle way between pleasure and asceticism. I had several close followers, particularly those interested in deeper meditation. But then came the legends about my birth and the theories about my previous lives, and accounts of future lives where I had become embedded in some good person. When I died, they built stupas around my remains and temples around the stupas. Then came the statues, some of them quite huge and, I am sure, very expensive. But I had no intention of being a founder of anything. It just happened."

Zhuangzi clears his throat to signal he would like to say something. "Nor was I a founder of anything, but thank you for inviting me to this interesting gathering. I simply wrote down my complicated ideas as they occurred to me, and others joined me. The better-known writing was the *Dao De Ching,* which was written by a number of different people who were also difficult to understand. We were all trying to describe an unknowable but partially knowable force that we saw within nature called Dao. But we were just poetic observers of a mysterious force. And out of this came something they called Daoism, with followers, rituals, temples, the yin-yang, *tai chi*, feng shui, and who knows what else. We were just writers, and frankly not so easy to understand, and they made a religion out of us, like Hemingwayism or Tolstoyism."

Moses glances at Jesus who signals back with a nod for Moses to go first. "I admit that I have often been called the founder of Judaism, but really there were many ancestors before me and brilliant kings and prophets to follow me, so I'm not sure why I am here today. But I am happy to be part of this discussion. Judaism is not about any one person; it is about a people. They were people who believed that God had some special power in their lives, and they were followers of this faith even when they were scattered all over the world, even when they knew that being identified as a Jew could bring them sudden death. No, I was not a founder, a lucky leader perhaps, escaping from Egypt, setting up a new society for the Promised Land, but I was just trying to help my people find their way in the wilderness and get organized.

Jesus sits forward, folds his hands, and rests them on the table. "Many of you had the good fortune to continue your work over many years. Whatever it was that I was trying to do only lasted three years before I was...before my life was cut short. Because of my rather dramatic crucifixion, people seemed to remember my death rather than my life, and they forgot many of my teachings. Apparently, they found it easier to worship me as a God than to follow me as a teacher. Maybe that is understandable because the teachings were about building a new kingdom, and they weren't easy. People whom I had never met when I was alive, took my death and built it into a system of salvation, a somewhat dubious one at that, some would say. If I am a founder, I have to say that the religion that grew up around me was not what I intended. Maybe you can hear a little disappointment in my voice." He crosses his arms across his chest and looks down.

"And I as well," adds Muhammad. "In the early years we had our fights for survival with neighboring tribes. Yes, there was defensive fighting even in the beginning, but we were trying to build a new kind of peaceful community at Medina. We were mostly successful and much of it seemed to work. We even wrote a constitution. But when I died, that's when the real fighting started around who was most fit to be my successor. Muslims assassinating Muslims. I admit to trying to found a special community in the name of Allah at Medina, but not an empire. I have some disappointment as well."

Plates of food arrive just in time to alter the pensive mood and the guests begin to exclaim:

"Such a festive way to break our fast."

"Manna from heaven."

"Such a special meal."

"I'm glad I didn't have to read the menu."

"A love feast, indeed."

"And all so spontaneous. Did you order this for us, Rāmakrishna?" Zhuangzi asks.

"I confess that I did. I hope it will be all right. Something tasty for everyone." Rāmakrishna is pleasantly surprised to find that the "founders" are such humble, ordinary people, able to delight in simple secular pleasures. He begins to relax.

Plates are filled, the food is sampled, and after a few moments, Rāmakrishna raises another question. "Tell me what you think may have happened. There appears to be some gap between what you intended and what actually took place among your followers. How do you explain it?" At first, no one responds. Perhaps the food is more interesting than the question. He admits it's not an easy question.

Finally, Moses pats his mouth and brushes his beard with his cloth napkin and says, "Let me take a stab at that. As we know, people tend to do the wrong thing even when they know it's wrong. My people appeared to struggle with that, so this is nothing new. I think people are so mystified by life, so confused about who they are, so troubled about what life to lead, that they will latch on to anything that gives them security, even if they have to invent it."

"Yes, certainly, Moses, and they are persistently anxious as well," Jesus suggests. "I sensed it among my disciples and followers, so anxious about their lives, what to eat and what to wear, confused about who I was, and ambivalent about what we were trying to build. And, of course, they were troubled by the mystery of death. Those who came after me wanted to believe that I had somehow answered that timeless question, reducing it to a few simple beliefs, so that everyone could be assured of their salvation."

"And there is so much suffering and sadness," Buddha adds. "Real suffering that comes from the conditions of existence, but then also the suffering we create for ourselves. People often feel quite hopeless, so instead of the difficult path to Enlightenment, they choose to build pagodas and huge statues to induce a sense of power and peace. They are, in fact, deeply troubled, and many do not want to live another life like the one they have just experienced."

"If I may add a word," Rāmakrishna enters the discussion himself, "I think that people have a strong desire for a greater power, one that can be called on in a time of need. We imagine that power in different ways, and that is what gives us so many gods in the Hindu tradition. Each person craves some place to turn to for help, not only for the major things in life, but for the small details as well; and so, we create temples, stupas, churches, and mosques with icons, paintings, statues, and designs to help envision this greater power. People create a way to be close to god so that they can be sure that god will hear them when they cry for help."

Confucius and Zhuangzi have been listening closely, but they don't enter into the discussion. Confucius leans over to Zhuangzi and whispers, "But worshipping me in a temple? It makes no sense."

"And reducing the mystery of Dao to 'go with the flow' is a great oversimplification." His eyes flutter like leaves quaking in the breeze.

The servers have returned to bring additional plates of bread and rolls and to refill water glasses. They have been hovering nearby like drones, as if to observe and overhear the discussion. Christy leans over to Jesus and asks, "Are you guys who my boss says you are?"

"And who does he say we are?" Jesus asks, remembering how he had posed that question to his disciples about himself.

"Religious guys. The founders."

"Many of us do not think of ourselves as founders of anything," Moses points out.

"You can deny it, I guess, but if you are what the boss says you are, how come there aren't any women?"

The question was spoken loud enough for all to hear and it created an embarrassing silence for everyone, including Christy, who says, "I didn't mean to interrupt, but I actually would like to know where the women are." Sarah has drifted over to stand beside Christy and says only, "Me, too."

"Well," Rāmakrishna begins, "difficult as it may be to understand how a gathering like this could even occur, these are the figures we usually associate with the major religions of the world; and, of course, they lived centuries ago, in very different times. They come from patriarchal societies, where women played a different role than they do now, but there were efforts, even then..."

"We had women nuns as well as male priests in our religious community, "Buddha says.

"And I even defended prostitutes," Jesus adds, trying not to sound defensive. "Women played an important role in the development of the early church. Look at the respect there is for my mother Mary."

"In Hinduism we have goddesses as well as gods, and I was very devoted to a female god, Devī, the Mother," Rāmakrishna adds.

"Except for Jesus," Muhammad mentions, "we were married and cared for our wives, sometimes more than one."

Christy raises her eyebrows, then turns to Sarah and whispers, "It sounds like the usual bunch of excuses, but I think we've made our point." They gather up the water pitchers and hustle back to the kitchen.

Everyone is silent for a moment, and finally Rāmakrishna says, "I'm always uncomfortable trying to explain the absence of women in our traditions."

Moses looks up at him and says, "Perhaps it cannot be explained in a satisfactory way today, like slavery, which we also had. The present is so different from the past."

"But the injustices remain," Rāmakrishna replies. "That's what they were asking about: being left out. You could hear it in their voices." He runs a hand through his straight dark hair. "Maybe we ought to move on. I have so many questions." He pulls the small notecard from his pocket to check his list. "Let me ask you this. We've heard what you think about what your followers did to you, but I'd like to know your thoughts about what they did to each other."

Muhammad begins, "There's been a lot of fighting and

disagreement that often leads to violence. The followers seem to have created irreconcilable differences in Islam. It's not a pretty picture."

"Every country where we settled," Buddha adds, "had problems that led to violence. I think violence is the problem itself, and I have said so, many times."

"My people," Moses reminds them, "have often been victims of unimaginable violence. We got blamed for everything."

"It is rather surprising," Jesus suggests, "that religious movements that start out with good intentions can cause so much division and hostility, often in the name of one of us, or of God. One group divides itself from another, each one claiming to have the truth, and that creates serious conflict with those who disagree. People start wars that turn into religious crusades. I've just been reading a book by that atheist, Christopher Hitchens, which, by the way, I think you would enjoy. It's called *God is Not Great: How Religion Poisons Everything,* and he has assembled a shocking list of shameful things. Great damage has been done in the name of religion. Sometimes I have to wonder if religion has done more harm than good."

Rāmakrishna enters the discussion again. "I've tried to get people to understand that each religion grasps some aspect of the truth, but in a limited way." But he can't continue. He takes a deep breath and sighs. "Perhaps we need to discuss the good things that have happened, wouldn't you agree?"

"The progress has been slow," Confucius begins, "but over the centuries there has come to be a clearer vision of the good leader and the just society. The development of democracy, though some still call it an experiment, is promising. The challenge is that all over the world, today as well as in my time on earth, political power is easily corrupted to serve the leader rather than the people. But, yes, I think an approximation of the Confucian ideal has been put into practice in many countries, through differing forms of social order, and that is heartening." He sounds tired but hopeful.

Buddha leans forward and pulls on one of his long earlobes. "I think one of the remarkable developments of modern times is the emergence of science. I know that Islam played an important role in this, Muhammad, and our understanding of the natural world is greatly enhanced by science. One of my current followers, the Dali Lama from Tibet, has gone out of his way to learn about science and we have had some very interesting conversations about neuroscience and astronomy."

"But I'm not sure we can take much credit for science," Zhuangzi observes. "We saw Dao in nature, but science has different assumptions, a unique mission."

"Yes," Buddha responds, "the assumptions about how to speak of reality are radically different. Today, the scholars say we spoke in myth, and I would say that's a good word if you understand that the meaning behind myth can be true. We definitely spoke a different language— well, actually many different languages—but then, we had a different agenda. We were dealing with the great mysteries of human existence. Perhaps that was our strength."

"But what has been achieved directly through religion?" Rāmakrishna asks, trying to get the discussion back on track.

Moses speaks up boldly. "A tremendous amount of human good comes from religion through service, the caring of individuals for each other. Perhaps we have not yet built the just society," he adds, "but we do a very good job of repairing the world and mending together the unjust society by seeing that the needs of the less fortunate are not forgotten."

"That has always been one of the great achievements of Islam," says Muhammad. "It is built into our faith through the *zakat,* the tithe."

Jesus adds, "And not only the care of individuals for each other, but institutionalized caring through hospitals, schools, and orphanages. Consider the founding of colleges, Martin Luther's ideas about universal public schools, and the many missionary hospitals like Doctor Schweitzer's. Religion has been the force behind a great amount of humanitarian effort."

"Some individuals choose charitable work as the good life," Buddha adds. "You call them saints; we say bodhisattvas, people who remain in this world intentionally to lead compassionate lives. It is not always easy to count all of the good that is done in this world, but I know that much of it grows out of a religious motivation."

"Yes, I think that's true of Hinduism as well," Rāmakrishna says. "But here's a different kind of question. I'm wondering what you might say about the influence of religion on art, broadly speaking, meaning all forms of artistic expression. It seems that the mysteries addressed by religion are often expressed in powerful ways through art.

"Yes, I know what you mean," Buddha says. We expressed some concern earlier about the cost and effort that goes into the building of temples, pagodas, and cathedrals, and..."

"At the expense of humanitarian efforts," Jesus says, "but please continue. I want to hear your view on this."

Buddha continues. "If there were some way to take us out of it as the so-called founders, and to look at the art as a human expression of the sacred and holy, then I could understand it better. The huge statues they made of me were essentially expressions of the mystery of the endless cycle of life and death. The calming effect of a serene sculpture of Buddha as an aid to meditation, to put the mind at rest, I think I understand that. But it's not about me, Siddhartha, it's about the need to express the profound peace of Enlightenment."

Turning to Buddha, Zhuangzi adds, "I have a deep appreciation of the ink painting that came from the Zen masters, so natural and spontaneous, and I love the meditation gardens of large stones surrounded with sand raked into patterns. The simplicity helps me experience Dao, if I may use them that way."

"My people have not always been so good at art," Moses admits, "unless you include film, and what we have inspired has often been done by Christian artists. What comes to mind is the creation of mankind on the ceiling of the Sistine Chapel. It is an image that is almost universally recognized today, God reaching over to touch the outstretched hand of Adam, the slight gap between their fingers allowing for the spark of life to jump across. The idea may have come from our scriptures, but the image is essentially about the mystery of the individual emerging from non-being into being. The artist Michelangelo captures it perfectly."

"Yes, that same artist," Jesus says, "was a sculptor as well as a painter, and he did a life-size statue of my mother and me called the *Pietà,* and it has become very famous. It shows my mother Mary comforting me after the crucifixion. It's one thing to portray a baby on his mother's lap, but a grown man? That's a challenge, but it works well the way he has proportioned and positioned us for this awkward moment. The image comes from the Bible, as Moses has suggested about the creation story, but it is really about the mystery of suffering— anyone's suffering—but particularly the suffering of a mother for the death of her child, and as sometimes happens, a grown child. In the sculpture, we are both suffering, but both comforting each other in our own way. It is portraying, as you have expressed so well, Siddhartha, that the mystery of suffering is at the center of existence."

"I'm not sure why we had such a strict prohibition of the use of images," Muhammad says, "perhaps to avoid idolatry and always respect the indescribable nature of Allah, but our decorative arts convey a sense of the beauty and the mystery of God. And don't forget that my people invented those different musical instruments, the guitar, lute, and flute. Certainly, we can include music among the arts?"

"Yes, of course," says Confucius. "Perhaps you don't know that I played the chimes and zither, and I loved to sing. I have always been a little shy about mentioning it. I believe that music touches that special place inside us when words fail. It can make us laugh or cry or get up and dance. You probably can't picture a dancing Confucius."

"Music is a form of god realization," Rāmakrishna says, "that can bring us closer to our gods. We have many different ways of making music in our cultures just as we have many ways of speaking of the holy. Music is the universal language that unites us." It sounds a little formal to Rāmakrishna as he says it, but it is what he believes.

"I have to say," Jesus begins, "that I have been completely amazed at how my followers through the centuries have created such beautiful works of music. It's like you say, Siddhartha, it's not about us. Take me out of it and just listen to the sadness and joy, the mystery, the reverence for the holy. It seems that for some people, sacred music is their only encounter with the sacred. I hardly know where to begin, but let's not forget Bach with his cantatas, meaning 'to sing,' and his motets, meaning 'word,' as well as his soul-stirring organ music. And Handel with his oratorio, meaning 'prayer,' presenting the vocal story of my life. Handel wrote it in twenty-four days, and when Haydn first heard the "Hallelujah Chorus," they said he wept like a child. The Catholic mass has attracted almost all of the great composers, and poor Mozart was writing the beloved "Requiem" as he was dying. The day before he died, his friends played some of it for him and he burst into tears. His own music for his own death! The requiem was unfinished when he died the next day." Jesus pauses.

"Tell us more," Rāmakrishna asks. "Tell us about the hymns."

"The Protestant counterpart to the mass was the hymn, and Martin Luther himself was musical and wrote thirty-six hymns, including the music for "A Mighty Fortress is Our God." And then there is the prolific English hymn writer, Isaac Watts, who teamed up with Handel to produce "Joy to the World," one of the best-known Christmas carols.

And speaking of Christmas carols, did you know that "Silent Night" was first sung on Christmas Eve, accompanied by guitar and a small choir of village girls because the church organ had broken down. Everyone loves Christmas carols, but I find it rather odd to hear an atheist humming "Oh, Little Town of Bethlehem." But, don't get me started on music; I think it is God's pathway into the human soul, a way of praying for those who can't."

From the expressions that Rāmakrishna reads on the faces of the guests, he perceives that this discussion of art and music could go on across many cultures and centuries, but he has another question he wants to ask, and to him it is the most important question of all. "I'm sorry to change the subject," he says, "because I can see that our experience with music and art is, indeed, universal and creates a special harmony among us. But I really want to hear what you have to say about this question: What is it you were really hoping to teach or build when you were on earth, and are there any words from your tradition that capture what your religion said or is still saying about life?"

"It is unusual for me to speak first," says Zhuangzi, "because the Daoist teaching is that those who know do not speak and those that speak do not know. This thought comes from my colleagues who contributed to the *Dao De Ching*, and there is great wisdom in those words. Therefore, I speak with humility and some hesitation. But there is a passage from that work that I believe sums up our teaching. It is this:

> If one looks for Dao, there is nothing solid to see;
> If one listens for it, there is nothing loud enough to hear.
> Yet if one uses it, it is inexhaustible.

Perhaps art helps us to see and music to hear, but I believe we were trying to say that even though the great spiritual force within the universe remains quite mysterious, when you draw on it, you will always find it. Just listen quietly and watch closely. The challenge is to temper our desire to acquire, and, instead, to build a simple life based on Dao. It won't disappoint when you do. It will always be there to help you find your way. Am I making any sense?"

"Yes, of course," Confucius says, "it is a simple but profound philosophy. I traveled a lot, as you know, and my teaching was mostly about how to provide effective government through good leadership.

But that comes about only as people try to understand each other. It is the essence of diplomacy. My followers and others put together a book of sayings, and it is not always easy to know which words are mine, but this passage sounds like something I would say. They are asking me questions. It goes like this:

'Is there one word' asked Tzu Kung, 'which could be adopted as a lifelong rule of conduct?' The Master replied: 'Is not sympathy the word? Do not do to others what you would not like yourself.'

"Yes," Jesus says. "I think most of us gathered here had that idea in one form or another.

The others nod in agreement.

Buddha adds, "We say that one should protect others as one protects oneself."

"It takes a slightly different form," Jesus points out, "in each tradition. My followers came to call it the Golden Rule, reflecting the value of gold in caring for one another in this way."

"It has always seemed to me so obvious," Confucius continues, "to begin with the individual as the point of reference, what that person would or would not want for themselves. To know what *others* want, one only needs a little sympathy. I guess they would call that 'empathy' today, but then you simply act accordingly."

Muhammad turns to Rāmakrishna and says, "Your question makes me re-examine what it was we were really trying to do at Medina. It was something like Confucius has suggested, building a just and strong social order. Beyond this, I think we were trying to help people recognize and acknowledge God, and in doing this, our place in his world. We wanted our people to stop whatever it was they were doing several times a day to remember Allah. It's easy to forget God. But if you remember God, that you are living before God, a lot of other daily decisions come more naturally. In the *Quran*, there is a well-known Surah (chapter) that sums it up:

Allah! There is no god
But he—the Living,
The Self-subsisting, Eternal.
No slumber can seize Him

Nor sleep. His are all things
In the Heaven and on earth.

The emphasis in this Surah is on the one God in whose presence we all live our lives in complete dependence. He is Self-subsisting; we are contingent. Think of living your life each moment before God, a God who neither slumbers nor sleeps. Our challenge is to be constantly aware because being aware of God makes a difference. All things are his. That means he is the owner of everything; we're just renting it while we are here."

"I've never been very good at thinking about God," Buddha says, "but I like this idea that we don't own anything and that we are only borrowing what really belongs to some greater power." He pulls on his earlobe and nods. "A perspective well-put. We don't own anything, not even our body. We occupy it while we are in our earthly life, or perhaps another in a subsequent life, and so forth."

He nods his head several times before he continues, "Let me try to explain to you, and perhaps once more to myself, what I was trying to teach. As you know, I had been born into a life of privilege and had a shock, an awakening, when I first encountered sickness, old age, and death. I was shaken by the suffering I saw, and the more I became aware of suffering, the more suffering I saw in its many different forms. Each time I experienced it and felt it deeply, my mind was greatly disturbed by it, my thoughts anxiously whirling around uncontrolled. I think that what I discovered, and then wanted to teach, was that the mind could be calmed, maybe not stilled completely, but managed in such a way as to go beyond the self in the moment, to a special mental and spiritual state we called nirvāna. Finding this enlightened mental state, I believed and still believe, is the most important thing a person can do, not only to reach personal fulfillment, but to develop a sense of compassion for others.

Those who came after me brought together my teachings, with some additions, I am sure, that eventually became called the Buddhist scriptures, and some of these that sum up my teachings are these:

What we are is the result of what we have thought,
Is built by our thoughts, is made of our thoughts.

Death carries off a person who is gathering flowers,
Whose mind is distracted, like a flood carries off
  A sleeping village.

Overcome anger by love
Overcome wrong by good;
Overcome the miserly by generosity
  and the liar by truth.

I think that in the transformed consciousness of Enlightenment we discover a new way of relating to others without hurting them and to the natural world without destroying it. One of my favorite sayings is:

As the bee collects nectar and departs without harming
the flower or its color or scent, so let the sage live in a village.

"Isn't that beautiful!" Moses exclaims. "Living without harming the flowers." He pauses, not wanting to disturb the special moment. He tugs on his long beard before he begins. "There are many lessons in our tradition, and I'm most remembered for the commandments and the law, but it was really those who came after me who gathered together our writings, stories, and songs, as well as the words of the prophets. I'm sure that one of the most widely known is one of the songs, which we called 'Psalms,' because it is recited often at funerals, both Jewish and Christian. But the Twenty-third Psalm is not so much about heaven as it is the broader message of being cared for, of not being left alone.

I love to picture the shepherd boy up in the hills above the town at nightfall. He has been responsible and reliable, taking care of the sheep that day, finding them pasture and water; but then the sun goes down, the clouds cover the stars and moon, and he is surrounded by darkness. Overwhelmed momentarily with a sense of fear and deep loneliness, he asks: Who is going to take care of *me*? And the answer comes to him:

The Lord is my shepherd,
I shall not want;
he makes me lie down in green pastures.
He leads me beside still waters,
He restores my soul.

He leads me in paths of righteousness
for his name's sake.

Then the shepherd boy gets badly frightened and asks himself: What if
I die up here all alone? Who will know? Who will care for me? What
about the sheep? Then he realizes:

Even though I walk through the
valley of the shadow of death,
I fear no evil;
for thou art with me;
thy rod and thy staff,
they comfort me.

Yes, my people believed that like a good shepherd, our god is with
us and cares for us. I think that is what they were trying to teach: living
with security, overcoming fear, having the courage to exist in the midst
of the darkest mysteries.

Rāmakrishna is moved and he swallows hard before he says,
"Your answers are so beautiful, all of you, so simple and direct. Turning
to Jesus, he says, "We haven't heard from you, Jesus. What was it you
were trying to teach?

"That question makes me wonder all over again what it actually
was and why we failed so miserably. The end of the world? Life in
the new Kingdom? Maybe I wasn't very good at making my point.
If you can, you need to set aside for a moment what people believed
about me, while I try to tell you what I believed about people. I was
Jewish, you know, in the tradition of Moses here, and I understand the
lonely shepherd boy, scared to death up on that hill in the darkness.
His need was great. One of the things I was trying to say is that God
cares most about those who most need his care. That spirit is captured
in the Gospel according to Matthew in what came to be known as the
Sermon on the Mount, although I remember it more as a hillside. The
section I am referring to is called the Beatitudes. We say be-at-i-tude for
a sense of great happiness. You may know some of them as statements
of blessedness.

Blessed are the poor in spirit, for theirs is the kingdom of heaven.

Blessed are those who mourn, for they shall be comforted.
Blessed are the meek, for they shall inherit the earth.
Blessed are those who hunger and thirst for righteousness, for they shall be satisfied.
Blessed are the merciful, for they shall obtain mercy.

There is another list of deserving people later on in Matthew's story, that makes it even clearer which people I was talking about.

I was hungry and you gave me food,
I was thirsty and you gave me drink,
I was a stranger and you took me in,
I was naked and you clothed me,
I was sick and you visited me,
I was in prison and you came to me.

"But God cares for everyone, is it not so?" Muhammad asks.
"Yes, of course, "Jesus replies, "I was trying to teach the people in the crowd that gathered around us that perhaps these are the very people that God most cares about, and the lesson is that we, therefore, should care about them, too. Call it a message of radical love, if you will, or maybe just simple ordinary love. How did the people who came after me make 'love one another' so complicated? Jesus wept.

Those at the table are nodding their heads in silence. Then Buddha says, "It seems so terrible that they would cause you such suffering, nailing you to a cross. For what? Your radical idea of love? Were you not angry?"

"Yes, being human I admit I was, but I was mostly disappointed. Why would so many choose the way of hatred instead of the path to love?"

"It continues to this day," Confucius notes.

Then Jesus, apparently wishing to take the focus away from himself, turns to Rāmakrishna and says, "Perhaps you could provide for us your view of what the many great teachers of the Hindu tradition were trying to say? Do you have a favorite passage that describes it?"

"Well, as you know, we have a variety of beliefs and teachings, but there is a well-known passage from the Bagavad Gītā, yes, from the Yajur Veda, that fits with what many of you have been saying.

> The one who loves all intensely begins perceiving
> in all living beings a part of himself.
> He becomes a lover of all, a part and parcel of
> the Universal Joy.
> He flows with the stream of happiness,
> and is enriched by each soul.

I know there are differences among us, but I have always believed that what unites us is greater than what divides us. The harmony we find is in the Universal Joy that comes when we see ourselves in others and flow together in the stream of happiness."

Rāmakrishna notices all of the participants nodding in agreement, as if what he has just said actually has occurred in this breakfast meeting. Everyone seems to enjoy this moment of silence and harmony. He glances at his watch and runs a hand through his hair. He feels that he needs to end the meeting without knowing exactly what to say next, but he hates to interrupt their happy time together. "Thank you all for accepting my invitation and for joining in the discussion today. I notice that it is the eleventh hour, and I promised that I would not keep you. So, we need to say good-bye for now. You inspired me. Maybe we can do this again sometime." They nod and smile as they begin to push back their chairs, stand, stretch, and begin to chat again informally with each other as they did when they arrived.

Rāmakrishna hears Confucius ask someone "If there is a God, and he had been listening to us today, what would he be saying to us right now?" Hearing only fragments of the answers drifting up from the group, Rāmakrishna is trying to identify who might be saying what, although he knows that it really doesn't matter.

> Don't be anxious and afraid.
> Enjoy life and be joyful.
> Go for more walks in the forest or along the beach.
> Sing and dance every day.
> Live like it is your last life.
> Or the last day of this life.
> It's not a rehearsal.
> I'm a little tired of being praised.

Stop expecting miracles.

You don't have to go far to find someone in need.

They linger, still chatting, as if it is difficult for them to break away and go back to...wherever it is they came from; but finally, there is a handshake, a bow, a gesture, and they disappear down the street.

The servers are back at the tables clearing away the plates, the glasses, and the flowers. Christy says to Rāmakrishna, "Well, how did you like the New Life Café?"

"It was a wonderful place for our meeting. I was a little nervous at first, but thank God it went well."

"I was taught to always thank God because she makes everything possible," Christy says.

Rāmakrishna smiles. She? Yes, she. He has no problem with that. Then he asks, "Why does the café have this name 'New Life'?

Sarah grins. "It is a little 'new age,' isn't it?"

"Well, yes, Christy says, "but people need a quiet place to talk about serious things, to get a new perspective on life. They look like they're feeling better when they leave here."

"Maybe it's the Bloody Marys," Sarah suggests.

"No, I think it's the conversation. Kind of brings them back to life." Christy says.

Now the manager is coming toward Rāmakrishna. The bill! He needs to ask for the check. "Excuse me, sir," he says, "I need to pay you."

"No problem. The older gentleman with the long white beard, took care of it."

"Holy Moses."

"Yes, I think that's the one."

Several weeks later in the early fall, as the professor was having lunch with a colleague at the Moulin Bistro over on Main Street, Alex walked by, spotted him, and popped over to say hello. The professor stood and they exchanged greetings.

"Don't let me keep you from your lunch," Alex said, "but I want to tell you one more time how much I enjoyed our conversations about the mysteries of life. Thank you, again."

"Oh, no need. You're quite welcome."

"And thanks for the copy of what you have written about the meeting at the New Life Café. Wow! I felt like I was there."

"And thank *you* for brainstorming with me. I hope you could see where I used your suggestions and questions."

"As usual, you tried to answer all of my questions."

"I tried, but, of course, there are no answers to the timeless questions."

"No, I know that, but now I have a better understanding of them. I'm starting to see what life is all about, you know, the big picture. And I'm having more serious conversations with my friends and family. I had a long talk with my grandpa before he died and I've grown much closer to my aunt, the nun. I'm even more open with my dad, and he said he likes that. Sometimes I feel like I'm a different person."

"Well, Buddha would be all over that, Alex. No permanent self, you know."

"Oh, and I have a new job."

"Congratulations."

"It involves more international contacts. I'm ready for that now. Alex nods, smiles, and raises one hand for a good-by wave. "So, enjoy your lunch, professor."

"It's good to see you again, Alex. And if you ever have any questions..." Alex vanished down the street before the professor could finish his sentence, disappearing as if only a fleeting figment of his imagination.

References

Abdullah, Yusuf 'Ali, *The meaning of the Holy Quran*. Brentwood, MD: Amana Corporation. This is an English translation of the Quran with commentary. The quotation "Allah! There is no god But He..." is Surah 2: 255 and is well known in Islam.

Aslan, Reza, *No god but God*. New York: Random House, 2011. Background on Muhammad's wife Kadija and their marriage is on p. 32. The reason for and number of other marriages is on p. 64.
Dalai Lama, *The Universe in a Single Atom: The Convergence of Science and Spirituality*. New York: Morgan Road Books, 2005. An articulate

effort to reconcile Buddhism and science.

Flood, Gavin, *An Introduction to Hinduism.* Cambridge: Cambridge University Press, 1996. Background on Sri Rāmakrishna is found on pp. 256-259. The reference to his worship of Kali, the Mother, is on p. 256. His dates are 1836–1886, found on p. 256.

Harris, Ian, *The Complete Illustrated Encyclopedia of Buddhism.* Leicester, UK: Anness Publishing, 2011. The background on the family life of Siddhartha, including his wife and son Rahula, is from p. 17. The quotation "the wider benefit of humanity" is from p. 15. His age of death is from p. 17.

Harvey, Peter, *An Introduction to Buddhism,* Second Edition. Cambridge: Cambridge University Press, 2013. Discussion of birth as the cause of death is on p. 71. The alternate version of the Golden Rule, "One should protect others as one protects oneself" is mentioned on p. 152.

Hitchens, Christopher, *God is not Great: How Religion Poisons Everything.* New York: Hatchett Book Group, 2007. A reasoned case against religious belief with a comprehensive exploration of all of the "bad things" produced by religion. Jesus refers to it in the discussion.

Holy Bible, Revised Standard Version. New York: Thomas Nelson & Sons, 1952. "The Lord is my shepherd..." is from Psalm 23, the Old Testament, p. 576. The Beatitudes, "Blessed are... are from Matthew 5: 3-10 in the New Testament, p. 5. The quotation "I was hungry..." is Matthew 25: 35-36, p. 32. "Love one another' is John 13: 34, p.122.

Rainey, Lee Diane, *Confucius and Confucianism.* Malden, MA: Wiley-Blackwell, 2010. Background on the family life of Confucius and his age at death are on pp. 18-20. The reference to the interest Confucius had in music is on p. 18. As for dance, that's poetic license.

Rainey, Lee Diane, *Decoding Dao.* Malden, MA: Wiley Blackwell, 2014. Background on the writing of Zhuangzi and his name are found on pp. 36-40.

Reddy, Helen, quoted in "Quotable to the End" in *The New York Times,*

Arts, December 28, 2020. What Christy says about God is drawn from an actual quote attributed to the recently deceased folk/pop singer Helen Reddy (born 1941), famous for her song "I am Woman." The actual quote is: "I would like to thank God because she makes everything possible."

Schmidt, Alvin J., *How Christianity Changed the World.* Grand Rapids: Zondervan, 2004. (Formerly titled *Under the Influence.*) A survey of Christian influence in many aspects of society. Separate chapters exist on Health, Education, Art, and Music. Luther's interest in schools is referred to on pp. 176-180. References to cantata, motet and oratorio are on pp. 318-319. Haydn's weeping upon hearing the "Hallelujah Chorus" is mentioned on p. 326. The account of Mozart's "Requiem" is on p. 328. Writing of hymns by Martin Luther and James Watt is on p. 322. Christmas carols and the first playing of "Silent Night" are described on p. 334.

Soothill, William Edward, Translator, *The Analects of Confucius.* London: Oxford University Press, 1951. Originally published translation, 1910. The quotation "Is there any one word..." is Chapter XXIII, p. 169.

Stegemann, Ekkehard, and Wolfgang Stegemann, *The Jesus Movement: A Social History of its First Century.* Minneapolis: Fortress Press, 1999. Section 13.1.3 'The Relationship of Jesus to Women and of Women to Jesus' describes the social association of Jesus with women, pp. 382-386. The reference to Mary of Magdala is on p. 381.

Waley, Arthur, *The Way and Its Power: A Study of the Dao Te Ching and Its Place in Chinese Thought.* New York: Grove Press, 1958. The quotation "If one looks for Dao..." is from the *Dao De Ching* XXXV on p. 186.

Zhuangzi, *Zhuangzi, The Essential Writings with Selections from Traditional Commentaries.* Indianapolis/Cambridge: Hackett Publishing, 2009. Translation by Brook Ziphorn. This is the book that Zhuangzi refers to as having his name on the title, and some of the sections are believed to have been written by a person of that name.

<chaplaincyinstitute.org/portfolio-items/20> This website lists well known quotes of ancient scriptures, including the Hindu Bhagavad Gītā. The quote "The one who loves all intensely..." is from the Yajur Veda, cited as 2 on the list of this collection.

Readers Guide

1. Alex, the hypothetical person asking the timeless questions in this book is not described, but by now you probably have such a person in mind. In your view, is this person young or old, male or female, educated to a certain level, a believer in religion or not? How do you picture the hypothetical professor who leads this exploration of timeless questions and the mysteries of life? What support is there for your view? Does it matter who these people are? Why do you think the author used them in this book?

2. Of the timeless questions explored in this book, which ones did you find most interesting and relevant to your life? Why?

3. Most of the proposed "answers" to the timeless questions come from the ancient traditions of seven prominent world religions. Which of these proposed solutions did you find more convincing or stimulating as a point of view? For example, "I liked the idea of..., but not..."

4. Most people, through no fault of their own, have very little structured opportunity to learn about religion as they are growing up. Did you find things in this book that were new to you or that you hadn't heard of before? What were they?

5. Some people hold the view that religious writings are "divinely inspired" and "infallible" and should be taken literally. Throughout this book, the scholarly methods for reading religious texts are explained, sometimes in detail, as the tools for the modern study of religion. Did you find these explanations helpful and liberating or distracting and upsetting? Can you share examples?

6. In several chapters, the concept of "myth" is presented and elaborated.

Did you find the idea of myth helpful or disturbing? Why?

7. Sometimes in this book, scientific explanations are presented side by side with religious explanations of the mysteries of life. Did you find this to be valuable or confusing? Why?

8. All of the ancient religious traditions have grown and developed through the years. What aspects of these newer developments did you find to be interesting, surprising, or even shocking? What examples come to mind?

9. Most religions have developed patterns of observance that their followers practice to some degree. What strikes you as interesting, odd, or baffling about religious observance?

10. The fictional breakfast meeting of the "founders" can be thought of as enjoyable, fun, humorous, instructive, uplifting, and illuminating; or it can be considered offensive, inappropriate, outrageous, or sacrilegious. For you, as the reader of this closing chapter, which of these words best describes your reaction to it? Do you have a better word for it? Why did you select the word you did?